LATIN AMERICAN THOUGHT

A HISTORICAL INTRODUCTION————————

Harold Eugene Davis

LOUISIANA STATE UNIVERSITY PRESS BATON ROUGE

To the memory of José Vasconcelos,
philosopher and inspiring teacher

ISBN 0–8071–0249–0
Library of Congress Catalog Card Number 78–181564
Copyright © 1972 by Louisiana State University Press
All rights reserved
Manufactured in the United States of America
Printed by Colonial Press Inc.
Designed by Albert R. Crochet

Contents

v

21132

Foreword

The historian of ideas chooses his basic approach in accordance with several different theories. He may treat ideas as a reflection of changing social and economic conditions and as generalizations that give an understanding of these changing circumstances. Or, adopting the position of the philosophical idealist, he may assume that ideas have an autonomous life and that thought is a vital force in history — "blown a red wind round the world, consuming the lies in its mirth," to borrow the vivid phrase of Vachel Lindsay. Or he may adopt various positions between these extremes, reconciling the dependence of ideas upon circumstances with a degree of autonomy of the intellect.

The author's view lies in some such intermediate position. The thought of a period clearly expresses changing conditions, conflicts, and aspirations, even if it is largely a reflection of them. Thought is part of the historical legacy and, as such, is one of the best guides to an understanding of the nature of the forces and circumstances of an era. At moments of critical change, however, when new revolutionary currents dominate the arena of history, ideas seem to assume a more active role, giving meaning and direction to new forces, attacking and destroying elites and power structures, while inspiring new ones.

The historian of thought must also choose among several levels of generality upon which to treat his subject. At the most general level he becomes the historian of philosophical systems (or non-systems). At the most specific and concrete level he is largely a recorder of public opinion, of accepted value systems, and of beliefs. Historians have generally tended to leave these

extremes of the intellectual spectrum to philosophers in the
first case and to social scientists and psychologists in the second,
concentrating on some area in between. But, as in the case of his
theoretical approach, the historian has a wide range of choice
between these extremes. He may focus on one or more of such
specific aspects of philosophy or theory as sociological thought,
economic theory, political theory, philosophy of religion, philosophy of law, anthropological theory, social ethics, or philosophy of education. On a more specific and concrete level, he
may concentrate upon the social and political issues and problems which seem to preoccupy the age he is studying. At this
level he will consider such questions as the extent and nature
of human rights, popular participation in government, the role
of industry and agriculture in society, social aspects of education, the social role of organized religion, the place of organized
labor.

In this book, the author has given major attention to social
and political thought, because Latin American writers have
done so. The major thrust of interpretation is upon the revolutionary character of this thought and upon the national quest
for identity that accompanies it. But he has also given attention
to more concrete concepts, such as those of history, law, economics, education, anthropology, and ethics as the latter relates
to social values. The reason for this combination of the philosophical or theoretical with the concrete lies partly in the very
nature of thought, in its autonomy as a vital part of being. It
also lies in the tendency of many of the Latin Americans with
whom this history is concerned to give their ideas a more philosophical or theoretical basis than is common in the more pragmatic and empirical writing of United States scholars.

This is not a complete and definitive treatise on the intellectual history of Latin America, for the author's modest ob-

jective has been merely to open up the subject to the thoughtful reader and to guide him to the growing literature in this subject so fundamental to an understanding of Latin American history, culture, and society.

Parts of this volume appeared in considerably different form in the introductory and critical notes of the author's *Latin American Social Thought*. Hence, the author owes a substantial debt to collaborators in the earlier work; he is particularly pleased to acknowledge this debt to Professors O. A. Kubitz and Harry Kantor. Some of the content of chapter one has appeared in *TOPIC*, published by Washington and Jefferson College, and is used here by the generous permission of the editors. A Spanish translation of this article has appeared in the *Revista de la Universidad de México*. But the greatest debt of all is to the scores of students with whom the author has pursued the study of this subject, and to whom he owes much of whatever understanding of it he has gained through the years.

H. E. D.

Chevy Chase, Maryland
October 26, 1971

LATIN AMERICAN THOUGHT

Sources and Characteristics

The student of Latin American thought, whether he is philosopher, social scientist, or historian, quickly discovers that the philosophy of this region has tended to be social philosophy in the broad sense — that its major concerns have been with questions of ethics, history, law, education, anthropology, and economics. Only recently has it come to emphasize such broader philosophical problems as those of ontology, axiology, and epistemology. This social emphasis was observed by Professor William Rex Crawford in the slim but challenging book which first opened the eyes of many North Americans to the exciting literature of Latin American thought.[1] More recently, Eduardo Nicol of Spain and Mexico has made a similar observation, in speaking of the thought of Latin American independence and revolution as "ideological." [2]

The literature of this social thought often reveals a dialectic, around which the Mexican philosopher Leopoldo Zea has developed his synthesis of Latin American intellectual history, especially as it relates to the nineteenth century. Zea views this dialectic in neo-Hegelian or Ortegan terms, seeing in it a kind

1. "Perhaps in a young country philosophy is bound to be social philosophy; such, at any rate, is the case with Latin America." William Rex Crawford, *A Century of Latin American Thought* (Rev. ed.; Cambridge, Mass.: Harvard University Press, 1961), 4.

2. Eduardo Nicol, *El problema de la filosofía hispánica* (Madrid: Tecnos, 1961), 33, *passim*.

of existentialist formulation of thesis, antithesis, and synthesis. Thus, Zea's interpretation precludes Hegel's assumption of inevitable progress through evolution, substituting the concept, derived from José Ortega y Gasset, of a historical rhythm which is essentially nonrecurrent. Zea insists, with Ortega, that history cannot be repeated; but he also asserts, as does Ortega, that it must be experienced or relived before it can be rejected.[3] Zea emphasizes this Ortegan dialectic in his treatment of the nineteenth century. But the necessity of experiencing history in order to reject or transcend it, and to a certain extent a process of doing so, can be seen throughout the history of Latin America, from its discovery to the present.

This dialectic, which Zea seems to see as the essence of the argument over social, cultural, and religious change in Latin America, resembles the concurrent argument in other parts of the modern world, especially in western Europe and North America. But the argument has had its own life, characteristic of Latin America and displaying distinctive attributes in various Latin American countries and linguistic-cultural areas. Such specific characteristics of individual countries, of sub-regions, and of the region as a whole, require the attention of the historian who is looking for the outlines of a Latin American historical-intellectual movement, in whatever terms he may conceive it. Certainly one of the characteristics of the Latin American movement, as Zea has perceptively noted, is a peculiar intensity with which Ibero-America rejected the Iberian heritage in the early nineteenth century. This heritage was rejected precisely because it was not thought to be a past out of which the future could grow, but rather an obstacle to that future.[4]

3. Leopoldo Zea, *El pensamiento latinoamericano* (2 vols.; México: Pormaca, 1965), I, Chap. 1.
4. "El pasado representaba lo que no se quiere y el futuro lo que no se

Like the intellectuals of the modern Western world during the past five to six centuries (some would say like all intellectuals since Plato and Aristotle), Latin Americans have argued basic questions. Are the values and objectives of human society derived from natural law? Is the source and basis of natural law God's will or does it derive from the natural world as expressed in the orderly character of this world and man? Is the tradition of religious belief merely a "mythology" that must be replaced by reason in human conduct? Or is this "mythology" a basic expression of truth? In a fundamental sense, one which reaches to the roots of Christian and especially Ibero-American culture, does man live for his self-realization, for the creation of the good society, or for the glory of God? What is the good society?

Latin Americans have also argued other basic questions on a more concrete sociological and political level. What is the relationship of the Church to the state and to society? What is the character and the social role of education? What is the nature of law, and what form should political constitutions assume, especially regarding popular participation in government? What role does the nation play in social and economic development or "modernization"? What is the nature and rationale of revolutionary as against evolutionary change? What is the extent and nature of individual freedom in modern society? What are the means for achieving and protecting it? How is social justice to be achieved in the highly class-stratified society inherited from colonial days and reinforced in some ways after

---

puede por obra de eso que no se quiere." Zea, *El pensamiento latinoamericano,* I, 5. Speaking at a meeting of United States and Mexican historians at Monterrey, Mexico, in 1950, Zea had remarked: "Tenemos que hacer de nuestro pasado algo que por el hecho de haber sido no tenga necesidad de volver a ser." (We must make of our past something which by the fact of having been does not need to be again.) *Memoria del Primer Congreso de Historiadores de Latino-América ... y Los Estados Unidos* (México D. F.: Cultura, 1950), 312–20, 318.

independence? One special question which has engaged attention in this connection is that of how a society may rise above
class stratification along ethnic lines, above a social stratification
that has produced a society in which Indians and Blacks form
the basis of the lower class.

Such questions as these have been considered by Latin American writers and political leaders within the various systems or
structures of social philosophy (including non-structures) in
Western thought. These structures, including systems of sociology, have differed from age to age, and each of the successive
formulations has contained the seeds of a system of ideas that
followed. When we know more about pre-Conquest thought, we
may be able to say that the sequence begins in Incan, Mayan, or
Aztec thought. But most Latin American scholars have seen it
beginning with the humanistic thought of the sixteenth century,
much of it included in the so-called scholasticism that confronted the debate over the nature of man and nature in the
New World.[5] This debate over the nature of man in America
continued during the following centuries, even as American
man became more European. In some respects the argument
continues to the present day.

A new set of controversies provided the nexus of the eighteenth century thought of the Enlightenment, later expressed
in the independence movements. These new controversies centered around the Newtonian theory of the universe and an increasingly rational or rationalistic (Cartesian) view of man,
society, law, and history. Such questions were argued within
systems of thought that are best understood as an emerging
sociology and political economy, and as "scientific" systems

5. It may well be argued that pre-Conquest thought is really the beginning.
See, for example, Lewis Hanke, *Aristotle and the American Indians* (London:
Hollis and Carter, 1959).

that found their basis more and more in laws observable in nature rather than derived from God.

Yet even as the Latin American independence movements took form during the early years of the nineteenth century as the third phase of the greater American-French revolutionary movement (earlier in Haiti), this structure of thought was assuming a new character in the western European world, a character quickly transferred to the New World. The romantic, revolutionary liberalism and utilitarianism of the second quarter of the nineteenth century was developing on the basis of underlying concepts of "scientific" history and of a historical philosophy of law, combined with German idealism, French eclecticism, and sensationalism. A new political economy was taking shape, derived from British laissez-faire and French physiocratic doctrines, combined with a utilitarian ethic. This thought produced the varied Liberalism of France, Spain, Portugal, and Latin America. Paradoxically, it also gave rise to the Christian traditionalism of France and Spain, a form of romantic idealism that produced distinct yet similar expressions in Latin America. Pablo González Casanova has studied this traditionalism of Spanish colonial thought as it opposed the tide of the Enlightenment religious thought in the eighteenth century, chiefly showing how it perforce yielded to the new currents, but in a pattern different from that in Spain.[6]

By the mid-nineteenth century, evolutionary and "scientific" Comtian and Spencerian positivism and Marxist socialism were beginning to replace the more idealistic revolutionary formulations of the earlier years. This new trend was so pervasive that even the traditionalists, who still had important influence in Latin America, though less than in Europe, often tended to

6. Pablo González Casanova, *El misoneismo y la modernidad cristiana en el siglo xviii* (México: El Colegio de México, 1948).

recast their thought within this evolutionary trend in their search for the best basis for maintaining the old order. A significant difference is to be noted, however. Positivists and Marxists rejected the metaphysical basis of knowledge. Traditionalists, in the main, merely neglected it.[7]

The revolutionary thought of the twentieth century, in its reaction against nineteenth century evolutionary thought, bears a certain resemblance to the romantic liberalism and idealism of the early nineteenth century. But it differs strikingly in being a rebellion against formal systems as such. The contemporary rebellion has been directed particularly against the formalism of positivist and Marxist systems. Adopting being or existence as the fundamental reality in a way that earlier rationalism and idealism had evaded or rejected (but without agreement on the nature of being), twentieth century thought has assimilated the relativism of physics and behaviorism, drawing on various European sources — Spanish, French, Portuguese, Italian, Russian, German, British — as well as upon North American ideas. But, in this process of assimilation, Latin American intellectuals have also contributed notes of originality drawn from their own American experience. As in the Western world in general, the new systems (or nonsystems) that emerge in Latin America infuse political trends running the gamut from a revolutionary anarchism to native varieties of fascism.

As earlier suggested, Leopoldo Zea has succinctly pointed out

7. See the interesting study by Henry Paul on Catholic thought in nineteenth century France, "In Quest of Kerygma: Catholic Intellectual Life in Nineteenth Century France," *American Historical Review*, MLXXV (December, 1969), 387–423. On traditionalism in eighteenth century Spain, see Francisco Puy, *El pensamiento tradicional en la España del siglo xviii (1700–1760); introducción para un estudio de las ideas jurídicos-políticos españolas en dicho periodo histórico* (Madrid: Instituto de Estudios Políticos, 1966). See also José Luis Romero, *El pensamiento político de la derecha latinoamericana* (Buenos Aires: PAIDOS, 1970), *passim*.

that in the twentieth century, as in the past, one of the key issues running through Latin American thought is that of the nature of historical and social change. Defining history as an ontological preoccupation, as man's assessment of his human experience, Zea argues that "history, the form in which the American man understands his history, has been and continues to be one of the keys to this assessment of conscience." [8] This historical preoccupation, it may be added, has roots in the close identification of America with the history of utopianism in Western thought since the days of Thomas More. But it derives a special emphasis in Latin America from the fact that Europeans of all nationalities came to America with the idea that a New World could be developed in the shape of whatever image they brought with them, or of some new image evolved from that model. Thus, for more than four centuries Americans in Latin- as in Anglo-America have conceived their history in one of its basic respects as a conflict between the Old and the New Worlds.

Aboriginal (American Indian) and African (Negro) thought and value systems have received some attention by students of the history of Latin American ideas, but not to the extent or in the ways that they deserve. Too often, such studies have been left to sociologists and cultural anthropologists, partly because historians have failed to find the kind of documentary materials with which they are accustomed to work. Numerous studies have been made on the Negro and slavery, and upon Indian society, economy, and culture, both pre-Conquest and post-Conquest. These studies have produced an important literature on Indianism (*indigenismo*.) But historians of thought have not to any large extent searched out ideas that have their sources in

8. Zea, *El pensamiento latinoamericano*, I, 2. Translation by author.

the aboriginal and Afro-American cultures or that have arisen from the experiences of ethnic assimilation. This lack of historical study has a special importance since the question of Indian and African influences is one of key significance in considering the autonomy of Latin American thought, as the reader will see repeatedly and in more detail in several of the following chapters.

European religious influences, and to some extent those of North America, have also left their mark on the Latin American mind. The major European religious influence appears in a persistently Roman Catholic spirit inherited from Portugal and Spain. This religious influence is reinforced by a heritage of Roman Law that gives a rational and authoritarian natural law cast to the political and legal thought of all peoples of Spanish and Portuguese speech. Protestantism quickly lost the initial foothold gained in sixteenth century Spain through the writing of Juan de Valdés and through the humanism of Luis Vives. Thereafter, although theology and philosophy achieved extraordinary consistency under the Catholic counter reform, they lost some of the vigor produced in northern Europe by philosophical controversy. The success of the Counter Reformation doubtless explains why certain aspects of "scholastic" philosophy survived with more strength in the Spanish and Portuguese worlds than in northern Europe.

By the eighteenth century, however, a significant change was occurring in the Iberian world. Rationalistic thought penetrated Portugal and Spain slowly under French cultural and political influence, finding expression in such eighteenth century Spanish writers as Fray Benito Gerónimo Feijoó y Montenegro. Traditional cultural and intellectual obstacles retarded acceptance of some of these new ideas in the Spanish-Portuguese world, as González Casanova has pointed out,[9] but ultimately they were adopted. In the nineteenth century, likewise, Latin America received the currents of romantic historicism, traditionalism, evolutionary idealism, positivism, and socialism as they developed in Europe. In the twentieth century they were followed or replaced by trends of relativism, psychologism, and existentialism, including varieties of neo-idealist thought.

In the New World, however, and in all these periods, these European concepts assumed different form and took on different meanings as they were affected by the American environment. In colonial days one such manifestation frequently noted by travelers was an exaggerated consciousness of being Spanish or Portuguese that upper-class criollos displayed. This criollo hispanicism was partly the product of a feeling of class superiority traceable to the consciousness of having subjugated the Indian and enslaved the Negro. In later years, this class-conscious criollo mentality found such widely differing expressions as sympathy for the Anglo-American planters in their eighteenth century revolt against Europe and acceptance of Pan Hispanism in the twentieth century.

As noted earlier, the criollos tended to reject European intellectual and cultural influences when they rebelled against overseas political domination. European immigrants came to the New World with a spirit of optimism that contributed to this criollo revolt against authority. It was the essence of the spirit of the independence movements. Thus, because the rebel criollos regarded Spain and Portugal as moribund, they modified their French Revolutionary rationalism and anticlericalism, giving these concepts a tone more like that of the earlier United

9. González Casanova, *El misoneismo*, 103–29.

States movement. It was an optimism in respect to things American and a rebellion against things Spanish and Portuguese that bears a striking resemblance to the anti-British feeling in the United States.

In the nineteenth century, Latin Americans also tended to reject the newly developing scientific and deterministic views of history coming to them from Europe, while asserting a historical basis in American experience for the principles they defended, like those described in the United States as "an American proposition." As it emerges in the twentieth century, the criollo attitude tends to be ambivalent and paradoxical. It is both an attraction toward and a repulsion against European culture — a psychological ambivalence of love-hate that seems to have deep roots in social class consciousness. It is this author's view that an understanding of this criollo mentality is essential if the reader is to understand how Latin American social thought could be consistently and aggressively preoccupied for a century and a half with problems of social reform and yet escape a close identification with European class-conscious socialism, at least until the twentieth century.

A basic sociological fact also helps to explain this seeming paradox. Nineteenth century society in Latin America differed essentially from that of Europe in respect to what has been euphemistically called the "social problem." Because Europe was rapidly urbanizing, this European problem was that presented by the demands of the rising working class and the workers movement of which the verbal and political expression was socialism. But Latin America remained more rural than Europe. Moreover, Latin America had a constant labor shortage in relation to its undeveloped resources, despite having a large depressed population of conquered Indians and liberated slaves.

The Latin American "social problem," therefore, was a more complicated social process than Europe's. It was a process of socioethnic change. the essence of which was the emergence of a proletariat of characteristically landless agricultural workers having an amorphous and mixed ethnic background, Indian, mestizo, or Afro-American. This social phenomenon contrasted sharply with the rise of the European working class whose ethnic character was fixed by centuries of social and cultural evolution.

Yet, despite this difference, social thought in Latin America and Europe has found common ground in the twentieth century in a preoccupation with the fundamental socioeconomic-political movement which José Ortega y Gasset termed the revolt of the masses — the rise of the common man to sociopolitical power; this preoccupation embraces the materialism and the demagogic politics accompanying that rise. Thus, in both hemispheres, the basic themes and problems of social thought in the twentieth century have been those of democracy, industrialization, urbanization, socialism (or its obverse, social Christianity), nationalism, and internationalism. The populist form given to these problems by politicians expresses a central process of modern history, of course, and has deep roots in all American countries. At an earlier stage, the American and French Revolutions provided much of the dynamism of this thought; in its later phases Latin American contributions have been notable, as we shall see. In fact, Latin America has been a great laboratory for this democratic experiment — the "revolt of the masses" — for more than a century. Democratic successes in this experiment have reinforced the American optimism which the all-too-obvious failures that have occurred at times have never entirely dissipated. Both the successes and the failures have contributed more than is often realized to the contemporary social thought of the area, even when Latin Americans have seemed to be merely lisping the sentiments or adopting the poses of European philosophers.

Utopianism was a major element in the New World optimism, in the form of an assumption that America was destined to be the scene of a society free from the evils of the Old World. The Christian prototype of this idea — the concept of the Kingdom of God and even of the imminent second coming of Christ — found a kind of expression in the Christian communities organized by Spanish missionaries in Chiapas and Michoacán, in Mexico, and by the Jesuits in Paraguay. The incipient rationalism of the Renaissance, building on earlier Christian concepts, easily conceived of America as a land uncorrupted by civilization in which a better social order could be achieved, if indeed it did not already exist. Later, in Latin America, as in the United States, the nineteenth century brought a rash of utopian socialist thought — Saint-Simonism and Fourierism — and of efforts to establish such utopian communities. In a more pragmatic sense this utopian spirit may be seen as a major continuing motive for the growing stream of migration to America.

This concept that America was to be the scene of a great social experiment was connected, of course, with the idea that the New World was different from and superior to the Old. It included not only the persistent European view that America was the land of hope where a new and better civilization could be achieved, but the opposite concept as well — that America was an inferior continent with inferior flora and fauna, a view that was also frequently expressed in Europe. This latter view originated in some of the first contacts of Europeans with the New World; it seemed to find scientific verification in the writings of the French scientist Buffon and philosophical expression in the view of Hegel that America was a land without a history. Latin

Americans rebutted this view in much the same way that Thomas Jefferson answered Buffon in his *Notes on Virginia*,[10] and in doing so reinforced the idea of a superior America.

Directly and indirectly, the example and the revolutionary ideology of the United States strengthened this Latin American utopian trend. During the independence movements in Latin America, North American political concepts had wide circulation. Mariano Picón Salas of Venezuela has written of that "anxious curiosity which surged from one region of America to another from the moment the young Yankee democracy took shape."[11] Ariosto D. González of Uruguay, in a similar vein, has written of the influence of United States constitutional concepts on José Artigas,[12] while Augusto Mijares of Venezuela and others have examined the influence of these concepts on Simón Bolívar.[13]

A decade or two after independence the ideas of Ralph Waldo Emerson and the New England Transcendentalists were known by the "Generation of 1837" in Argentina, by the "Generation of 1842" in Chile, and by similar intellectual and literary

10. See the several works of Lewis Hanke on Las Casas, particularly the *Spanish Struggle for Justice in the Conquest of America* (Philadelphia: University of Pennsylvania, 1949); Silvio Zavala, *Filosofía política de la conquista de América* (México: Fondo de Cultura Económica, 1947); Edmundo O'Gorman, *The Invention of America* (Bloomington: Indiana University Press, 1961); Francisco Larroyo, *La filosofía americana* (México: Universidad Nacional Autónoma, 1958); Leopoldo Zea, *El pensamiento latinoamericano*; and Pablo González Casanova, *Una utopía de América* (México: El Colegio de México, 1953). See also the comment on Buffon and others by Francisco Miró Quesada, "Realidad y posibilidad de la cultura latinoamericana," *Revista de la Universidad de México*, XXVI, Números 6 y 7 (febrero y marzo de 1972), 3–13.

11. Mariano Picón Salas, "Historia hispano-americana," in *Obras selectas* (Madrid-Caracas: Edime, 1953), 834.

12. Ariosto D. González, *Las primeras fórmulas constitucionales en los países del Plata (1810–1814)* (Nueva edición; Montevideo: Barreiro y Ramos, 1962).

13. See, for example, Augusto Mijares' biography of Bolívar, *El Libertador* (2nd ed.; Caracas: Arte, 1965).

groups elsewhere. The ideology of the Horace Mann common school revival was translated into Argentine thought by Domingo F. Sarmiento and by the school teachers he invited to Argentina from the United States. Latin Americans read and admired the poetry of Edgar Allen Poe and Walt Whitman and other United States writers of the nineteenth century. In the twentieth century these cultural contacts between the United States and Latin America have become even more frequent and extensive. The psychology of William James and the educational philosophy of John Dewey have had wide Latin American circulation. The anthropological thought of Franz Boas and the vitalism and scientific organicism of the Anglo-American Alfred North Whitehead have also had their Latin American interpreters. In general, however, North American influences in other aspects of the thought of Latin America have been small in comparison with those stemming from European thought.

Finally, we may note that one of the most distinctive aspects of Latin American thought has been its revolutionary and ideological quality, evidenced since the days of independence. Basically, this revolutionary character has appeared in the tendency to reject traditional European forms and values as forms of colonialism. In the twentieth century this revolutionary tone has become even more evident, as may be seen in the currents of thought accompanying the Mexican Revolution, Uruguayan *Batllismo,* Peruvian *Aprismo,* and similar political movements in other countries. In the early years of this century, revolutionary thought found a principal focus in an attack on the evolutionary positivist sociology and philosophy. As the twentieth century progressed, however, the thought lost some of this anti-positivist emphasis. But it continued to be broadly humanistic, was occasionally Marxist, and was often influenced by the doctrines of social Christianity expressed in the series of Papal Encyclicals that began with the *Rerum Novarum* and in the writing of Jacques Maritain and other neo-Thomists. By mid-century it had become a more basic challenge to the assumptions and belief of the "American Proposition" which had long been the essential core of ideas imbedded in the national histories. Today, even Christian Democrats sometimes join the chorus of voices of the new generation that aims to shake to its foundation the structure of all inherited beliefs and values. Despite the highly polemical tone of this contemporary debate, however, it may be noted, as Eduardo Nicol has pointed out, that it expresses something quite significant and universal in tendency.[14]

14. Eduardo Nicol, *El problema,* 33.

Pre-Conquest and Colonial Antecedents

Throughout the colonial era the population of Latin America remained largely indigenous. Spanish migration in the sixteenth century was measured in tens of thousands while the native population was measured in millions. Native population seems to have declined in absolute numbers in the sixteenth and seventeenth centuries, however, largely because of epidemics of smallpox and measles. Spanish immigration increased in volume in the seventeenth and eighteenth centuries. Yet, at the end of the colonial period the population was still predominantly Indian, as Baron Alexander von Humboldt observed when he traversed many parts of the New World early in the nineteenth century.

African immigration (the slave trade) had practically equalled that from Europe, with the result that Latin America had a large population of African or mixed Afro-European origin, especially large in some areas, and that colonial culture in these areas was highly Africanized. Both Spanish and Portuguese colonists (as well as those of French, Spanish, English, and Dutch America) were influenced by the religious beliefs, value systems, and modes of thought of both their indigenous and their Afro-American subjects.[1]

1. Mariano Picón Salas has written of the religious hybridism of the colonial population. See his *De la conquista a la independencia* (México: Fondo de Cultura Económica, 1944), 101–102; also his *Pedro Claver, el santo de los esclavos*, in *Obras selectas* (Madrid-Caracas: Edime, 1953), 575–700.

THE INFLUENCE OF INDIGENOUS AND AFRICAN ELEMENTS

The influence of Indian and African cultural elements was no doubt great in shaping colonial as well as later modes of thought and opinion, although relatively little study of indigenous thought and its influence, or of the influence of African ideas has been made, except in connection with indigenous religious ideas and law. Miguel León Portilla in *El reverso de la Conquista*[2] brings out the pre-Conquest and Conquest literary survivals of the Aztecs, Mayas, and Incas. Their literary survivals, he says, have preserved something of the origin myths and the cult of such native deities as Quetzalcoatl and Viracocha. These survivals have also preserved a vivid sense of the trauma and tragedy of the Conquest. Pre-Conquest concepts of law and politics survived in the native institutions of local government that continued to govern the Indian communities under Spanish rule and that still influence Indian community structures today.[3]

Missionaries imbued with the humanism of the sixteenth century, such as Bartolomé de las Casas and Bernardino de Sahagún, were greatly impressed by the values and ideas they encountered in the native cultures and made heroic efforts to record them. Much of what has been preserved of the pre-Conquest cultures we owe to them. Even a rough soldier like Bernal Díaz del Castillo showed this influence of native thought in his *True History of the Conquest of New Spain*. More signifi-

2. Miguel León Portilla, *El reverso de la Conquista* (México: Joaquín Mortiz, 1964).

3. See, for example, Luis Chávez Orozco, *Las instituciones democráticas de los indígenas mexicanos en la época colonial* (México: Instituto Indigenista Interamericano, 1943); Carlos H. Alba, *Estudio comparado entre el derecho azteca y el derecho positivo mexicano* (México: Instituto Indigenista Interamericano, 1949); Jorge Basadre, *Historia del derecho peruano* (Lima: Antena, 1937); Manuel Gamio, *Hacia un México nuevo* (México, 1935), 39–50.

cant influences appear in the work of such mestizo writers as the
Peruvian, Garcilaso de la Vega (1539[?]–1616), author of *Comentarios reales de los Incas.*

Twentieth century Mexican agrarian reform appears to have
got some of its ideas from these surviving pre-Conquest concepts.[4] Pre-Conquest thought also inspired twentieth century
indigenismo (Indianism). Contemporary Peruvian thought, for
example, shows this indigenous influence in the classic work of
Hildebrando Castro Pozo, *Nuestra comunidad indígena.* Castro
Pozo spoke of the spirit of the Indian as part of the spirit of
Peruvian nationality, pointing out the continuing influence of
pre-Conquest cults on the way in which present-day Indians of
Peru think and react to many things.[5] Novels of the Guatemalan
Nobel prize winning author, Miguel Asturias, express the influ-
ence of ideas from the *Popul Buk,* the Maya-Quiche "bible,"
in the contemporary Guatemalan mentality. In this author's
Hombres de Maíz, maize retains an indigenous religious significance.

Considering the culture and thought of the Maya area (Yucatán, Chiapas, Guatemala) in his work on the civilization of the
Mayas,[6] Alberto Ruz Lhuiller tells us that we must reckon with
an earlier (pre-Conquest) rejection of theocratic domination
that had undermined the value system of the culture. By way of
contrast, Daniel Valcárcel of Peru has pointed out that the sub-
stantive content of the well organized Incaic educational system
was intuitive rather than logical. It was, he says, normative,

---

4. Jesús Silva Herzog, *El agrarismo mexicano y la reforma agraria* (México:
Fondo de Cultura Económica, 1959), 28, 37.

5. Hildebrando Castro Pozo, *Nuestra comunidad indígena* (Lima: El Lucero,
1924), vi, 183f., 197ff.

6. Alberto Ruz Lhuiller, *La civilización de los antiguos mayas* (Santiago de
Cuba: Universidad de Oriente, 1957), 77.

civic, and ethical.[7] Rodolfo Kusch has written that knowledge among the Aymará and Quechua is "ritualistic and revealed." It is not objective but transcends the object. It is concerned with causes of community and life, aiming to maintain a cosmic balance.[8]

In one of the few really significant studies of pre-Conquest thought, Miguel León Portilla writes that "from the point of view of the history of ideas" Mayan thought "offers the possibility of an approach to distinct and certainly extraordinary concepts of an old theme — time." The Mayan calendar was in itself an extraordinary achievement in respect to time, but its major significance, as León Portilla sees it, lies in its revelation of the great preoccupation of Mayan thought with the idea of time. Nothing and no one could escape the control of time incorporated in the calendar. Time and space were inseparable, the Mayans believed; thus, nothing could exceed the importance attached by the priestly caste to reading the problems and possibilities of the future as a function of the completion of distinct periods of time. One of the major objectives of religious practice was to put one's self under the protection of deities who were the bearers of time.[9]

According to Jacinto Quirarte, Mayan astronomers and mathematicians thought time was infinite, having no beginning and no end. They believed that the world had been created and destroyed various times by the gods and would be destroyed again. The reason for the destruction each time was the imper-

7. Daniel Valcárcel, *Historia de la educación incaica* (Lima: Universidad de San Marcos, 1961).

8. Rodolfo Kusch, "Pensamiento aymará y quechua," *América Indigena*, XXI (1971), 389–96.

9. Miguel León Portilla, *Tiempo y realidad en el pensamiento maya* (México: Universidad Nacional Autónoma de México, 1968), 15, 108.

fection of the world resulting from failure of the gods to create men capable of venerating their progenitors. The only exception to this belief in the inexorable passage of time appears in a view of history represented in Mayan steles commemorating certain historical persons.[10]

Terence Grieder has recently written, citing Miguel León Portilla in support of his views, that the Inca and Aztec arts differed greatly in the concept of social control. The Aztecs, he says, accepted the principle that esthetic experience is the only ultimate reality and that, hence, they should seek exaltation in their art. "To have lived meant to have experienced esthetic exaltation, which is not a social experience but a profoundly individual one." Grieder argues that this philosophy was linked to the excessive Aztec devotion to human sacrifice. In another article Grieder has argued that prohibitions and sanctions of a religious character were applied principally to the exploitation of natural resources.[11]

Aztec proverbs gathered by Fray Bernardino de Sahagún and others embody folk wisdom not unlike the proverbs of Western Christian culture, as these examples illustrate:

> Ayoppa in pilthua, ayoppa in tlacatihua.
> One lives only once.
>
> Cuix aca ticneliz, ca ah ticmoneliz?
> Who will be useful to another when he is not useful to himself?

10. Jacinto Quirarte, "Diferencias arquitectónicas en dos ciudades mayas: Uxmal y Chichén Itzá," *Boletín del Centro de Investigaciones Históricas y Estéticas*, Universidad Central de Venezuela, No. 5 (Mayo, 1966), Caracas, Venezuela. Also published as Offprint No. 89, Institute of Latin American Studies, University of Texas, Austin, 57–58.

11. Terence Grieder, "Demons and Discipline in Ancient Peru," *Art News*, LXVII (Oct., 1968). University of Texas, Institute of Latin American Studies. Offprint Series #71. Also, "Ecología Precolombiana," Offprint #99 in the same series, originally published in *Américas* of the Organization of American States.

In yuhqui cichi, in yuhqui mehua.
As one goes to bed, so will he arise.[12]

Other parts of the Aztec literature resemble in spirit the skeptical wisdom of the book of *Ecclesiastes*. For example, Sahagún reports these words of a king speaking to his daughters:

The earth is not a place of pleasure: there is in it neither joy nor happiness. Of old they said:

> So that we should not go on weeping forever, so that we should not always be sad, God gave us laughter, sleep, food, our strength and courage and that sweet pleasure of the flesh with which men are propagated.[13]

In general it may be observed that as long as the native languages continue to be the major means of communication of millions of Latin Americans, as they still are in the late twentieth century, indigenous concepts of religion, ethics, art, community relations, law, and politics will have a significant place. Among these various influences the symbolism and language of the plastic arts and of the Indian peasant architecture may well be the most durable survivals. But religious and ethical values will also continue to have an important role in forming the minds of the contemporary generation.

Twentieth century authors, consciously or unconsciously seeking a more autonomous thought, provide the modern emphasis on *indigenismo* (Indianism), that is to say on "redeem-

---

12. The English version is translated by this author from the Spanish of Sahagún as it appears in Angel M. Garibay K., *La literatura de los Aztecas* (México: Joaquín Mortiz, 1964), 101–102.
13. Translated by the author from the Spanish version of Sahagún in Garibay, *La literatura de los Aztecas*, 117.

ing" the Indian populations in America.[14] This autonomous "Indianist" tendency has found strongest expression, of course, in countries of Indian and mestizo populations. The literature on the subject is voluminous, and the number of authors is too great even to list here.[15]

The influence of the Africans who were brought to America as slaves was quite different from that of the Indians. Yet the Africanism which has appeared in the literature of Brazil and of the Caribbean regions in which Negroes form an important segment of the population is similar in influence to that of *indigenismo.* Of this influence, the writings of Arthur Ramos and Gilberto Freyre of Brazil, of Fernando Ortiz of Cuba and of Aimé Cesaire of Martinique, provide examples. We know much less than we should about the survival of African ideas in slave societies of America. But certainly much of the strength of such Haitian leaders as Toussaint L'Ouverture, Henri Christophe, and the contemporary François Duvalier derives from their understanding of this heritage. "Negritude," Voodoo, and the spiritism of popular Brazilian religion (not the more sophisticated spiritualism) are meaningless without this understanding.[16]

14. On *indigenismo* see Alejandro Lipschutz, *Indoamericanismo y la raza india* (Santiago, Chile: Nascimento, 1937) and his *Indoamericanismo y el problema racial de las Américas* (Santiago: Nascimento, 1944); Juan Comas, *Ensayos sobre indigenismo* (México: Instituto Indigenista Interamericano, 1953); the excellent introduction to Aida Cometta Manzoni, *El indio en la poesía de América española* (Buenos Aires: Joaquín Torres, 1939); Luis Villoro, *Los grandes momentos del indigenismo en México* (México: El Colegio de México, 1950); and Manuel Gamio, *Consideraciones sobre el problema indígena* (México: Instituto Indigenista Interamericano, 1948).

15. Juan Comas, *Bibliografía selectiva de las culturas indígenas de América* (México: Instituto Panamericano de Geografía e Historia, 1953) is a convenient guide to the literature as of the date of his survey. Much has been written since that date, of course.

16. Aimé Cesaire, *Cahier d'un retour au pays natal (Return of the Native),* trans. Mazisi Kunene (Baltimore: Penguin Books, 1969). See also Irene Jackson, "Negritude: A Study in Outline," in Berrian and Long (eds.), *Negritude: Essays*

What is indeed surprising is to find expressions of both Indian and Negro influence in a country like Argentina, which has a predominantly European immigrant population. Yet the Argentine Ricardo Rojas, calling for a new and essentially American aesthetics to be erected around values derived from American geography and indigenous cultural elements, provides one such expression.

HUMANISTS AND SCHOLASTICS

The discovery and conquest of America gave an impetus to Renaissance humanism in Spain, as in Europe generally, through the expansion of geographic knowledge. Portuguese discoveries had a similar, in some respects even more striking effect in that country. In Spain, this influence, which was both religious (Christian) and secular, found notable voices in Juan Luis Vives (1492–1540), contemporary and peer of Erasmus, in Francisco de Vitoria (1480[?]–1546) who initiated the study of international law by discussing the rights of the Indians,[17] and in the Jesuit scholar Francisco Suárez (1548–1617). In the New World, this humanism inspired the great missionaries of the sixteenth century, such as Bartolomé de las Casas, Bernardino de Sahagún, Pedro de Gante, and Motolinia (Toribio de Bena-

---

and Studies (Hampton Institute Press, 1967). See also papers on Afroamerica by Jean Price Mars, Melville Herskovitz, Gonzalo Aguirre Beltrán, William R. Bascom, Suzanne Comhaire-Sylvia, Rhoda Metraux, Roger Bastide and Richard Alan Waterman in Selected Papers of the XXIX International Congress of Americanists: Acculturation in the Americas, Sol Tax ed. (Chicago, University of Chicago Press, 1952), 143–218; Gilberto Freyre, The Masters and the Slaves, trans. Samuel Putnam (New York: Knopf, 1946) and The Mansions and the Shanties, trans. Harriet de Onís (New York: Knopf, 1963).

17. See volumes I and II of the series El pensamiento político hispano-americano: Bernardo G. Monsegu, C. P., Filosofía del humanismo de Juan Luis Vives (Madrid: Instituto Luis Vives de Filosofía, 1961); Guillermo A. Lousteau Heguy and Salvador M. Lozada (eds.), Francisco de Vitoria (Buenos Aires, Depalma, 1966).

vente). The ideas of the humanist Erasmus were debated in the first university established in America, that of Santo Domingo. It was also in Santo Domingo that Friar Antonio de Montesinos spoke out bravely for the protection of the Indians. This was the pro-Indian campaign that Las Casas took up so vigorously in his remonstrance to the Spanish crown and in his *True History of the Conquest*. The spirit of humanism also characterized Las Casas' *Apologetic History* and other historical works. Bernardino Sahagún's studies of the native culture of New Spain produced the richest single source of our knowledge of the religion, history, customs, and ideas of the native peoples of Mexico. In passing it may be noted that Luis Nicolau d'Oliver's study of Sahagún as a historian has thrown light on the attitude of the Inquisition toward such humanistic studies and toward Sahagún's theory and method.[18] In Brazil the Jesuit missionary Manoel da Nobrega expressed a similar humanist spirit.

After the Council of Trent (and especially during the days of Philip II in Spain), the increasing rigidity of Spanish and Portuguese intellectual life was reflected in the New World. But the seventeenth century was nevertheless the golden age of Spanish literature and art, and the growing Spanish intellectual rigidity did not prevent the appearance of some notable intellectual figures in the colonies. Among these was Juan de Cárdenas of the University of New Spain, whose *Problems and Secret Marvels of the Indies* (1591) combines the fantastic with scientific knowledge. Another outstanding seventeenth century intellectual was the astronomer-mathematician Carlos de Sigüenza y Góngora. The poetess Sor Juana Inés de la Cruz (1651–1695) wrote some of the most beautiful lyrics in Spanish literature on

18. Luis Nicolau d'Oliver, *Fray Bernardino de Sahagún (1499–1590)* (México: Instituto Panamericano de Geografía e Historia, 1952).

themes of both sacred and secular love. The University of San Marcos in Peru had the eminent scientist Pedro Peralta Barnuevo Rocha y Benavides. The lively book trade in colonial Spanish America, as we learn from the studies of Irving Leonard, is further evidence of a vigorous intellectual life there.[19]

THE ENLIGHTENMENT

The Enlightenment came to Spanish America in two fairly distinct currents. One of these currents, as Mariano Picón Salas of Venezuela and Enrique de Gandía of Argentina have made us aware, was that of the Jesuit scholars who shaped colonial social consciousness by spreading rational and humanist ideas through their schools and monasteries, which were the centers of intellectual life in many provincial towns in both Spanish America and Brazil. Some historians, for example, Bernabé Navarro of Mexico and Guillermo Furlong of Argentina, suggest that this Jesuit rationalism and humanism, because it expressed a populist and republican spirit in its sympathy for the growing criollo desire for political power, may have been one of the reasons for the eighteenth century expulsion of the Jesuits from the Spanish and Portuguese empires.[20]

John Tate Lanning has shown the extensive acceptance of Enlightenment thought, as exemplified in the Newtonian concept of the universe, in theses presented at the University of

19. See Irving Leonard, *Books of the Brave* (Cambridge, Mass.: Harvard University, 1949); and *Baroque Times in Old Mexico* (1959); as well as his numerous journal articles.

20. Magnus Mörner (ed.), *The Expulsion of the Jesuits from Latin America* (New York: Alfred A. Knopf, 1965); Guillermo Furlong, *Nacimiento y desarrollo de la filosofía en el Río de la Plata* (Buenos Aires: Guillermo Kraft, Ltd., 1952), 597; Bernabé Navarro, *Cultura mexicana moderna en el siglo xviii* (México: Universidad Nacional Autónoma Mexicana, 1964), 188; and Jean Sarrailh, *L'Espagne éclairée de la seconde moitié du xviii siècle* (Paris: Imp. Nacionale, 1954).

San Carlos de Guatemala. Guillermo Furlong has demonstrated the prevalence of Enlightenment ideas in Córdoba, Argentina, where the Franciscan José Elías de Carmen (b. 1760) was teaching a Cartesian philosophy and a Newtonian view of the universe, and has suggested its probable influence on the independence leader, Gregorio Funes. Writing in *The Americas,* Antonine Tibesar has described the circulation of Enlightenment ideas in Trujillo, Lima, and Arequipa, Peru — ideas that included the principles of Newtonian physics. Hernani Cidade's study of the Enlightenment in Portugal and E. Bradford Burns' research on the circulation of the works of European writers of the Enlightenment in Brazil show that the new ideas had spread widely there in the years prior to the uprising known as the *Inconfidencia.*[21]

In a recent excellent survey and summary of the Enlightenment in Latin America, Arthur P. Whitaker has criticized the persistent tendency of historians to consider Enlightenment thought only in relation to the ideologies of independence. He takes issue with the view expressed by Robin Humphreys and John Lynch in the introduction to their book of readings, *The Origins of the Latin-American Revolutions, 1808–1826* (New York: Alfred A. Knopf, 1965), which treats the Enlightenment largely as the ideological background of independence. The view of Professor Whitaker and John Tate Lanning, with which this author must agree, is that the Enlightenment in Latin

21. John Tate Lanning, *The Eighteenth Century Enlightenment in the University of San Carlos de Guatemala* (Ithaca, N.Y.: Cornell University Press, 1956), especially Chaps. 6 and 7; Guillermo Furlong, *Nacimiento de la filosofía,* Pt. II, Chap. 3, and Part III, Chaps. 1 and 3; Antonine Tibesar, "The Peruvian Church at the Time of Independence in the Light of Vatican II," *The Americas,* XXVI (April, 1970), 349–75; E. Bradford Burns, "The Enlightenment in Colonial Brazil," *Journal of the History of Ideas,* XXV (July–September, 1964), 430–38; Hernani A. Cidade, *Ensaio sobre a crise moral do século xviii* (Coimbra: Imprensa da Universidade, 1929).

America was a revolutionary cultural development significant in itself.[22]

The second current was that of direct contact with European scholars, either through their visits to America, as in the case of Alexander von Humboldt, or through studies abroad by Latin Americans. Three notable examples, among many others that could be cited of Latin Americans whose ideas were influenced by European study, are José Bonifacio de Andrada e Silva of Brazil, Simón Bolívar of Venezuela, and Bernardo O'Higgins of Chile.

If further proof is needed of the prevalence of Enlightenment ideas in the Spanish world in the eighteenth century, it is furnished in an interesting study by Marcelo Bitar Letayf entitled *Spanish Economists of the Eighteenth Century*. Bitar Letayf analyzes the concepts of political economy in the writings of some thirty Spanish writers and political figures, ranging from the Marqués de Villadarias of the early decades of the century to the Count of Floridablanca and José Canga Argüellos of the later decades. Almost universally, he finds them receptive to the new concepts of greater freedom in international trade.[23]

From whatever source they may have come, the ideas of the Enlightenment were discussed by Spanish and criollo scholars in Mexico City, Buenos Aires, Córdoba, Caracas, Bogotá, Lima, and in many provincial cities as well, with much the same freedom as in Europe. Perhaps the circulation of new ideas was more limited in the New World than in the Old, because the criollos and Spanish were so small a minority in most parts of

22. Arthur P. Whitaker, "Changing and Unchanging Interpretations of the Enlightenment in Spanish America," *Proceedings of the American Philosophical Society*, CXIV (August, 1970), 256–71. See also A. Owen Aldridge (ed.), *The Ibero-American Enlightenment* (Urbana: University of Illinois, 1971).

23. Marcelo Bitar Letayf, *Economistas españoles del siglo xviii* (Madrid: Ediciones Cultura Hispánica, 1968).

the colonial empire. Moreover, the minority status of the criollos may have made them less susceptible to the influence of the
new ideas that seemed to challenge the authority of the Church
and of the monarchy — the two essential bases of the criollo
domination.

The Age of Reason and the Independence Movements

The thought of the independence movement tends to be concerned largely with ideologies, but it is important to notice the theoretical basis of these ideologies. The leaders of independence drew their ideological orientation from a variety of sources, many but not all of which shared in some degree the basic Cartesian position that reason is the central reality of human existence (*Cogito ergo sum*). Thus, except for the concepts derived from Christian natural law, and to a degree even in these ideas, the basic appeal was to human reason in this Cartesian sense. Yet the Enlightenment did not provide just a single pattern of thought, but rather a rich and exciting variety. So far as this variety had a common denominator of reason, however, it was that intellectual leaders of independence saw the natural world through the eyes of Isaac Newton and the other scientists who followed in his footsteps. They looked for reason in religion, rather than superstition or authority, and for reason in law and politics, applying reason as a measurement of the legitimacy, justice, and effectiveness of society and government. Most of the intellectual leaders of independence assumed that the movements they directed were the reasonable actions of reasonable men, and argued with Condorcet that society tended to become progressively more rational. For them, and even for the Jesuit exponents of the ideas of Francisco Suárez, political independence was part of the process of perfecting man and society.

In a more immediate sense, it should be observed that the independence leaders derived their ideas from the thought of
the Enlightenment as it had entered such Spanish American
Universities as those of New Spain, Guatemala, and Chuquisaca,
as well as private libraries in the eighteenth century.[1] O. Carlos
Stoetzer, in a paper on "The Intellectual Background of Latin
American Independence" presented at the American Historical
Association meeting in Boston (1970), stressed the Spanish background of Spanish American independence thought, minimiz-
ing the importance of non-Spanish elements of the Enlightenment.

The influence of Enlightenment thought on the independence movements takes on a unique aspect, however, when it is
remembered that Latin American independence was the final
act of a drama of which the preceding acts had been played in
the United States and France earlier and by other actors. Hence
the thought that accompanied the independence movements
seems to be a reconsideration of what had been previously
thought. Even though the ideas of the leaders were basically
those which had excited the participants in the North American
and French Revolutions, these ideas appear prematurely skeptical when expressed by Latin American independence leaders
who have not gone through the initial stages of revolutionary
exuberance. What this occasionally pessimistic quality of the
independence thought shows chiefly is disillusion with Europe
and its culture. But it also shows that the Latin American lead-

1. See Whitaker, "Interpretations of the Enlightenment"; Aldridge, *The
Ibero-American Enlightenment*; Lanning, *The Enlightenment in the University
of San Carlos de Guatemala;* Enrique de Gandía, *Las ideas políticas en la Argentina* (Buenos Aires: Depalma, 1960), Vol. I of his *Historia de las ideas políticas en la Argentina* (5 vols.; Buenos Aires: Depalma, 1960–1968); and Guillermo
Furlong, *Nacimiento y desarrollo de la filosofía en el Río de la Plata, 1536–1810*
(Buenos Aires: Guillermo Kraft, 1952).

ers could not escape reflecting the momentous development of reactionary ideas in Europe and North America during the Napoleonic and Metternich eras.

Since the scientific and social thought of the Enlightenment began its assault on the traditional philosophy in the Spanish American universities during the eighteenth century, our consideration of the thought of independence may appropriately begin then. The studies by Lanning, noted in the previous chapter, have shown that the ideas of Cartesian and Lockian rationalism were widely accepted and discussed by students. Such scholars as the Portuguese Luis Antonio Verney (1713–1792), the Spanish priest Benito Gerónimo Feijóo, and the Peruvian Pedro Peralta Barnuevo had introduced discussion of Newton's law of universal gravitation, Etienne Bonnot Condillac's sensationalism, the natural moral philosophy of Nicolas de Malebranche, and even the pantheism of Baruch Spinoza.[2] Guillermo Furlong, as noted, has shown that prior to the expulsion of the Jesuits from the Spanish empire, they had created an atmosphere of rational inquiry in the University of Córdoba, Argentina. His studies have also shown that the thinking of the sixteenth century Jesuit theologian and writer on natural law Francisco Suárez had stimulated the writing of treatises in Córdoba which expressed the new natural law scientific and philosophical concepts. The role of Azeredo Coutinho in the Brazilian Enlightenment has been studied by E. Bradford Burns.[3]

The teaching of these ideas was at times prohibited by

2. John Tate Lanning, *Academic Culture in the Spanish Colonies* (London and New York: Oxford University Press, 1940), 61–89.

3. Guillermo Furlong, *Nacimiento de la filosofía*, 159–84. E. Bradford Burns, "The Role of Azeredo Coutinho in the Enlightenment in Brazil," *Hispanic American Historical Review*, XLIV (May, 1964), 154–60.

Church authorities, but they continued to be discussed in some respects; at least these ideas prepared Latin American leaders to accept the social and political thought of the Enlightenment — of Voltaire, Montesquieu, John Locke, Benjamin Franklin, Thomas Paine, Thomas Jefferson, and the Abbé Raynal, among others. Brazil had no university until after the arrival of the Portuguese Court, fleeing from Napoleon's armies, in 1807–1808. But the Jesuit and other *colegios* had helped modestly to spread the ideas of the Enlightenment there, and such Brazilian students as José Bonifacio de Andrada e Silva, the "Patriarch" of Brazilian independence, had encountered the thought of the Enlightenment in the Portuguese university of Coimbra. E. Bradford Burns, studying the contents of two private libraries of colonial Brazilians, has shown that they included works of Montesquieu, Diderot, Raynal, Beccaria, Mably, Adam Smith, Condorcet, and French, English, and United States histories. These latter included Robertson's *History of America*. They also included such works in science as the two volumes of Linnaeus's *Species Plantarum* (1764), the fifty-two volumes of Buffon's *Histoire Naturelle*, and Lavoissier's treatise on chemistry. The research of Burns, it may be said, emphasizes the influence of non-Iberian writers. The Brazilian historian João Cruz Costa[4] says that the 800-volume library of one prominent Brazilian priest-philosopher, Luis Vieira da Silva, in addition to theological works, contained works of Diderot, D'Alembert (the Encyclopedia), Voltaire, and Montesquieu, but also the *Disputations Metaphysical* of Silvestre Aranha and some of the works of the Spanish priest, Benito Feijóo.

How these ideas of the Enlightenment had reached the lead-

4. See Burns, "The Enlightenment in Colonial Brazil"; and João Cruz Costa, *Panorama of the History of Philosophy in Brazil* (Washington: Pan American Union, 1962), 25, 26.

ers of Haitian independence is somewhat less clear. But the ideas of Abbé Raynal were apparently known even to the relatively untutored Toussaint L'Ouverture. Agents of the French Revolutionary government must also have disseminated such ideas.

The traditional thought imbedded in Iberian religiosity was too deeply intrenched, of course, to be easily and completely replaced by the new science. Thus, many Guatemalan scholars insisted on qualifying Newton's law, and Guatemalan Thomists and Scotists still disputed as late as 1816, according to José Manuel Mestre. The Cuban philosopher Félix Varela y Morales found scholasticism still firmly intrenched in Cuba as late as the early years of the nineteenth century.[5] Charles Griffin, writing on the relationship of the Enlightenment to the independence movements, concluded that the political concepts of the French philosophers were received with considerable hostility in Latin America before independence, but became quite important once the movement began.[6]

It has generally been assumed that Rousseau was the major influence in shaping the thought of Latin American independence leaders. In the United States this theory was developed by Jefferson Rhea Spell in his classic work, *Rousseau in the Spanish World before 1833*.[7] Augusto Mijares, in his biography of the Liberator, has shown that Bolívar had a preference for the works of Rousseau, including the *Émile* and the *Social Contract*.[8] Among others, according to Guillermo Furlong, the

5. José Manuel Mestre, *De la filosofía en la Habana* (Habana: Ministerio de Educación, 1952; originally published 1851), 33–40.

6. Charles Griffin, "The Enlightenment and Latin American Independence," in A. P. Whitaker (ed.), *Latin America and the Enlightenment* (2nd ed.; Ithaca, N.Y.: Cornell University, 1961).

7. Jefferson Rhea Spell, *Rousseau in the Spanish World before 1833* (Austin: University of Texas, 1938).

8. Augusto Mijares, *El Libertador* (2nd ed.; Caracas: Arte, 1965), 101, *passim*.

Colombian historian Rubén Darío Restrepo insists Rousseau was the greatest influence on independence thought.[9] Enrique de Gandía has shown that Rousseau was read in Buenos Aires as early as 1793.[10]

Other scholars, both North American and Latin American, have called attention to Anglo-American influence, especially the influence of works on the British constitution, of *The Federalist,* of the writings of Thomas Paine, and of the state and federal constitutions of the United States. Ariosto D. González of Uruguay, Enrique de Gandía of Argentina, and Pedro Grases of Venezuela (and Spain) have shown that Manuel García de Sena's 1811 publication in Spanish, *La independencia de la Costa Firma justificada por Thomás Paine treinta años ha,* spread the Anglo-American political theory and knowledge of United States constitutions in the Spanish American world. Ariosto D. González has also written of the influence of Paine and the ideas expressed in *The Federalist* upon José Artigas of Uruguay and Mariano Moreno of Rio de la Plata. In recent decades a notable group of Venezuelan historians has studied various aspects of the history of Spanish American independence. Among them is Pedro Grases who has made particularly important contributions to an understanding of the intellectual background of the movement through his studies of Andrés Bello, German Roscio, Francisco Miranda, Simón Rodríguez, Simón Bolívar and others, including the later liberal Christian, Fermín Toro.[11]

9. See Guillermo Furlong and others, *Presencia y sugestión del filósofo Francisco Suárez y su influencia en la Revolución de Mayo* (Buenos Aires: Kraft, 1959), 76. Furlong cites Rubén Darío Restrepo, *Causas filosóficas y políticas de la independencia,* which the author has been unable to locate in Washington.

10. Enrique de Gandía, *Las ideas políticas en la Argentina,* 308–309.

11. See Ariosto D. González, *Las primeras fórmulas constitucionales en los paises del Plata (1810–1814)* (2nd ed.; Montevideo, Barreiro y Ramos, 1962).

Still others, such as Guillermo Furlong, and more recently O. Carlos Stoetzer, have pointed to the influence of the natural law writings of Francisco Vitoria and Francisco Suárez, including the latter's formulation of the social contract. However great or small the direct influence of this inherited Catholic tradition of natural law may have been, it certainly affected the meaning that Latin American leaders gave to the concepts imported from abroad. Enrique de Gandía insists that while some Latin Americans were attracted to the ideas of the social contract expressed by French, British, and North American writers, it may well have been because the Thomist tradition had already established the basic concepts in the Hispanic American mentality.[12] Thus, one may well ask, when Dean Gregorio Funes referred to the social contract in the Cathedral of Córdoba in 1790, was he referring explicitly to the idea in Rousseau's work, which he probably had not read but had certainly heard of? Or was he referring to the earlier, more familiar contract concept of Suárez based on the traditional Christian natural law? [13]

Pablo González Casanova of Mexico has shown us the strength of what he calls *Misoneismo* by pointing out how certain little-known writers of New Spain, influenced by traditional ideas,

See also Enrique de Gandía, *Las ideas políticas en la Argentina*, Chap. 24, for the influence of Manuel García de Sena in introducing the ideas of Thomas Paine and *The Federalist* in Rio de la Plata. For the wide-ranging intellectual work of Pedro Grases, see *La obra de Pedro Grases* (Caracas: Arte, 1969).

12. Enrique de Gandía, *Las ideas políticas de la independencia* (Buenos Aires: Depalma, 1968), 712, Vol. V of his *Historia de las ideas políticas en la Argentina*.

13. See Furlong, *Nacimiento de la filosofía*, 585–607; and Enrique de Gandía, *Las ideas políticas en la Argentina*, Chap. 24. See also Antonio Gómez Robledo, *El origen del poder político según Francisco Suárez* (México, 1948), and O. Carlos Stoetzer, *El pensamiento español durante el período de la emancipación (1789–1825); las bases hispánicas y las corrientes europeas* (Madrid: Instituto de Estudios Políticos, 1966).

opposed the introduction of such modern ideas as those of Fray
Benito Gerónimo Feijóo. An important body of traditionalist
thought in Spain gave intellectual support to this opposition, as
the Spanish scholar Francisco Puy has shown.[14]

By the time of Latin American independence, it is well to
remember, the currents of thought coming to America from
Europe already signaled in some respects the dawning nineteenth century romantic liberalism and utilitarianism. Insofar
as these new concepts of the nineteenth century expressed the
aspirations of a rising urban middle class, or constituted a
formative influence on them, they encountered a less-solid basis
in the economic interest groups of Latin America than in those
of Europe or Anglo-America. Latin America had almost no
middle class of the European and North American variety. In
the British colonial society of North America the interests of
fishing, trade, shipping, and industry occupied an important
place and supplied a kind of elite commercial power to the
independence movement there. Latin America had relatively
little of this kind of "middle-class" leadership.

Throughout Spanish and Portuguese America, the leaders of
independence were class-conscious, land-owning criollos (American born Europeans) who thought chiefly of liberating themselves from the "tyranny" of a decadent Spain by taking over
the power of the crown. This was true even of those who went
to Spain as representatives in the Cortes of Cádiz. They found
the rationale for this power revolution in natural law theories
of politics, economics, and social morality as expressed in the
writings of Condorcet, Locke, Montesquieu, the Physiocrats,
and Adam Smith; but this rationale modified, as we have seen,

14. Pablo González Casanova, *El misoneismo y la modernidad en el siglo xviii*
(México: El Colegio, de México, 1948), especially Chap. 3. For Spanish traditionalism, see Francisco Puy, *El pensamiento tradicional en la España del siglo xviii*.

the Hispanic natural law tradition. The ideas of Jeremy Bentham also had strong following.

The political economy of the independence leaders was that of the Physiocrats and Adam Smith, modified by Bentham, but their concept of the ideal society in America, as of the nature of power, also embraced traditional Spanish elements. Some of these Spanish elements were derived from studies that took place in colonial universities of the great code of Spanish colonial legislation, the Laws of the Indies. Another source was the "liberal" Spanish Constitution of 1812, a document that amalgamated Spanish tradition with the prevalent French liberalism. At times, as when Fray Servando Teresa de Mier gave a new and American version of the appearance of the Virgin of Guadalupe in his notable sermon of December 12, 1794, the leaders even sought more strictly American origins for colonial society and culture within the indigenous cultures of America. Mier argued that it was not the Spaniards who first brought Christianity to America, because Saint Thomas had Christianized the Mayas in the first century A.D.[15]

Even more significant than this role of Mier is the more widespread role of priests, especially criollos, who embraced and propagated liberal ideas. Francisco Hidalgo and José Morelos of Mexico are outstanding examples. But there were many others. Antonine Tibesar, for example, has written of the prevalence of liberal sympathies among Peruvian priests at the time of independence.[16]

Most of the independence leaders, like Francisco Miranda and Simón Bolívar of Venezuela and José Cecilio del Valle of

---

15. Fray Servando Teresa de Mier, *Memorias* (México: Porrúa, 1946), I, 5–98.
16. Antonine Tibesar, "The Peruvian Church at the Time of Independence in the light of Vatican II," *The Americas*, XXVI (April, 1970), 349–75.

Central America, sounded a note of conscious Americanism. But their Americanism included very little nationalism. Nationalism, particularly in Spanish America, developed later, in the course of the struggle for national stability after the tragic dissolution of the former Spanish empire. Leopoldo Zea has pointed out what he believes to be the awakening of criollo American consciousness in defending America against the charges by French naturalist Count Buffon (1707–1788) that the Americas produced inferior forms of life. This spirit, he says, animated such eighteenth century writing in Spanish America as the *History of Ancient Mexico* by the Mexican Francisco Clavijero, the *History of Chile* by the Chilean priest and botanist Juan Ignacio Molina, and the works of the Peruvian physician and independence leader José Hipólito Unanúe. Rather than nationalism, this spirit was a New World consciousness similar to that of Thomas Jefferson's *Notes on Virginia*.[17]

The optimism that often, but not always, characterized the thought of the independence leaders, their general belief in the natural goodness of men, and their commitment to a theory of a natural progress in human affairs, may be considered characteristic of this Americanism. But the gravity of the social and ethnic problems they faced occasionally led them to expressions of a deep pessimism, also of American origin. Moreover, even as they optimistically assumed that American leadership could solve their problems, their tendency to blame colonial difficulties on the Conquest and on Spanish (or Portuguese) misrule added another, a paradoxical, element to their pessimism. Thus, when Latin Americans accepted at face value, as they often did, eighteenth century Europe's criticism of the Iberian nations as

17. Leopoldo Zea, "Introducción," in Abelardo Villegas, *Antología del pensamiento social y político de América Latina* (Washington, D.C.: Unión Panamericana, 1964), 11.

retrograde, they were adding to their argument for independence an opinion that the very sources of their institutions and culture were decadent.

In applying their ideas of natural law — that a natural order of freedom in politics, economics, science, and morality would bring progress — independence leaders displayed sharp differences in their assessment of social and political realities. They differed even more as to the policies and measures that should be adopted and their most heated arguments concerned this latter question. But this debate over measures also revealed fundamental diversities in social and political outlook.

Many independence leaders, perhaps most, were monarchists who hoped the Spanish empire could be reconstructed as a group of closely linked but autonomous constitutional monarchies. Bishop Manuel Abad y Quiepo (1751–1825), who patronized the seminary in Valladolid, New Spain, that Miguel Hidalgo directed, was such a liberal monarchist; he died a prisoner of Ferdinand VII. José San Martín, the Argentine leader, preferred liberal monarchy to republicanism; he believed Spanish American leadership, unsupported by the forces of tradition represented in monarchy, would be unable to control popular violence and anarchy. As late as 1829, when San Martín was invited by emissaries of Juan Lavalle, then in control of Buenos Aires, to assume the governorship of the province, he rejected the offer, as he had earlier rejected a similar offer of the Federalists, on monarchist grounds. "My opinion is known," he said, "that the country will find neither quiet, freedom, nor prosperity, except under the monarchical form of government." [18]

18. Eduardo Trolé and Juan Andrés Gelly to Juan Lavalle, April 15, 1829, quoted in Carlos Ibarguren, *Juan Manuel Rosas* (Santiago, Chile: Empresa Letras, 1936), 153–54.

Monarchism was the position adopted by the masonic or similar lodges through which San Martín, Carlos de Alvear, and Bernardo O'Higgins worked in Argentina and Chile, José Bonifacio de Andrada and Pedro I in Brazil, and Agustín Iturbide in Mexico. Sergio Villalobos has shown that most of the leaders of independence in Chile were monarchists, at least during the early stages of the movement.[19] These monarchists, in addition to being masons, were the so-called Girondists of the early independence movements in Chile, Argentina, and elsewhere. Like the French Girondists, they were also advocates of liberal reform. Sometimes, but not always, they became federalists.

Republicans, at first a small minority among the leaders, gradually became the majority. Moved by the example of the United States, most of them believed that a federal republic was the form of government best adapted to the Latin American need for decentralizing the government and limiting the absolutism that characterized Spanish colonial administration. The leaders of the first Venezuelan republic incorporated federalism in the first Venezuelan constitution, as did José Morelos and his followers in the first constitution of Mexico, the constitution of Chilpancingo (1813). José Artigas and Mariano Moreno held similar federalist views.

Some of the early republican-federalists were conservative provincial criollo leaders who welcomed the freedom from Spanish control but at the same time feared the reforming tendencies of the more radical independence leaders, the so-called *exaltados*. Yet some of these radicals or *exaltados* were also federalists: Mariano Moreno and Bernardo Monteagudo of Argentina, the Carrera brothers and Ramón Freire of Chile,

19. Sergio Villalobos, *Tradición y reforma en 1810* (Santiago: Universidad de Chile, 1961), 115.

Miguel Hidalgo, José Morelos, and José Joaquín Fernández de Lizardi of Mexico, the priest José Matías Delgado of El Salvador, and Francisco Morazán of Honduras. It is paradoxical that so many of these *exaltados* were federalists, since to such a large extent federalism came to express the conservatism of local power groups and caudillos. It is a paradox that helps to explain many of the subsequent difficulties of Spanish American federalism.

SIMÓN BOLÍVAR (1783–1830)

Simón Bolívar is one of the most challenging, though in some respects a contradictory, representative of the thought of the independence period. His republicanism contrasts sharply with the monarchism of San Martín. But it also contrasts with the federalism of many of his republican contemporaries. Bolívar admired the British constitution and believed its principles could be reconciled with those of a presidential system. He was convinced, however, that Latin America was not prepared for the federal form of political organization. His skepticism concerning the capacity of the *castas* (the illiterate masses of Indians, mestizos, and Africans) to share in the government revealed his class-conscious "aristocratic" temperament. Yet he had confidence in the ability of the independence leaders to close ranks in an aristocracy of merit and virtue in order to create a stable and prosperous republic. In this respect his thought suggests that of Montesquieu, Burke, and Hobbes more than that of Rousseau, Paine, or Jefferson.

Bolívar brought independence to northern Spanish South America and was the founding father of five republics. After seven years of bitter frustration and defeat, he initiated the successful movement in 1817 that led the armies of Colombia and Venezuela in brilliant victories, wresting those two countries, as well as Ecuador and ultimately Peru and Bolivia, from Spanish control. After his death (1830) his influence continued in a generation of leaders who had been his lieutenants in the war for independence. Of all the independence leaders, he left the strongest impression in the minds of Spanish Americans, so that even in the twentieth century a kind of cult of *Bolivarismo* continues.

Born in Caracas, Venezuela, on July 24, 1783, Bolívar was the son of a wealthy marquis who owned copper and silver mines, cacao plantations, and many Negro slaves. While young Simón broke sharply with the older political interests of his family, he never completely escaped the influence of his class. Hence, as noted, his ideas often contain a tone of aristocratic *noblesse oblige*.

Bolívar displays little originality as a thinker except in the striking and often original way in which he applied ideas to practical situations, especially in the political realm. But this lack of originality in theory should not stand in the way of our seeing that his constitutional ideas and his concept of the role of Spanish America in the world have been central to the political dialogue in Latin America ever since his day. He showed an extraordinary grasp of the nature of the social revolution accompanying political independence and of its bearing upon the problem of creating new political institutions. This understanding appeared in various ways. It may be seen in his urging Negro emancipation, in his sense of the dangers involved in the sudden "liberation" of landless agricultural workers (*castas*), in his understanding the need for revolutionary changes in political institutions, and in his acceptance of impending change in the relationship of the Church to Spanish American society.

Because of this intuitive understanding of the revolution he led, he was troubled by the political difficulties he saw lying ahead. His amazing political intuition also explains his two principal proposals for achieving political stability: the lifetime presidency and a league of the Spanish American republics. In both he may well have been influenced, as has been suggested by Augusto Mijares, by the proposal made to William Pitt by Francisco Miranda in 1790 to create "one vast constitutional monarchy" in America, governed by an emperor descended from the Incas, with a Senate appointed by the Inca for life and a lower legislative house elected by popular suffrage.[20] Although Bolívar rejected the monarchism of Miranda and his contemporaries rejected the Bolivian proposal of a lifetime presidency, these ideas left an imprint upon such leaders as Andrés Santa Cruz of Bolivia, Juan José Flores of Ecuador, and José Antonio Páez of Venezuela, as their later actions show.

The twentieth century has brought a clearer realization of the extent to which Bolívar grasped the realities of his day and understood the political needs of the revolutionary movements that had emancipated the *castas,* freed the slaves and abolished most of the traditional guardianship of the Indians, and which required new political structures to provide the kind of stability formerly provided by Church and Crown. We now see that although his thought was mainly the product of the natural law utopianism of the Enlightenment, it was colored by the emerging romantic liberalism of the early nineteenth century and by an emphasis upon Americanism. He accepted the compact theory of the state, though whether it was the Rousseau concept or something more traditionally Spanish is not entirely clear, as

---

20. Ricardo Piccirilli, *San Martín y la política de los pueblos* (Buenos Aires: Gure S.R.L., 1957), 100–101. Augusto Mijares, *El Libertador* (2nd ed.; Caracas: Arte, 1965), 54ff., 147, and *passim,* brings out the close resemblance of Bolívar's thought to that of Miranda, as well as a certain socio-theological note in the concept "Brothers in Jesus Christ, equal before God."

Mijares suggests. In his address to the Congress at Angostura (1819) he called on the "representatives of the people" to confirm or to suppress "whatever may appear to you worthy of preservation, modification or rejection in our social compact." Society, he believed, was a product of liberated minds and wills, cemented together by good customs and by sentiments of honor, love, and loyalty.

Economics played a minor role in his thought as a whole — a major weakness. Such economic ideas as he expressed seem to have been phrased largely within French physiocratic concepts. But he had imbibed enough of the emerging British utilitarianism to think that the structure of the state must correspond to the economic interests of individuals and groups. Upon them, he believed, rested the responsibility for developing the essential morality and customs of all institutions. He was willing to agree with his colleague, Francisco de Paulo Santander, that this responsibility was best met by developing systems of laws as suggested by Jeremy Bentham.

Manuel Pérez Vilá has argued that the works of Montesquieu made the greatest intellectual appeal to Bolívar, while Rousseau appealed to his sensibility.[21] Lamentably, in his otherwise excellent *The Age of Democratic Revolution,* R. R. Palmer makes no significant reference to the ideas of Bolívar.[22] If Palmer had examined Bolívar's thought he might well have seen that Bolívar, like Montesquieu, saw in the British House of Lords the essential mediating power between monarchical authoritarianism and a demagogic House of Commons. Thus, his lifetime

21. Manuel Pérez Vilá, *La formación intelectual de Bolívar* (Caracas: Sociedad Bolivariana de Venezuela, 1964), 442–43. Cited in Augusto Mijares, *El Libertador,* 103.

22. R. R. Palmer, *The Age of the Democratic Revolution* (Princeton, N.J.: Princeton University Press, 1964).

presidency proposed for Bolivia, far from being conceived as an instrument of tyranny, was intended to be a unifying and stabilizing center of the nation. It was also conceived as an essential part of an aristocratic republic. What Bolívar appears not to have seen is that Latin America lacked the powerful middle-class commercial interests which in Britain, as Montesquieu saw, permitted an aristocracy to be a powerful mediator between them and the crown. Perhaps, also, he did not properly evaluate the "psychological" handicap under which an uncrowned monarch would operate.

In his last years Bolívar was accused of ambition to become another Napoleon. This view has recently been revived by Hal Draper, commenting on Karl Marx' article written on Bolívar for the *New American Encyclopedia.* Marx characterized Bolívar as an "aristocratic Bonaparte" and "a Napoleon of the Retreat," and many Marxist writers since then have echoed this judgment. As late as 1951, William Z. Foster repeated this view in his *Outline Political History of the Americas.* It is interesting to note, however, that recent Soviet historical scholarship rejects this view, arguing that Marx was too much influenced in his judgment by prejudiced sources, and presenting Bolívar as an "authoritarian liberal reformer." [23]

Historians will doubtless conclude that despite his lack of faith in Latin American readiness for democracy, Bolívar was true on the whole to his republican view that monarchy was not suitable to America, just as he remained consistent in his devotion to the abolition of Negro slavery. The proposal for an hereditary senate and a fourth, or moral, power of government

23. The Hal Draper comment appeared in "Marx and Bolívar: A Note on Authoritarian Leadership in a National Liberation Movement," *New Politics,* VII (Winter, 1968), 64–77. The Foster *Outline Political History of the Americas* was published in New York by International Publishers, 1951.

was based on reasoning similar to that of Montesquieu. "But what democratic government has simultaneously enjoyed power, prosperity, and permanence?" he asked in his address to the Congress of Angostura in 1819.[24] The obvious implication of this question is that the only successful governments are those in which a natural aristocracy mediates between the tendencies toward absolute executive power and demagogic anarchy.

Thus, it would be a mistake to attribute Bolívar's advocacy of the lifetime presidency or his anti-federalism to a philosophy of social reaction. Rather, it should be understood as a proposal to consolidate in the national structure all of those who had led and supported the revolutionary movement, whatever their political views, in support of reforms to deal with the ethnic and social problems of national life. It was this concern for unity that led Bolívar to urge a strong presidency in a limited democracy. He had been encouraged to renew the fight for independence by the support he received from the Haitian president Petion and to proclaim the abolition of slavery. In the lifetime presidency of Haiti he professed to see "the most democratic republic in the world," [25] the model for the presidency he proposed in the Bolivian constitution.[26]

24. Vicente Lecuna and Harold Bierck, *Selected Writings of Bolívar* (New York: Colonial Press, 1951), I, 178.

25. *Ibid.*, II, 599.

26. Bolívar's writings have been edited in twelve volumes, *Cartas del Libertador*, by Vicente Lecuna (Caracas and New York: 1929–1930, 1947, 1959). The two volumes of *Selected Writings of Bolívar* (Caracas and New York: Colonial Press, 1951) present the best of these writings, selected by Lecuna and translated and edited by Harold A. Bierck, Jr. Lecuna edited or wrote many other works on Bolívar, including his notable and controversial *La entrevista de Guayaquil* (Caracas: Ministerio de Educación, 1952). The biography by Augusto Mijares, previously cited (n. 20) is especially useful for its analysis of Bolívar's thought. But see also Daniel Guerra Iñíguez, *El pensamiento internacional de Bolívar* (Caracas: "Ragón," 1955). Among numerous biographies in English, the best is that of Gerhard Masur, *Simón Bolívar* (2nd ed.; Albuquerque, N.M.:

MARIANO MORENO

Mariano Moreno (1778–1811) had a tragically brief but brilliant political career. Commonly misunderstood, despite his clarity of literary style, he was one of the most revolutionary and clear-sighted spokesmen of the Argentine Revolution of May (1810), a movement notable among the Spanish American independence movements of that year, not only for its unique success, but also for the clarity of its economic and political ideas and objectives.

Moreno was a criollo from a good but not wealthy family of Buenos Aires. His legal education, acquired in the Caroline Academy of the University of Chuquisaca, in present-day Bolivia, prep:.ed him to play an important role in the 1810 revolution. Chuquisaca was the only real university in the viceroyalty, and the Caroline Academy had become a center for critical study of the Laws of the Indies. There he acquired the basic ideas of the natural law economic principles which dominated the rising political groups in France, Britain, and the United States; he earned degrees in both law and theology. His thesis presented to the Caroline Academy in 1802 was a critical study of the colonial forced labor systems of the *mita* and the *yanaconazco*. Practicing law in Buenos Aires, he sharpened these

---

University of New Mexico, 1969). But see also Víctor Andrés Belaúnde, *Bolívar and the Political Thought of the Spanish American Revolution* (2nd ed.; Baltimore: The Johns Hopkins University, 1966); Daniel A. Del Rio, *Simón Bolívar* (New York: The Bolivarian Society, 1965); Carlos E. Chardón, *Estudios sobre el Libertador Simón Bolívar* (Rio Piedras, Puerto Rico: Universidad de Puerto Rico, 1966); and Manuel Fraga Iribarne, "La evolución de las ideas de Bolívar sobre los poderes del estado y sus relaciones," *Revista de Estudios Políticos* (Madrid), Nos. 117–18 (May–August, 1961), 225–62. John J. Johnson with the collaboration of Doris M. Ladd, *Simón Bolívar and Spanish American Independence (1783–1830)* (Princeton, N.J.: W. Van Nostrand, 1968), is a good brief summary with selected readings.

ideas in frequent contacts with the older Manuel Belgrano, an
official of the Merchant's Guild and a major leader of the
Argentine movement.[27]

Extensive British trade, much of it contraband from Brazil,
had helped to create an atmosphere in the Plata area favorable
to freedom of thought, freedom of commerce, and the encouragement of agriculture. Moreno's first important work, a *Memoria,* reflected this atmosphere as he recounted the Argentine
defeat of the British expeditions of 1806–1807. His later
Representación de los labradores y los hacendados, a vigorous
plea for free trade, originally submitted as a legal brief to the
Viceroy, paved the way for the prominent role he soon played in
the stirring events of 1810–1811.

After the May, 1810, uprising, the liberal-aristocratic elite of
Buenos Aires, whose interests Moreno represented, attempted
at first to govern through a triumvirate. For a brief time,
Moreno was its secretary and moving spirit. This triumvirate
was soon overthrown, however, partly because its liberal political and economic views aroused opposition, partly because
Moreno objected to including provincial representatives in the
governing junta, and partly because of radical measures under-
taken to suppress a conspiracy against the revolutionary regime.
Sent to England on a political mission in 1811, Moreno died
aboard ship.

Ariosto D. González of Uruguay has brought to our attention
the writings of Moreno on political structure, and especially
his defense of federalism in the *Gaceta* of Buenos Aires, a journal which he founded and wrote for while secretary to the

27. Enrique de Gandía, *Las ideas políticas de los hombres de Mayo* (Buenos
Aires: Depalma, 1965), Chaps. 16 and 17, Vol. III of his *Historia de las ideas
políticas en la Argentina.*

Junta. But Moreno's influence on Argentine economic thought was at least equally great. His *Representación de los labradores y los hacendados* made him a pioneer in Latin America in this respect. It was an inspired application of the principles of Anglo-French political economy to the economic situation of Argentina, as seen through the eyes of the landowners of Buenos Aires province and the merchants of this rising and ambitious colonial center of commerce on La Plata. The freedom of commerce he advocated meant a loss of income to the viceregal government, but was in accord with the new ties of Buenos Aires commerce with British merchants.

Moreno's was the last of a series of petitions addressed to the Viceroy of La Plata during the years just before independence, at a time when the involvement of Spain in the French Revolutionary and Napoleonic wars had brought severe economic dislocation and disruption throughout the Spanish Empire. An earlier petition (1793) had asked only for the free importation of grain. Just prior to the Napoleonic invasion of Spain (1808), however, the British had invaded the Banda Oriental of Uruguay (1806–1807), with economic consequences which Moreno utilized effectively in his argument. By 1809, conditions in Buenos Aires made the time ripe for Moreno's broader proposal to open the port of Buenos Aires to free trade. Less than a year after the appearance of this *Representación de los labradores y los hacendados* trade was freed by viceregal decree from the restrictions and quotas with which it had been fettered in the past. Moreno had utilized every argumentative technique that he could muster, including reason, flattery, sarcasm, philosophy, irony, and satire. His plea to the viceroy was chiefly directed against the injustices done to the landowners and merchants of Buenos Aires and the "Vanda [sic] Oriental" (Uruguay). But it also aimed at rallying support from provincial landowners and clergy, giving it a broader revolutionary basis.[28]

MIGUEL HIDALGO Y COSTILLA (1753–1811) AND JOSÉ MARÍA MORELOS Y PAVÓN (1765–1815)

The two priests who were the major leaders of Mexican independence in its early and unsuccessful stage were much alike in their beliefs and ideas, though differing greatly in their background. Miguel Hidalgo came from a prosperous criollo family. The son of a plantation owner who had married the daughter of another criollo landowner, he received a good education, subsequently becoming a professor in the seminary in Valladolid, present-day Morelia in Michoacán. There, both as student and as teacher, like other young intellectuals of his day, he read and discussed the forbidden works of the Enlightenment. He might have continued to rise through clerical ranks

28. The full title of the legal brief is *Representación del "Apoderado de los Labradores y Hacendados de las Campañas de la Vanda Oriental y Occidental del Río de la Plata."* It appears in the two-volume collection of Moreno's works edited by Ricardo Levene, *Mariano Moreno: Escritos*, volumes VI and VII of the Biblioteca de Clásicos Argentinos (Buenos Aires: Estrada, 1943). An earlier collection was edited by Norberto Piñero, *Escritos políticos y económicos* (Buenos Aires: La Cultura Argentina, 1915). There is a still earlier edition (Buenos Aires: La Biblioteca del Ateneo, 1896). Ricardo Levene published a limited selection in *Pensamiento vivo de Mariano Moreno* (Buenos Aires: Losada, 1942). An excerpt from the *Representación de los labradores y los hacendados* in English translation will be found in Harold E. Davis, *Latin American Social Thought* (University Press of Washington, D.C., 1961 and subsequent editions). Biographical studies include Sergio Bagú, *Mariano Moreno* (Buenos Aires: Claridad, 1939), Guillermo F. Elordi, *Mariano Moreno, ciudadano ilustre* (Buenos Aires: La Facultad, 1938), and Ricardo Levene, *Ensayo histórico sobre la revolución de mayo y Mariano Moreno. Contribución al estudio de los aspectos político, jurídico y económico de la revolución de 1810* (2 vols.; Buenos Aires: Facultad de Derecho y Ciencias Sociales, 1920–1921). See also Eugene M. Wait, "Mariano Moreno: Promoter of Enlightenment," in *Hispanic American Historical Review*, XLV, (August, 1965), 359–83, and Harold F. Peterson, "Mariano Moreno: The Making of an Insurgent," *Hispanic American Historical Review*, XIV (May, 1934), 450–76.

in his association with this seminary if his increasing commitment to ideas considered radical at that time had not involved
him in difficulties with the Inquisition. He escaped severe
punishment, partly through the influence of his family, and
partly because these ideas were so widely accepted, even among
officials of the Inquisition. Instead, he was exiled to the remote
Indian village of Dolores, where as curate he promptly began to
promote a remarkable development of village economic life.
In 1810, he became the center of the independence movement.

José María Morelos, the child of poor parents, came out of a
more modest social background. His father was a carpenter, his
mother the daughter of a school teacher. Although José was
baptized as a legitimate child of pure Spanish descent, both parents were probably *casta* — of mixed Indian-(possibly Negro-)
white origin. As a boy he received the most meager education.
He learned to read and write, but from an early age was forced
to earn his living, first as a shepherd and then as a muleteer.
Hence it was as a mature man that he entered the seminary at
Valladolid to begin the elementary studies leading to prepara-
tion for the priesthood. After completing his studies, he was
assigned to serve a poor country parish, where Hidalgo's proc-
lamation of the movement for independence in September,
1810, found him. Morelos immediately joined Hidalgo, becoming his major lieutenant in Indian southern Mexico. After the
capture and execution of Hidalgo in 1811, Morelos continued
to lead the rebellion in southern Mexico until his defeat, capture, and execution in 1815.

In his ideas Morelos was a disciple of Hidalgo, and both were
creatures of the rational thought of the Enlightenment. Strictly
speaking, neither thought in terms of racial warfare, yet both
were spokesmen of the downtrodden Indians and Afro-Ameri-
cans and both Indian and African soldiers of dark skin pre-

dominated in Hidalgo's and Morelos's armies. Like the other
Spanish American leaders of 1810, Hidalgo professed loyalty to
monarchy, while directing opposition to the "gachupines" or
peninsular Spaniards. Morelos likewise was a monarchist until
after Ferdinand returned to the throne in Spain and rejected
the Constitution of 1812. Only then did Morelos accept the
principle of republicanism soon to be incorporated in the Constitution of Apatzingán (1814). At his trial, he said that this
constitution was influenced both by that of the United States
and by that of the liberal (monarchical) Spanish Constitution of
1812.[29] Both Hidalgo and Morelos advocated the abolition of
slavery and of all social distinctions based upon race. They
urged measures to improve the social and educational condition
of the Indians, agrarian reform, prison reform, measures to encourage the development of industries, and popular participation in government.

José Joaquín Fernández de Lizardi (1776–1827)

Fernández de Lizardi, the well-known author of the first Mexican novel, *El Periquillo Sarniento* (*The Itching Parrot*), is also
the author of a revolutionary series of pamphlets published in
1812–1814 entitled *El Pensador Mexicano* (*The Mexican
Thinker*). In social thought, as in literature, Lizardi expressed
a transition from the earlier natural law rationalism of the
American and French Revolutions to the newer romantic and
revolutionary liberalism which was taking shape in the Western
world as Latin America acquired independence. Thus, in many
ways he was a spokesman of the emerging Liberal parties and
the reformers among the dominant criollo class who triumphed

---

29. Ubaldo Vargas Martínez, *Morelos siervo de la nación* (México: Porrúa,
1966), 152.

politically in Mexican independence. The criollos were finding that their position was threatened, not only by the Spanish authority against which they were rebelling, but also by the unrest of the masses stirred by the Hidalgo uprising. This unrest might have been expected to decline after Hidalgo's defeat, but it increased instead. Thus the vitriolic attacks of the "Mexican thinker" upon the shibboleths of criollo society, published at this time, together with his proposals for social reform, had the special significance of stirring the criollos to an understanding of the popular discontent. His objective was to spread the doctrines of liberalism among the criollos, but his democratic thought, like that of Bolívar, had aristocratic overtones that often disclosed an attitude of *noblesse oblige* and expressed the prejudices and interests of his social class.

Later as a member and an ardent defender of the Masonic order, he was anticlerical. But his Scottish Rite (Grand Orient) anticlericalism was mild, if anything from his sharply critical pen may be described as mild.

On the whole, Lizardi was more vitriolic in language than radical in thought. Like many other independence leaders, he favored Mexican autonomy within the structure of Spanish monarchy, fearing the social revolutionary effects of a sudden transition to a republic. Thus, he supported Iturbide's plans for Mexican independence under the Plan of Iguala, with a European prince, until Iturbide made the fatal decision to play the role of an American Napoleon and had himself proclaimed emperor. In changing his attitude toward monarchism at that time, Lizardi gives us one of the most typical, one might almost say artless, expressions of the thought and prejudices of the class-conscious criollos of his day. Threatened on the one hand by what they believed to be blind and inefficient Spanish authoritarianism and on the other by their fear of native uprisings,

the liberals among them, in seeking a middle course, moved
from their earlier monarchism to republicanism under the
influence of liberal social thought with its overtones of the
dawning utopian socialism. Lizardi is significant for his expression of this change.

Lizardi's class consciousness may be seen in his *Conversations
of the Peasant and the Sacristan,* first published shortly after
Iturbide's overthrow in the midst of the constitutional discussions preceding the Constitution of 1824. It is a work full of
tongue-in-cheek humor and is sharply critical of the bigotry,
superstition, and authoritarianism characteristic of Mexican
society. Interspersed among his satirical comments, sometimes
in them, the author expresses a romantic-liberal and utopian
concept of the good society that relies upon the natural virtue
and goodness of man, believes in freedom of the will, and emphasizes moral education, the abolition of monopolies, and
the adoption of simple humanitarian and political reforms.
These included reforms of the penal, agrarian, and educational
systems as well as a system of rewards for civic virtue. The
influence of Bentham's utilitarianism appears at many places
in the work. But its major impact is that of social and economic
utopianism, as in suggestions for reform of the land system
and the establishment of agricultural colonies. Echoes of Lizardi's earlier monarchism also appear in this later work, linked
with numerous suggestions of his aristocratic distrust of popular
tendencies. All in all, Lizardi presents one of the best examples
of the persistent paradox of Latin American independence
thought, that of political and social reform filtering down from
the top, under the direction of a class-conscious elite.[30]

30. *El periquillo sarniento* is available in English as *The Itching Parrot* (New
York: Doubleday Doran and Co., 1942). The *Conversaciones del payo y el
sacristán* was published in two volumes of some 200 pages in Mexico by D. Ma-

José Cecilio del Valle (1780–1834)

José Cecilio del Valle was a prominent leader of independence in Central America, though also playing a role in Mexico. He is linked with Bernardino Rivadavia of Argentina and Francisco Santander of Colombia as one of a trio of Bentham's predilect disciples in America. Valle's letters to Bentham reveal much of his thought. They show his acceptance of the economic principles of free trade and free capitalism, as well as the utopianism which the union of eighteenth century rationalism and nineteenth century romanticism was beginning to produce in the Western world. They also show, in a broader sense, his acceptance of the social ethic underlying the evolving British political economy of his day.

By nature Valle was conservative, and his optimistic concept of progress was one of evolution rather than revolution. Like many other "liberals" of his day, he rejected the then emerging nineteenth century concept of "scientific" history insofar as it

---

riano Ontiveros, in 1824. As of 1970 the National University of Mexico had published four volumes of the *Obras completas*. Selections from the writings of Lizardi are available in the Biblioteca del Estudiante Universitario series, under the title *El Pensador Mexicano* (México: La Universidad Nacional Autónoma, 1940), with a critical study by Agustín Yáñez. Excerpts in English translation from the *Conversaciones del payo y el sacristán* are in Harold E. Davis, *Latin American Social Thought*, 39–55. *Don José Joaquín Fernández de Lizardi*, a biography by Luis González Obregón, was published by the Secretaría de Fomento in Mexico, in 1888 (Rev. ed.; México: Botas, 1938). Jefferson Rhea Spell published *The Life and Works of José Joaquín Fernández de Lizardi* (Philadelphia: University of Pennsylvania Press, 1931), and Paul Radin edited, as a W.P.A. project, a series of critical bibliographical studies: *An Annotated Bibliography of the Poems and Pamphlets of J. J. Fernández de Lizardi*, published in three parts, the first two in mimeograph by the California State Library in San Francisco (1940) and part three in the *Hispanic American Historical Review*, XXVI (May, 1946), 284–91. Paul Radin also edited, under the imprint of the Latin Branch of the California State Library, two volumes (mimeograph) of "Occasional Papers" relating to Lizardi, one in 1939, the other undated. A brief biography appears in Harold E. Davis, *Latin American Leaders* (New York: H. W. Wilson Co., 1949; reissued in 1968 by Cooper Square Publishers), 111–18.

seemed to imply a deterministic influence of the past. Rather, he asserted a firm belief in a view of history that was consistent with the free exercise of the human will. In an essay on "America" he expressed the anti-Spanish feeling of the criollo leaders and their insistence on breaking with the past. "America," he wrote, "will not march a century behind Europe." The most distinctive aspect of his Americanism, however, was his defense of the Indian. "The Indian and the ladino, who abandoned themselves to criminal pursuits," he said, "will in the future make the sacrifices which honor demands." In this discussion of the Indian and his rights, Valle also gave one of the earliest expressions to an American principle of international law — one that reflects the view of the sixteenth century Francisco Vitoria, however — that "force gives no right." He also gave early expression to the concept of American sovereignty in terms of international law and to the American principle of non-intervention. Like Bentham, Valle saw the role of the state chiefly as that of ensuring justice in accordance with the principle of "the greatest possible good to the greatest possible number." [31] It may be important to note at this point that Leopoldo Zea has characterized as "concubinage" (*contubernio*) the union of American conservatism and utilitarian reformism that Valle seems to express.[32]

Valle was born in Choluteca, Honduras, on November 22, 1780, and died in the city of Guatemala in 1834. The son of prosperous criollo parents, he was educated in the Tridentine College in Comayagua and in the University of San Carlos de Guatemala, where he graduated as a lawyer. There he absorbed the new scientific and philosophical thought of the Enlighten-

31. See English translation of this essay in Harold E. Davis, *Latin American Social Thought*, 81–92.
32. Leopoldo Zea, "Latinomérica en la formación de nuestro tiempo," *Sobretiro de Cuadernos Americanos* (Septiembre–Octubre, 1965), 11.

ment which, as we have seen, permeated the university.[33] He held several important political posts. In 1809 he was chosen a deputy to the Cortes called by the Supreme Central Junta of Spain, the revolutionary body established to oppose Napoleonic rule. Subsequently he was a professor in the university in Guatemala, giving lectures on political economy. In 1820 he began publishing a journal entitled *El Amigo de la Patria* (Friend of the Fatherland) to express his liberal views. When the Iturbide-Guerrero Plan of Iguala (1821) precipitated the independence of Mexico, Valle drafted the declaration of Central American independence, supporting the union of Central America with Mexico, and he was elected a deputy to the Mexican Congress. Within the Congress he opposed Iturbide after the latter was declared emperor, yet finally became a minister in the transitional cabinet in order to work out the arrangements for the emperor's abdication. When Central America thereupon resumed her independence, Valle became one of the triumvirate executive which ruled the new nation until a federal constitution was adopted and a president elected.

In 1822 he anticipated the Bolivarian proposal for a continental congress in a book with the picturesque title *Soñaba el Abad de San Pedro y yo también sé soñar*. In it he proposed a plan for an American (Hispanic) congress to meet in San José, Costa Rica, or León, Nicaragua. All the provinces of Spanish America were to be invited to send representatives to report on political, economic, fiscal and military conditions, to prepare a plan of continental defense, to form a federation, and to adopt an economic plan.[34] Twice he was defeated for the presidency of Central America, but he continued as a deputy in Congress.

33. See John Tate Lanning, *The Enlightenment in the University of San Carlos de Guatemala.*
34. José Salvador Guandique, *Proyecciones* (San Salvador: Ministerio de Cultura, 1957), 65.

During his last years, he was director of the *Sociedad Económica* (Economic Society), devoting himself to advancing the study and teaching of economics. These *Sociedades Económicas* had been established in most countries of Latin America at this time, or earlier in the eighteenth century, and became important centers for the dissemination of physiocratic, utilitarian, and laissez-faire political economy.[35]

A FINAL COMMENT

It may be said that independence thought, while displaying considerable variety, found a common denominator in the generally rationalistic pattern of the Enlightenment. A republican current was derived from the French and North American revolutions; but constitutional monarchism predominated, even in Haiti, in which independence was tied most closely to the French Revolution. Most Spanish American leaders were liberal, constitutional monarchists until it became clear that monarchy was not a realistic solution to the political problem, because Spain would not accept American independence, even in monarchical form. Monarchism predominated in the Masonic lodges through which much of the planning for independence went on.

35. The *Obras* of José Cecilio del Valle were published in 1914 in Tegucigalpa, Honduras, and in 1929–1930 in Guatemala (2 vols.; Tipografía Sánchez de Guise). The late Rafael Heliodoro Valle published a *Bibliografía de don José Cecilio del Valle* (México: Ediciones de Número, 1934) and edited a volume of selections entitled *Valle, Prólogo y Selección,* published by the Secretaría de Educación Pública (México, 1943). Ramón Rosa has written a *Biografía de don José Cecilio del Valle* (Tegucigalpa: Talleres Tipográficos, 1934), containing a critical bibliographical introduction. See also *José Cecilio del Valle and the Establishment of the Central American Confederation,* by Franklin Dallas Parker, published by the University of Honduras (in English) in 1954; also José Salvador Guandique, "José Cecilio del Valle, precursor de la sociología centroamericana," in his *Proyecciones,* 63–70. Brief selections from Valle's writings, in English translation, are included in Harold E. Davis, *Latin American Social Thought,* 80–94. On the economic societies, see Robert Jones Shafer, *The Economic Societies in the Spanish World (1763–1821)* (Syracuse University Press, 1958).

Even Bolívar began as a monarchist, though he ended as one of the clearest examples of republicanism. In Brazil, of course, monarchism was largely taken for granted, although republicanism was represented by an aggressive minority.

It is generally assumed that the mainstreams of thought in Spanish America came from British, French, and North American sources, including the federalism and presidentialism of the United States. But Spanish sources are also apparent, notably in the attention given, as in the Caroline Academy at Chuquisaca, to the legal precepts of the Laws of the Indies, but also in the continuing influence of the teachings of Vitoria and Suárez and the provisions of the Spanish Constitution of 1812.[36] Much of the importance of this Hispanic background, reinforced by the Enlightenment in Spanish and Portuguese America, lies in the fact that the exotic Anglo-American and French concepts were often reinterpreted within the framework of Hispanic legal and constitutional thought. More radical "leveling" tendencies appeared in some places, most notably in the Haitian slave insurrection, in the earlier uprising of Túpac Amaru in Peru (1780), and in the Hidalgo-Morelos movement in Mexico. But the liberalism of the criollo leaders of Hispanic America was generally expressed in less revolutionary terms.

The disillusionment and pessimism often encountered in independence leaders, and their rather obvious doubts as to their ability to control the social forces they were releasing, remind us that these leaders in Hispanic America were speaking, for the most part, in the days of Bonaparte, Talleyrand, and Metternich. Yet beneath this pessimism, and contrary to a view often

36. On the influence of the Constitution of 1812 see the Preface in Russell H. Fitzgibbon (ed.), *The Constitutions of the Americas* (Chicago: University of Chicago Press, 1948). Also Arnold R. Verduin, *Manual of Spanish Constitutions, 1808–1931* (Ypsilanti, Michigan: University Printers, 1941).

expressed by historians, lay concepts of profound social and economic change. Even loyalists, it may be added, seem to have adopted the ideas of the British and French political economy of free capitalism. Some independence leaders advocated agrarian reforms having an obvious source in French physiocratic thought. The *exaltados* advocated abolition of slavery as well as repeal of all the special laws which made wards of the Indians.

Their most radical proposals, however, were to reduce the wealth of the Church and its role in society. Thus Lizardi urged that the clergy should be required to teach that true liberty arises from civil society. Liberal leaders in Chile, after overthrowing the provisional regime of Bernardo O'Higgins, proceeded to seize the wealth of the clergy and to banish the Bishop of Santiago. In general, the liberals among the independence leaders worked to reduce the role of the Church in social life by putting its wealth into private hands, taking away its monopoly of education, and eliminating its legal control of the family. Some were religious freethinkers, and even an occasional note of atheism is to be heard. But by and large, independence leaders asserted that they were Christians, even while urging quite fundamental changes in the place of the Church in their societies — objectives that almost invariably led to political reverses.

In general, as we have seen, the thought of Latin American independence served as a passage between the rationalism of the Enlightenment and that of the "time of troubles" that followed independence. The appearance during this period of some of the concepts of romantic liberalism, ideologism, utilitarianism, historicism, utopian socialism, and traditionalism that came to fruition later is important to note in understanding this transitional aspect of independence thought.

Revolutionary Liberalism, Utilitarianism, and Traditionalism

Although the thought of the three decades or so following independence shows no abrupt change and is best understood indeed, as an outgrowth of the previous period, new ideas continued to come from Europe, and new intellectual influences arose in Latin America in connection with the conflicts and uncertainties of the post-independence years. Among these intellectual influences were the new "scientific" history, the historical philosophy of law, utilitarian ethics and social philosophy, romantic liberalism in literature and political thought, including utopian socialism, the new emphasis on sensualism in philosophy, and especially the eclectic philosophy of Victor Cousin (1792–1867). Politically, these years were a "time of troubles" in Latin America, with social and political difficulties arising from a variety of sources. But they derived in large measure from the common challenge of forming new political structures under such difficulties as that of a depressed mining industry, drastic dislocations in international trade, and recurring financial crises in the new governments. These problems tempered the trends inspired by European movements and ideas in the New World with a more American character than in the preceding years.

Important American nuances in the thought of the period also arose from the fact that romantic liberalism, utilitarianism, utopian socialism, and the historical view of law — even

63

the Cousin philosophical eclecticism — generally expressed social attitudes and prejudices of the criollo landowners. More
than during the independence years, such class-conscious attitudes seemed to color the thought of Latin Americans of the
oligarchic ruling class. A professional and commercial urban
class, emerging more slowly in Latin American cities than in
those of more highly urbanized Europe, seems to have been
influenced by these European trends still more than the landowners.

FIVE STREAMS OF EUROPEAN INFLUENCE

Five streams of European influence during these years may be
distinguished. The first is that of British political economy, es-
pecially the utilitarianism of Jeremy Bentham and James Mill.
Utilitarianism had a profound influence upon the Venezuelan-
Chilean Andrés Bello during his long stay in London, and upon
José María Luis Mora of Mexico, Juan Bautista Alberdi of
Argentina, José Cecilio del Valle of Central America, Francisco
de Paula Santander, and many others. Bentham's theories were
taught as early as 1821 in the university founded in Buenos
Aires by Bernardino Rivadavia.[1]

The French utopian socialism of Count Henri de Saint-Simon, François M. C. Fourier, and their followers, was a second
and, if anything, a more significant stream of influence. It found
Spanish American expression, for example, in the Argentine Association of May and in Esteban Echeverría's *Dogma socialista,*
the creed of the Association. Among many others who could be
mentioned as revealing this influence is Francisco Bilbao of
Chile. The *Revue encyclopédique* and *La globe,* both of which

1. Rafael Heliodoro Valle, *Valle, Prólogo y Selección* (México: Secretaría de
Educación Pública, 1943), xxxiii–xli.

diffused the ideas of Saint-Simonism, were widely read through-out America, especially in Chile, Argentina, and Uruguay.

Both Bilbao and Echeverría also reflect the ideas of the liberal French priest, Félicité Robert de Lamennais (1782–1854), indi-cating a link between utopian socialism and other romantic-liberal trends in thought. This romantic liberalism so often characterized revolutionary Liberal movements that it may well be called a third trend, although it embraces elements of most of the others. Bilbao and his circle of young Liberal friends in Chile also took up the literary and political thought of the Romantic French poet, Alphonse Lamartine. Under this influ-ence they called themselves *Los Girondinos,* adopting the names of the leaders of the *Gironde* as pen names.

A fourth stream of influence is that of Victor Cousin's eclec-ticism, and of Count Destutt de Tracy's "ideology," a French school of thought which combined idealistic and "scientific" philosophies of history. Eclecticism helped to introduce the ideas of German idealism and the Jansenism of Blaise Pascal (1623–1662). In Cuba its effect may be seen in the lectures on philosophy delivered there by José Manuel Mestre y Domínguez in 1861.[2] Guillermo Francovich and others have noted the spread of Cousin's ideas in Brazil.[3]

Latin American literary production of all kinds, in its gen-erally romantic tendency during these years, embraced the last two trends of thought. On occasion this Latin American roman-tic idealism also exhibited some of the traditionalist expressions of French literary romanticism. This literary romanticism re-minds us that romantic idealism embraced a wide range of

2. José Manuel Mestre y Domínguez, *Estudio preliminar, notas por Humberto Pinera Llera, De la filosofía en la Habana* (La Habana: Ministro de Educación, 1952).

3. Guillermo Francovich, *Filósofos brasileños* (Buenos Aires: Losada, 1943).

social principles and ideologies, ranging from those of Liberal reformist tendencies to those of the French traditionalism of Joseph de Maistre and the Spanish traditionalism of Jaime L. Balmes. In this latter form, as we have seen, it was sometimes brought to America by traditionalist priests fleeing from revolutionary regimes in Spain or Portugal.[4]

This traditionalism is a fifth major stream of influence. A number of Latin American leaders, such as Lucas Alamán of Mexico, Dr. Francia of Paraguay, Juan Manuel Rosas of Argentina, Diego Portales of Chile, and Bernardo Pereira de Vasconcellos of Brazil, expressed varieties of traditionalist thought that had antecedents, if not an actual source, in de Maistre, Balmes, or Juan Donoso Cortes (1809–1853). To many students the thinking of these American traditionalists has seemed merely a reflection of the European conservatism of the Metternich Era. But it is much more. These American traditionalists certainly shared with their European counterparts an opposition to the romantic-liberal-socialist revolutionary movement of the day. Yet, upon closer examination, they also reveal close ties with American experience, as Juan B. Alberdi of Argentina pointed out to his generation in his *Fragmento preliminar al estudio del derecho*,[5] when it was presented originally to his youthful colleagues in the Argentine Association of May. Moreover, as we shall see, the traditionalism of these Americans significantly lacked the European element of defending the old social order presided over by a nobility; and it often differed from that of Europe in assimilating the principles of the Liberal political economy.

4. Antonine Tibesar, "The Peruvian Church at the Time of Independence in the Light of Vatican II," *The Americas*, XXVI (April, 1970), 349–75.

5. Juan B. Alberdi, *Fragmento preliminar al estudio del derecho* (2nd ed.; Buenos Aires: Librería Hachette, 1955).

PREDOMINANCE OF UTILITARIANISM AND LIBERALISM

The combination of romantic revolutionary idealism and utilitarianism produced a heady mixture for Latin American Liberal intellectuals of the political elite from which most of them came. These revolutionary philosophies emphasized the importance of individual liberty in a free society and assumed that free individuals would be moved by ideals of virtue, honor, and patriotism to seek glory and the respect of their fellow men. Such an essentially romantic theory had special appeal within the Iberian culture because of its tradition of honor and chivalry. The ethics, political economy, and philosophy of law of the utilitarian made him judge action, both individual and social, on the basis of its social usefulness and assume that society should always seek the greatest good of the greatest number. The generation of youth emerging within the dominant elite at the time of independence saw a combination of these two systems of ideas — romantic idealism and utilitarianism — a revolutionary and nationalist ideology through which they could achieve the most complete realization of themselves. They also viewed this possibility of self-realization as one linked with the opportunity of creating a society in which all individuals would have freedom to develop their capabilities and realize their own destinies.

Several factors in the American hemisphere environment of this era led these young Latin Americans to combine utilitarian concepts with varieties of idealist or romantic and revolutionary Liberalism. One factor was the success of the republican experiment in the United States, a success which Latin Americans tended to see as an expression of such a combination of ideas. A second factor was an abundance of undeveloped land and resources in Latin America that called for policies to encourage the immigration of workers and capital from Europe. A free trade (utilitarian) policy was the natural corollary of any such encouragement. This belief in a policy of freedom of international trade was a heritage from the independence movements, in which it had been almost as fundamental a doctrine as that of the self-determination of peoples. But it now achieved a new prominence in the thought of Latin American Liberals.

Two other elements in the ideological heritage from the independence movements supported this blend of utilitarianism and revolutionary Liberalism. One was the political concept of federalism, a theory which, like that of the republican experiment, enjoyed prestige because of its success in the United States. In Latin America, however, federalism was interpreted to mean the decentralization of political and economic authority, rather than the creation of new central (federal) powers. Anticlericalism was also inherited from the independence movements. A product of the rationalism and skepticism of the Enlightenment, with overtones acquired from the French Revolution, this anticlericalism had American (anti-Spanish) sources; but it was also in some respects a counterpart or part of the contemporary Spanish and Portuguese Liberal anticlericalism. It also had links with the French Liberal Catholic thought of Felicité de Lamennais.

THE PROBLEM OF HISTORY

One of the most notable aspects of the Latin American thought of this period was a concept of history expressed in its spirit of American rebellion against the authority of Europe. The anti-Spanish movement (*desespañolización*), one of the striking aspects of the period, was not merely a political phenomenon. It also embraced profound cultural and philosophical trends. Thus, Andrés Bello (1780–1865), in inaugurating the University of Chile in 1842, called for a national educational program and a culture which would be American and Chilean in every aspect. Another Chilean, José Victorino Lastarria, speaking in language like that of Channing and Emerson in the United States at this time, called for American literary independence. Juan B. Alberdi (1810–1884) of Argentina, explaining the constitutional problem of his country upon the basis of such American realities as the caudillo, proposed to eliminate "all which is least contemporary and least applicable to the social needs of our countries, the means of satisfying which should furnish us with the materials of our philosophy." [6] The other members of this Argentine "Generation of 1837," including Bartolomé Mitre, Domingo F. Sarmiento, and Esteban Echeverría, spoke in similar terms.

One new element of European thought that was often rejected by this generation was the tendency to historical determinism they saw in the scientific philosophy of history. The theory of a "science" of history was one of the major intellectual currents of the nineteenth century, one which Latin American thinkers could not avoid. But they could and did express different and sometimes contradictory positions on the possibility and meaning of such a "scientific" history. José Luz y Caballero (1810–1862) of Cuba, while accepting much of the eclecticism of Victor Cousin, attacked Cousin's Hegelian idea that history had an inevitable or determined evolutionary form. Such historical determinism, argued Luz y Caballero, would make it intellectually impossible to think of a genuine revolutionary movement for Cuban independence. Yet his contemporary, Lucas Alamán,

6. Juan B. Alberdi, *Ideas para presidir a la confección del curso de filosofía contemporánea en el Colegio de Humanidades* (Montevideo, 1849), quoted in Leopoldo Zea, *Dos etapas del pensamiento en Hispanoamérica* (México: El Colegio de México, 1949), 138.

the Mexican historian and organizer of the Mexican Conservative party, would have disagreed. For while Alamán accepted much of the Liberal thought, and particularly its political economy, he wrote his history of Mexican independence on the premise that independence was a mistake because of its rejection of traditional colonial institutions.

In his *Dos etapas del pensamiento en Hispanoamérica* Leopoldo Zea has pointed out the paradoxical character of the Liberals' adoption of this new scientific historicism as it applied to law and institutions. Even while they were explaining their own reality historically, writes Zea, they were rejecting the Spanish (and Portuguese) historical past which they were determined to destroy. Thus, he says, the Latin American engaged in "a difficult, practically impossible task: that of tearing out or amputating a very important part of his being." [7] Most other scholars may well agree with him to the extent that Liberals used the argument of the survival of the past ("the dead hand of the past") to reinforce their demands for its destruction, and that some even went so far as to claim that the movement for independence was not really revolutionary — that it had not really been animated by liberty but by Spanish traditionalism. Zea has subsequently made this theory even more explicit, in terms that suggest the historical theory of José Ortega y Gasset that "the past represented what was not liked and the future that which can not be [achieved] by means of that which is not liked." Most scholars would doubtless agree with Zea that the real revolution, as these Liberals were saying, was still to be accomplished and could not be built upon the past.

Whether or not we agree with Zea's interpretation, we must see that the new generation of emancipators after 1825, with

7. Leopoldo Zea, *Dos etapas del pensamiento*, 19–23.

the courage and zeal of Spaniards, undertook to extirpate the Spanish past, including its close association with the Church, and to "make a new history." We must also see that they soon discovered that the past is not so easily disposed of. Political parties took different names, new philosophies appeared, yet the past still remained alive. The romantic liberals might deny this Hispanic past, but they were unable to escape it, as Zea rightly points out, because they had not accepted it by actually experiencing it as history.[8]

THE ARGENTINE GENERATION OF 1837

The most distinctively American thought of this period came in the "Generation of 1837" in Argentina and in the "Generation of 1842" in Chile. In Argentina the dictatorship of Juan Manuel Rosas, extending roughly from 1829 to 1852, resulted from a victory of the Conservative and Federalist hacendados of Buenos Aires province over the reforming Unitarists. In Chile, the contemporary triumph of the Conservative party under Diego Portales was the triumph of an oligarchy of landowners and merchants that continued to dominate Chilean politics for over three decades. In both countries, the leaders of thought who emerged in the middle years of the century were Liberals nurtured in the opposition to these regimes.

Esteban Echeverría and the young men of his generation in Argentina had believed at first that they could give intellectual guidance to the Rosas dictatorship. They were quickly disillusioned, however, and in the travail of exile lost much of the basis for their previous optimism — their unconscious loyalty to the landowning families from which they came. This break with the past contributed an element of rebellion to their de-

8. *Ibid.*

veloping spirit of romantic Liberal nationalism. In Chile the nationalist note of this Liberal party was equally strong, even in the more socialistic Bilbao.

The authors that influenced the thinking of these young men as they read in the National Library founded by Mariano Moreno in 1810, or gathered in such literary salons as the bookshop of Marcos Sastre, were many and varied. Vicente Fidel López (1815–1903), in his *Autobiography*, mentions the following among such authors: Victor Cousin, Francisco Renato de Chateaubriand, Alejandro Dumas *(Père)*, Edgar Quinet, Count Henri Saint-Simon, François Guizot, Pierre Leroux, Claudio F. Jouffroy, Walter Scott, Madame de Staël, George Sand, François Villemain, Lord Byron, Désiré Nisard, Félicité Lamennais, Victor Hugo, and Alexis de Tocqueville. The young man read such periodicals as *Revue de Paris, Revue Britannique, Revue Encyclopédique, Revue des Deux Mondes,* and *The Edinburgh Review.*[9]

Esteban Echeverría (1805–1851) was a romantic poet, a utopian socialist, an intellectual leader of the Argentine Generation of 1837, and the major founder of the Association of May that became the center of opposition to the dictatorship of Rosas. Born in Buenos Aires in 1805, he died at the age of forty-six, an exile in Montevideo. The Argentine dictator who had been the major target of Echeverría's writing was overthrown a year after Echeverría's death.

In France, where Echeverría completed his education, he came under the influence of the romantic movement in literature, reading the works of such authors as Goethe, Schiller,

9. Vicente Fidel López, *Autobiography,* cited by Felix Weinberg in *El Salón Literario de 1837* (Buenos Aires: Hachette, 1958).

Byron, and Lamartine. He also absorbed the socialist ideology of Saint-Simon. From the *New Science* of Giovanni Battista Vico, he seemed to derive the concept of society that led him to describe the May Revolution of 1810 as an historical process of which the essence was certain ideals — ideals that were, essentially, those he set forth in his *Dogma Socialista*. Another and perhaps greater intellectual influence upon his formation, as it appears in his writings, was the nationalism of Mazzini's *Young Europe*. The Association of May, which Echeverría organized in opposition to Rosas, brought together a group of young intellectuals, often spoken of as the Generation of 1837. These youths were dedicated to the principles of freedom that had been expressed in the May, 1810, revolution. In their philosophy of romantic idealism they bear some resemblance to the New England Transcendentalists.

Echeverría's social and political liberalism had an obviously romantic cast, the product of his literary romanticism. Probably because of his literary inclination, he showed less interest in economics than his brilliant young colleague in the Association of May, Juan B. Alberdi. Echeverría believed that the chief purpose of society was to provide the greatest individual freedom, and he thought society was an association bound together by such social sentiments and feelings as love and honor. In this, and other respects of his thought, we may see that he was influenced by the innate aristocratic and chivalric sense of *noblesse oblige* noted in other leaders of his day.

Echeverría combined with his literary romanticism the rationalism of the eighteenth century Enlightenment. Thus he argued against the adoption of Saint-Simon's socialism on the grounds that Argentines were not yet prepared for it. And although he urged the equality of classes, he rejected universal

suffrage. He argued that it was not the people but their reason
that was sovereign. This quality of rational intelligence, he believed, was found only in those who were educated and owned
property. Similar rationalist considerations led him to oppose
unlimited freedom of the press. On the other hand, and unlike
many of his anticlerical contemporaries, he considered religion
an incentive to morality and thought of Christianity as essentially civilizing and progressive.

The major significance of Echeverría, of course, is that his
Dogma Socialista (Socialist Creed) became the revolutionary
platform of the Association of May.[10] But, as the theory of Argentine republicanism and democracy, it also became in some
respects the ideology of an entire age of Latin American democratic Liberalism.

Juan Bautista Alberdi (1810–1884) was born in Tucumán in
1810, the son of one of the early proponents of Argentine independence, and was educated largely in Buenos Aires. He was
already a well-known figure among Buenos Aires young intellectuals and in musical circles (as a pianist and composer of waltzes
and minuets) when he attracted attention in 1837 by the brilliant theory of law and politics expressed in his *Fragmento*

10. The *Obras completas* of Echeverría were published in five volumes
(Buenos Aires: C. Casaralle, 1871–1874). Editions of the *Dogma Socialista* have
been published by Alberto Palcos (La Plata, 1940) and by Salvador M. Dana
Montaño (Buenos Aires: Estrada, 1948). Bibliographical and critical studies of
Echeverría are numerous: Rómulo Bogliolo, *Las ideas democráticas y socialistas
de Esteban Echeverría* (3rd ed.; Buenos Aires: La Vanguardia, 1937); An-
tonio J. Bucich, *Esteban Echeverría y su tiempo, y saintsimonismo* (Córdoba:
Rossi, 1934); and Alberto Palcos, *Echeverría y la democracia argentina* (Buenos
Aires: El Ateneo, 1941). William Rex Crawford included a good brief sketch in
English in *A Century of Latin American Thought*, 12–18. Other studies include
Oreste Popescu, *El pensamiento social y económico de Esteban Echeverría*
(Buenos Aires: Americana, 1954) and Pablo Rojas Paz, *Echeverría* (Buenos Aires:
Raigal, 1953).

preliminar al estudio del derecho.[11] As a member of the Association of May, Alberdi subscribed to the views expressed in Echeverría's *Dogma Socialista*. But, as the years went by, his views became more realistic than those of the more romantic leader. By the time Alberdi wrote his *Bases y puntos de partida para la organización política de la República Argentina,* when Rosas was being overthrown in 1852, he had rejected some of the utopian ideas of Echeverría's *Dogma Socialista*. Thus, for example, his historical philosophy of law and politics had led him to accept the reality of the caudillo system in the provinces as the basis of Argentine federalism — a major step away from the idealism of Echeverría and other colleagues of the Association of May.

Alberdi was both a natural realist, in the Scottish philosophical sense, and a Comtian positivist. But he may be better understood as an Americanist, for the realism that was his outstanding characteristic was based on his understanding of the effects of American experience upon law and institutions.[12]

11. Juan Bautista Alberdi, *Fragmento preliminar al estudio del derecho,* "Introducción" by Bernardo Canal Feijóo (Buenos Aires: Librería Hachette, 1955). The first edition was published in Buenos Aires by Imprenta de la Libertad in 1837.

12. Alberdi's works are published in *Obras Completas* (8 vols.; Buenos Aires: Nacional La Tribuna, 1886–1887), *Escritos póstumos* (16 vols.; Buenos Aires: Imprenta Europa, 1895–1901), and *Obras selectas* (18 vols.; Buenos Aires: Librería de la Facultad, J. Roldán, 1920). The famous *Bases* is available in numerous editions, including that of L. J. Rosso, 1933. Alberdi's *Autobiografía* was published with a prologue by Jean Saures (Buenos Aires: El Ateneo, 1927). Among the studies of Alberdi are the following: Miguel Angel Carocano, *Alberdi, su doctrina económica* (Buenos Aires: Roldán, 1934); Harold E. Davis, *Juan Bautista Alberdi* (Gainesville: University of Florida, 1958); Martin García Mérou, *Alberdi, ensayo crítico* (Buenos Aires: Rossi, 1937); Pablo Rojas Paz, *Alberdi, el ciudadano de la soledad* (Buenos Aires: Losada, 1941), and Luis Alberto Murray, *Pro y contra de Alberdi* (Buenos Aires: Coyoacán, 1960). Guillermo A. Lousteau Heguy and Salvador María Lozada, in Volume VI of their series, *El pensamiento político hispanoamericano,* devoted to Alberdi and Sarmiento, have included the *Bases y puntos de partida* and the *Constitución de la*

Domingo F. Sarmiento (1811–1888) was a man of extraordinary talent and of many professions. He was a journalist, a sociologist, a school teacher, a soldier, a diplomat, a state governor, and the president of his country. The difficulties he encountered in securing an education in the midst of poverty doubtless motivated the later successful battle for the public education of his nation, that won him the sobriquet, "the school teacher president." With the slogan "to govern is to educate," he made of the fight to free men's minds his basic strategy to achieve in Argentina the larger objectives of economic, social, and political freedom and, on the basis of these freedoms, the economic and cultural progress toward which they looked. His pugnacious spirit, frustrated during long years of exile, found expression in an explosive, vitriolic style of writing. It was a literary style implicit in the activist posture of his generation, a generation which insisted that the written and spoken word should lead to action. Thus, in a letter written in 1862, shortly after his election as governor of San Juan, Sarmiento wrote, ". . . in three years of government I will show them the fists that God has given me. You will see if I do not do what I say." [13]

Sarmiento was born in San Juan, in western Argentina, February 14, 1811. His father had been a soldier with General San Martín, and his mother came from a family that had long played a prominent role in the religious, political, and economic life of the province. As a boy, he studied in the local school and with a

---

Confederación Argentina (Buenos Aires: Depalma, 1964). For brief sketches in English see William Rex Crawford, *A Century of Latin American Thought*, 18–37, and Harold E. Davis, *Makers of Democracy in Latin America* (New York: H. W. Wilson, 1945; reissued by Cooper Square Publishers, Inc. in 1968), 49–51, and "Juan Bautista Alberdi, Americanist," *Journal of Inter-American Studies*, IV (January, 1962), 53–65.

13. Domingo F. Sarmiento to Posse, San Juan, March 24, 1862, in Archivos del Museo Histórico Sarmiento, quoted in Allison W. Bunkley, *The Life of Sarmiento* (Princeton: Princeton University Press, 1952), 396.

maternal uncle who was a priest. In 1823 he applied for a scholarship, offered by the Rivadavia government for study in the newly established university in Buenos Aires; but local politics seems to have prevented his winning the award, one that would have given him direct personal acquaintance with the other young men of the then emerging "Generation of 1837." In 1831 his writing and teaching, directed against the political system introduced by Rosas, resulted in threats of punishment which forced him to spend most of the next twenty-two years in exile. During most of this time of exile he lived in Chile, although he also spent part of the time in Uruguay and also traveled in Europe and the United States. A meeting with the Horace Manns in the United States at this time had a lasting effect on his educational ideas. In Chile he achieved fame as a journalist and teacher, founded a national normal school, and in 1845 wrote his classic work *Civilization and Barbarism, The Life of Juan Facundo Quiroga.*

Facundo was a devastating criticism of the caudillo and "caudillismo." Basically it was a sociological study which described Facundo Quiroga as a product of barbaric influences derived from the *pampa* and expressed in gaucho life. Unlike Frederick Jackson Turner's explanation of the "frontier" in the United States, Euclydes da Cunha's analysis of the backlands of Brazil, and the twentieth century Bolivians' concept of a "mystique" of the land, Sarmiento considered the telluric element (the land) to be essentially malignant. He was led to this view by the historicism he had come to share with others of his generation, as well as by his own experiences of the evils of the caudillo system that Quiroga and Rosas represented. Hence, in reaction to these Argentine historical "realities," he arrived at an overly simplified equation of civilization with Europe and of barbarism with the American *pampa*. On this premise he explained all of Argentina's anarchy and bloodthirsty violence.

One may readily see that in some respects Sarmiento anticipated Darwinian social evolutionism and positivist racialism in explaining Argentine social reality. In other respects, however, he is more at home in a kind of demonic romantic rebellion against restraints on the free human spirit. One of his best biographers, Allison W. Bunkley, has dismissed this apparent contradiction in Sarmiento as a conflict between his objective of a society ruled by reason and his literary art of attack on social and political evils.[14] But Sarmiento's inner contradiction is more profound than Bunkley's overly simple explanation suggests. It expresses, rather, the romantic Liberal rebel's concept of a cosmic struggle between the forces of good and evil, one in which the Liberal's understanding of the magnitude of the historic forces that created the social realities drove him to strive to change the course of that history, even while taking his stand upon it.[15]

14. Bunkley, *The Life of Sarmiento*, 204.
15. The *Obras de D. F. Sarmiento* were published in 53 volumes in Paris, Santiago de Chile, and Buenos Aires by various publishers during the years 1889–1903. A centennial edition was later issued by the Argentine government in 1938, and a still later edition appeared in 1948 (52 vols.; Buenos Aires: Luz del Día, 1948). Ricardo Rojas edited *El pensamiento vivo de Sarmiento* (Buenos Aires: Losada, 1941). A convenient source for Sarmiento's thought is *Domingo Faustino Sarmiento, Selección, notas biográficas y comentario de Pedro Alba* (México: Imprenta Universitaria, 1944). *Facundo* has appeared in numerous editions. Other Sarmiento works particularly important for the student are *Comentarios sobre la Constitución* and *Argirópolis*, both of which are in the *Obras*.

Biographies include C. Galván Moreno, *Radiografía de Sarmiento* (Buenos Aires: Claridad, 1938), Leopoldo Lugones, *Historia de Sarmiento* (Buenos Aires: Babel, 1931), and Aníbal Ponce, *Sarmiento constructor de la nueva Argentina* (3rd ed.; Buenos Aires: Iglesias y Matera, 1950). Allison Williams Bunkley has written a good biography in English: *The Life of Sarmiento* (Princeton: Princeton University Press, 1952). Stuart Edgard Grummon and Bunkley have edited an anthology of selections in English: *A Sarmiento An-*

Bartolomé Mitre (1821–1906) was another member of this Argentine Generation of 1837. Like them, he was forced into an exile, spent first in Uruguay and later in Bolivia, returning to Argentina only at the time of the uprising which drove Rosas from power in 1852. Trained as a soldier, Mitre's greatest fame came from his leadership of the Province of Buenos Aires in the struggle against the Confederation and from his subsequent leadership of a United Argentina in the Paraguayan War. But, in addition to this notable political and military career, one that continued long after his presidency, he is one of Argentina's great historians. He also made a significant contribution to Argentine literature in his novel, *Soledad*. This novel was written during his exile in Bolivia, he explains in a prologue, to point the way to exploiting the possibilities of the American novel so sadly lacking in South America; one objective of the American novel, as he saw it, was to place moral man above the physiological.[16]

Traditionalism, at least in the European sense of Church, crown, and nobility, found little place among Argentine intellectuals of the independence and post-independence eras. The true Argentine traditionalism was to come much later as *Argen-*

---

thology (Princeton: Princeton University Press, 1948). See also William Rex Crawford, *A Century of Latin American Thought,* 37–51; and Harold E. Davis, *Makers of Democracy in Latin America,* 52–55, and *Latin American Social Thought,* 133–47.

16. See Ricardo Levene, *Mitre y los estudios históricos en la Argentina* (Buenos Aires: Academia Nacional de la Historia, 1944) and the same author's *Las ideas históricas de Mitre* (Buenos Aires: Institución Mitre, 1948). The complete works of Mitre have been published in Buenos Aires by the Institución Mitre, edited by Agustín P. Justo. Important historical works include a *History of San Martín* and a *History of Belgrano,* both in numerous editions. Enrique de Gandía, *Mitre, hombre de estado,* was published in Buenos Aires by the Institución Mitre in 1940. See also, José M. Niño, *Mitre, su vida íntima, histórica, hechos, reminiscencias, episodios y anécdotas militares y civiles* (2 vols.; Buenos Aires: Imprenta y Casa Editora de Grau, 1906), and a short sketch in Harold E. Davis, *Makers of Democracy in Latin America,* 56–60.

tinidad. Juan Manuel Rosas has often been called a traditional-ist;[17] but while his policies may be so interpreted in some re-spects at least, his is a much less intellectual voice than those of Echeverría, Sarmiento, Alberdi, and Mitre. Something similar may be said of Martín de Alzaga, one of the heroes of the defeat of the British invasion of 1806 who was executed as the leader of a presumably "Spanish" conspiracy against the revolutionary government in 1812. Alzaga was a monarchist, a good Catholic, and an anti-Mason in a day when Masons dominated the Argen-tine independence movement. The recent study by Enrique de Gandía points out that the abortive uprising of 1809 led by Alzaga and Mariano Moreno aimed to establish in Buenos Aires a popular revolutionary junta like the one already established in Montevideo to support the revolutionary juntas in Spain. The objective of the movement, the achievement of independ-ence as a monarchy tied to Spain, can be called traditionalist in only the most general sense. The movement was criollo and was defeated by Carlos Saavedra and other criollo leaders who were mostly, if not all, Masons who supported Viceroy Liniers and who seemed ready to turn the vice royalty over to Napo-leon, to Carlota in Brazil, or to Britain.[18]

THE CHILEAN GENERATION OF 1842

Raúl Silva Castro has pictured Diego Portales as a spokesman of Chilean traditionalism, and in the main this is a correct inter-pretation.[19] However, Andrés Bello (1781–1865) is a much more intellectual and distinctive voice of Chilean conservatism dur-ing these years of the romantic rebellion. Yet Bello's ideas were

17. See Carlos Ibarguren, *Juan Manuel de Rosas* (Buenos Aires: Ultra, 1936).
18. Enrique de Gandía, *Las ideas políticas de Martín de Alzaga* (Buenos Aires: Depalma, 1962), Vol. II of his *Historia de las ideas políticas en la Argen-tina.*
19. *Ideas y confesiones de Portales* (Santiago: Ed. del Pacífico, 1954).

different from the traditionalism of de Maestre or Balmes. Rather, Bello was a moderate who avoided the excesses of romanticism in either direction. He insisted upon the historical view of language (a radical departure for the times) and upon a rational-historical view of international law, while calling for a literature, culture, and political life that would be truly American. It would be difficult indeed to find a figure more representative than Andrés Bello of the best in the Spanish American intellectual life of the early years of the nineteenth century, whether in literature, grammar, history, or law. During the middle years of his life, in the late nineteenth century, he was sometimes regarded as an anachronistic voice. But that was because he had outlived his age. From the perspective of the present age, he is better understood as a historian-philosopher, one of the best minds of Spanish America, proclaiming that "a country cannot break the chain of time nor allow the roots of its tradition to dry up." [20]

Germán Arciniegas has given us a good portrayal of Bello as one of the great leaders of Spanish American independence and its greatest intellectual leader. He was a literary critic, an innovating poet, the author of an important book on Spanish grammar and of a standard textbook of international law, the principal author of the Chilean national law code, and a counselor for many years in the Chilean ministry of foreign relations. Above all else, he was the founding and directing intelligence of the University of Chile.[21]

Andrés Bello was born in Caracas, Venezuela, on November 29, 1781. His parents were of moderate means but devoted to music and learning. The education he received from them and

20. Pedro Lira Urquieta, *Andrés Bello* (México: Fondo de Cultura Económica, 1948), 207.
21. Germán Arciniegas, *El pensamiento vivo de Andrés Bello* (Buenos Aires: Losada, 1946).

from the schools of Caracas is evidence of the high state of culture there in the late eighteenth century. Rafael Escalona, one
of the notable teachers of his time, was his instructor in philosophy. Later, from 1810 to 1829, while representing the
Spanish American revolutionary movements in London, Bello
extended his studies in the British Museum and made the
acquaintance of such British intellectuals as Jeremy Bentham
and James Mill. His reading in the British Museum prepared
him for the demanding tasks later of preparing the Chilean
code and advising the Chilean government on international law,
as well as for his subsequent studies of Spanish grammar and
poetry.

The ideas Bello applied in these various fields are well represented in his inaugural address as the first rector of the new
university. The university, he urged, should be at the service
of the nation, which expected from it "practical utility, positive
results, [and] social improvements." It should not only concern
itself with its own curricula, but should sponsor a program of
primary education for all children and should conduct literary
and scientific studies at the highest level. In economics it should
be "completely Chilean," gathering and examining Chilean
statistics and studying Chilean society from the economic standpoint. In all other fields, such as medicine, the sciences, language, art, law, and literature, he pled for freedom from sub-
servience to European ideas in order to develop an autonomous
national culture.[22]

22. Bello's *Obras Completas* were published in 15 volumes by various pub-
lishers in Santiago, 1881–1893, and reissued by the press of the University of
Chile, 1930–1935. Works on Bello, in addition to the two cited, include Gabriel
Méndez Plancarte, *Andrés Bello* (Serie el pensamiento de América) (México:
Secretaría de Educación Pública, 1943); Miguel Luis Amunátegui, *Vida de Don
Andrés Bello* (Santiago: Ramírez, 1882); and Eugenio Orrego Vicuña, *Don
Andrés Bello* (3rd ed.; Santiago: Prensa de la Universidad de Chile, 1940).

Francisco Bilbao (1823–1865) expresses even more thoroughly the age of romantic idealism than does Andrés Bello. He is also one of the most typical Spanish American products of his times. He was born in Santiago, Chile, on January 9, 1823, into a family devoted on the paternal side to the tradition of the Encyclopedia and the French Revolution. When Francisco was eleven, his father was exiled to Peru because of his political activities. There, as a child, Francisco is said to have learned carpentry, to recite the Gospel according to St. John, and to "chant" a chapter of Rousseau's *Social Contract.*[23] When his family returned to Chile a few years later, Francisco entered the Instituto Nacional, the school famous for producing many of Chile's leaders. In his classes there he came to know the revolutionary ideas, among others, of the Liberal Christian, Félicité de Lamennais. By 1841 he was participating in a Literary Society organized by José V. Lastarria, who would later head the Faculty of Humanities in the University. Bilbao's controversial book, *La sociabilidad chilena,* grew out of his activity in this society. Published in 1844, it brought him a fine for blasphemy and forced him to depart for Europe. During this exile he established friendships with Lamennais, the historian Jules Michelet, and the poet Edgar Quinet, absorbing from them the revolutionary ideas of the year 1848. Later, writing between the years 1854 and 1856, he would recall that Lamennais lent him a book from which he "received . . . the scientific confirmation or revelation of eternal Republicanism."[24]

23. Manuel Blanco Cuartín, "Francisco Bilbao, su vida y sus doctrinas," *Biblioteca de escritores de Chile,* XI (1913), 677–88.

24. Francisco Bilbao, *Obras completas* (Buenos Aires: Manuel Bilbao, 1886), I, 123. The statement apparently refers to *Le livre du peuple* (1838) but does not exclude the possibility that Bilbao became acquainted with the same author's *Words of a Believer* (1834) and *On a Modern Slavery* (1840), as claimed by Diego Barros Arana in his *Un decenio de la historia de Chile, 1841–1851* (Santiago, Chile: Imprenta Universitaria, 1905), I, 494.

Returning to Chile in 1850, Bilbao shared in organizing the Society for Equality, whose activities brought him another exile, this time to Peru, France, and Argentina. This second exile proved to be his most productive period. His writings during these years include *The Law of History, America in Danger,* and the *American Gospel.* He died in Argentina in 1865.

In his *Sociabilidad chilena,* Bilbao sought a social belief based on a new philosophical, political, and historical synthesis. After an exposition and criticism of what he called the "old synthesis" of feudalism and Catholicism, he turned to this "new synthesis" of beliefs that he saw developing since the Middle Ages and which had culminated in belief in the "equality of liberty."

In the *Law of History,* written in 1858, Bilbao merged his concern for reform with that of the contemporary interest in philosophy of history. As early as 1836 Bello had urged a Chilean approach to constitutional problems through history, warning against disregard of the voice of experience in establishing democratic institutions in a society whose habits and outlook were colonial.[25]

Bilbao carried this historical argument to a much more radical position. After defining history and its conditions, he found that the laws of history were normative rather than descriptive. Like Lamennais, he interpreted the imperative of nature, destiny, and providence as not denying man's historical freedom. History, he insisted, gave man no excuse for resigning what was properly his own responsibility to some impassive, inevitable, automatic cosmic process. Rather, he believed, man found the true law of history, the command of his Creator and the norm of his action and judgment, in his awareness of duty. Duty required that man possess rights and laws, that he have liberty.

25. Speech at inauguration of the University of Chile, 1843, in Andrés Bello, *Antología,* ed. Pedro Grases (Caracas: Imprenta Nacional, 1949).

Social perfection, he held, supposed the complete development of each individual in harmony with the development of all. This ideal or principle enables man to judge history, to learn from his mistakes, and thus to be stimulated to further effort. Such a concept of social development, which Bilbao interprets to mean "sovereignty of the people," he further elaborates to denote sovereignty of reason and law, freedom, republicanism, and the incessant struggle for perfection.

It is not hard to see how Bilbao's thinking moves in the ambience of the social thought of his European idealist contemporaries, including Immanuel Kant. He sees, however, that no metaphysical system can be constructed to guarantee the ultimate success of democracy in the abstract, aside from human effort. Thus, to direct man's effort toward democratic ideals, he calls for a fundamental change of outlook in Latin America, a change to an outlook under which sovereignty of the people becomes the sovereignty of reason. As he conceives it, this is a change toward conformity to divine law — a theme he develops further in his *American Gospel*. From this point of view, "history is reason judging memory and projecting the duty of the future." [26]

José Victorino Lastarria (1817–1888) was the most brilliant disciple of Andrés Bello and one of the outstanding intellectuals of his country in the nineteenth century. He was protean, ex-

26. The author is indebted to Professor O. A. Kubitz of the University of Illinois for his interpretation of Bilbao in his article, "Francisco Bilbao's *Ley de Historia* in relation to the doctrines of Sarmiento and Lamennais," *Philosophy and Phenomenological Research*, XX (June, 1960), 487–502. The above paragraphs on Bilbao also rely heavily on Professor Kubitz's earlier contribution, chapter 12 in the author's *Latin American Social Thought*. Other useful biographical and critical studies include two works of Armando Donoso: *Bilbao y su tiempo* (Santiago, Chile: Zig Zag, 1913) and *El pensamiento vivo de Francisco Bilbao* (Santiago, Chile: Nascimento, 1940).

pressing many aspects of the evolving intellectual life of his times. Although he was a protégé of Bello and was nominated by him to make the address celebrating the first anniversary of the university in 1844, he used this occasion to propose one of the most profound rejections of the Spanish heritage as "three centuries of a gloomy existence without movement." Bilbao could hardly have put it more strongly. Lastarria condemned the Spanish system of government, its restrictions upon freedom of thought and belief, the mixture of races which its rule produced, and the class system under which Spaniards abandoned to Indians and mestizos the exercise of any mechanical arts they may have known. Spaniards, said Lastarria, made religion an instrument of despotism. He argued that this struggle between the Spanish past and the present was still going on and that Chileans should study both the past and the present in order to "destroy completely the resistance offered by the old Spanish system embodied in our society." [27]

Lastarria had had numerous discussions with Bello as to whether history should be narrative or interpretative and, if it were the latter, whether or not it was ruled by providential laws that imprison man in a fatalistic system. Lastarria rebelled against the latter interpretation, presumably that of Giovanni Battista Vico, though possibly that of Marx, while Bello merely observed that he thought it poor educational policy to replace the study of history with philosophy of history.[28] Responding to Lastarria's speech in 1844, Bello concluded that Lastarria, by criticizing the views of Vico and especially those of Herder,

27. José Victorino Lastarria, *Investigaciones sobre la influencia social de la conquista i del sistema colonial de los Españoles en Chile* (Santiago, Chile: Imprenta Barcelona, 1909), Vol. VII of his *Obras completas*, ed. Alejandro Fuenzalida Grandón (14 vols.; Santiago, Chile: Imprenta Barcelona, 1906–1934).

28. José V. Lastarria, *Obras completas*, X, 253.

had denied "general principles which were for many centuries the faith of the world." [29] Bello's statement suggests that in defending Vico's view of providentialism in history he interpreted it to mean an orderly historical process, and that he was profoundly disturbed by Lastarria's apparent readiness to adopt a more revolutionary (Marxist?) position. But history was on Lastarria's side. Exiled briefly for his radical views, he soon returned to become a prominent figure in Chilean cultural life, virtually the personification of the movement for Chilean intellectual and cultural independence.[30]

THE MEXICANS

Mexico produced a number of outstanding Liberal spokesmen during these years, as well as one of the best American representatives of traditionalist thought, the historian of independence and organizer of the Mexican Conservative party, Lucas Alamán. But first let us note the thought of three Liberal advocates of quite different types: José María Luis Mora, Ignacio Ramírez and Manuel Crescencio Rejón.

José María Luis Mora (1794[?]–1850), in his life and in his writing, gives us an expression of Mexican economic and political Liberalism during the troubled quarter century that followed independence. Mora spoke for that part of the Mexican elite who were willing to break with the authority of Church

29. *Ibid.*, 275. For Lastarria's discussion of the whole chain of events see chapters 25–28. See also his discussion of Herder in Vol. VII, 17–23.

30. In addition to works previously cited, see Sady Zañartu, *Lastarria, el hombre solo* (Santiago: Ediciones Ercilla, 1938); Alejandro Fuenzalida Grandón, *Lastarria i su tiempo: su vida, obras e influencia en el desarrollo político e intelectual de Chile* (Santiago: Imprenta Cervantes, 1893; second edition by Imprenta Barcelona, 1911); and Domingo Melfi, *Dos hombres: Portales y Lastarria* (Santiago: Nascimento, 1937).

and crown in trying to apply the Liberal principle of freedom in politics, religion, and economics.

His moderate Liberalism was characterized by an aristocratic or class-conscious temper. But it also breathed something of the spirit of the historicism of Friedrich Karl von Savigny and the Compte de Volney, as well as that of the liberal political economy of Adam Smith and Jeremy Bentham. He believed in progress and in the perfectibility of man and society; but when forced to choose between liberty and order, he chose order. His writing also reveals the race-consciousness characteristic of the social thought of his day. Recognizing the Indians as Mexico's greatest social problem, like Domingo Sarmiento in Argentina and Antonio Saco in Cuba, he believed that to develop, Mexico should emphasize her European character. "The name of Mexico is so intimately linked with the memory of Cortes," he wrote, "that while the latter exists the former will not perish." [31]

Mora was the theoretician of Mexican political Liberalism in the years immediately following independence, playing an active part in developing the federalist constitution of 1825 and in later restoring federalism after its abrogation by Santa Anna. As a minister in the Cabinet of Valentín Gómez Farías (1832–1834), he was identified with the short-lived anticlerical reforms of that administration. The anonymous *Catecismo político de la federación mexicana* (1831) is generally attributed to him.[32] This pamphlet presented federalism as a logical application of Liberal political principles which asserted that decentralization lessened the danger of generating arbitrary political power. In a spirit somewhat similar to that of the authors of the United

31. Quoted by Arturo Arnáiz y Freg, in *José María Luis Mora* (México: Universidad Nacional, 1941), xvi–xvii.
32. Samuel Ramos, *Historia de la filosofía en México* (México: Imprenta Universitaria, 1943), 109.

States federal constitution, Mora wrote that federalism was a means of preventing the demagogic forces (the local caudillos) from capturing control of the state. Federalism also appealed to him as a hierarchical structure of the state through which the criollo leaders might govern with law and order, holding in restraint the threat of social revolution ever present in the sub-jugated Indian masses. In accordance with this view of limited democracy, he advocated a suffrage limited to property owners. His principal reform objectives were to destroy the privileges of the two most powerful institutions in Mexican society, the Army and the Church.

Consequently, Mora displays much of the Liberal, but little of the romantic, even in his historicism. Supremely confident in the power of reason, he rejected Bolívar's dream of a united Spanish America as "the greatest of deliriums." Mexico, he was sure, would have its own future as a separate nation. The memory that his family had been ruined financially by the destruction attending the Hidalgo uprising may have caused him to fear popular movements that might bring the repetition of such a violent mass movement. This fear was not unusual among his social class, whether or not they had suffered personally. The distinctive thing in Mora's case was that his keen social perception led him to see that in order to avoid such revolutions the governing class must rule democratically, extending the realm of freedom by progressive measures.[33]

33. The author has not been able to determine whether the complete works of Mora have been published. Some of his writings are found conveniently in *Ensayos, ideas y retratos*, edited with a prologue by Arturo Arnáiz y Freg (México: Universidad Nacional, 1941); *El Doctor Mora Redivivo. Selección de sus obras. Estudio crítico de Genaro Fernández MacGregor* (México: Botas, 1938); and *José María Luis Mora, Ensayos, ideas y retratos* (México: UNAM, 1964). *México y sus revoluciones* (3 vols.) appeared in Paris in 1836, and two volumes of *Obras sueltas* were published there in 1937 by Rosa. Biographies and critical studies include *El Doctor José María Luis Mora, Homenaje de la Universidad Nacional*

Manuel Crescencio Rejón (1799–1849), another of the Mexican Liberals, was the principal originator of the broad judicial process called the *amparo,* a Mexican juridical innovation subsequently copied elsewhere in Latin America. Under this process an individual may defend his constitutional rights against governmental action of almost any kind. It has sometimes been compared in its scope and importance to the writ of Habeas Corpus, and the comparison is not inappropriate, much as the two procedures differ.[34] Rejón was also one of the early Mexican proponents of freedom of the press. Known as one of the *Puros* among the Liberals, he was a federalist, an advocate of direct elections, and like Mora a collaborator with Valentín Gómez Farías in restoring the federal constitution of 1824. In 1840 he was a minister in the Gómez Farías government. Yet in 1844, as minister of foreign affairs, Rejón supported Santa Anna in his opposition to the United States in the Texas question, later (1846) defending this action in what is one of his more important written works.[35]

His full name was Manuel Crescencio García Rejón y Alcalá, though he was usually known as Manuel C. Rejón or Crescencio Rejón. Born in the year 1799 in the village of Bolonchenticul, near Mérida, in Yucatán, he was the son of Manuel García Rejón, descendant of an old Yucatán family and Bernarda de

de México (México: Universidad Nacional de México, 1934), Salvador Joscano, *Vida del Dr. Mora* (México: Biografías Populares, No. 1, 1936), and Charles A. Hale, *Mexican Liberalism in the Age of Mora (1821–1853)* (New Haven: Yale University Press, 1968). William Rex Crawford gives a good brief sketch in *A Century of Latin American Thought,* 247–50.

34. Ignacio Burgoa, *El juicio de amparo,* quoted in *Manuel Crescencio Rejón: pensamiento político.* Prólogo, selección y notas de Daniel Moreno (México: Universidad Nacional Autónoma de México, 1968), xxviii.

35. Manuel Crescencio Rejón, *Justificación de la conducta de Manuel Crescencio Rejón, desde 1841 hasta la fecha* (New Orleans, 1846); reproducido en Daniel Moreno (ed.), *Manuel Crescencio Rejón: pensamiento político.*

Alcalá, of the Canary Islands. In Mérida he studied in the Seminario Conciliar de San Ildefonso and pursued studies under two Yucatán philosophers who had embraced ideas of the Enlightenment: Vicente María Velásquez and Pablo Moreno. He was encouraged in his studies and aided financially by a wealthy young priest, José María Guerra, who later came to be bishop of Yucatán. Both Velásquez and Moreno were ardent defenders of the Indians of Yucatán and espoused the ideas of Bartolomé de las Casas. A group of young men who gathered around them included, in addition to Rejón, Andrés Quintana Roo and Lorenzo de Zavala. The group, most of them destined to national fame, came to be known as the San Juanistas, a name derived from Velásquez's parish of San Juan Bautista.

Rejón completed his studies in philosophy in 1819 at the age of twenty. Two years later he participated in the independence movement of 1821, working through the Masonic Lodge in support of the Iturbide movement. He then went to Mexico as a member of the national Congress. But he soon became a critic of Iturbide and was one of those members who absented themselves from the Congress that approved Iturbide as emperor. He was a member of the commission which drew up the Constitution of 1824, becoming one of a trio of early federalists with Ramos Arizpe and Prisciliano Sánchez. In this connection he defended the principle that the judicial authority emanates not from the executive or legislative, but "directly from the people" *(inmediatamente del pueblo)*.[36] Rejón also urged the adoption of Liberal economic and fiscal policies, especially in foreign commerce and in respect to a merchant marine. His greatest influence, however, was in the fields of law and politics.

His thought shows a number of intellectual influences in

36. *Ibid.,* xiv.

addition to those of his teachers, Moreno and Velásquez. To the eclectic Victor Cousin, he owed some of his moderate characteristics. John Locke and the eighteenth century British jurist Sir William Blackstone, both of whom he cites in defending his action in issuing certain controversial decrees of 1844, influenced his political and legal thinking. He was also familiar with the Constitution of the United States, to which he frequently refers.

In the final analysis, the essentials of Rejón's thought may be summed up in five basic principles, all characteristic of the evolving liberal ideology: (1) the popular basis of the judicial authority, (2) the constitutional right of the individual citizen for protection against arbitrary action of government, (3) the fundamental importance of freedom of the press, (4) the essential need for decentralizing political authority to prevent authoritarianism, and (5) the fundamental importance of national loyalty (and of the nation) as the basis of all rights.[37]

Ignacio Ramírez (1818–1879) was Mexico's Voltaire. A generation later than Mora, Rejón, and Ramos Arizpe, he speaks for a mid-century Mexican Liberalism in full vigor. As Minister of Justice and Public Instruction under President Benito Juárez, he was responsible for carrying out the Laws of Reform, including the suppression of monasteries. In this connection, as well as in other ways, his anticlericalism, verging on atheism, earned him the popular sobriquet, *El Nigromante* (The Necromancer). Diego Rivera may have overdramatized this religious nonconformity of Ramírez by putting his phrase *"Dios no existe"* (God

37. In addition to Daniel Moreno's collection, *Manuel Crescencio Rejón: pensamiento político,* see Rejón's speeches in Carlos A. Echánove Trujillo (ed.), *Manuel Crescencio Rejón. Discursos parlamentarios (1822–1847)* (México: Secretaría de Educación Pública, 1943).

does not exist) in a controversial mural in the Hotel del Prado in Mexico City, a painting depicting leaders of Mexican reform. Yet, although the text of the address has been lost, this appears to have been what he said in a speech in the Academy of Letrán.

There is no question that he pursued the rationalism of his age to a position of pantheism, if not atheism. It is unfair to his thought as a whole, however, to confine its significance to this one, somewhat exceptional position. Atheism, as a not unnatural accompaniment of Liberal romantic thought, deserves special attention. But what Ramírez and his like really meant was that reason (the science or reason of the universe) was the supreme good. His speech is best understood as a violent protest against the Church's opposition to the Liberal reforms, especially in the field of education, *El Nigromante's* special concern.

Ramírez was much more than an anticlerical. A mestizo by birth, but Spanish (criollo) in culture, he sympathized with the Indians and admired those Spaniards, such as Bartolomé de las Casas, who had defended them. His Liberalism included vigorous advocacy of universal suffrage, freedom of speech, and religious freedom.[38]

Miguel Ramos Arizpe (1775–1843) was another of the early Mexican intellectual Liberals coming out of the generation of independence. His career exhibits several aspects interesting for the thought of his time. A revolutionary priest, he was excommunicated for his heretical ideas, yet served for years as Dean of the Cathedral of Puebla, and in his later years was for a time Minister of Justice and Ecclesiastical Affairs.

Born in San Nicolás de la Capellanía, now Ramos Arizpe,

---

38. Ignacio Ramírez, *Ensayos, Prólogo y selección de Manuel González Ramírez* (México: Ediciones de la Universidad Nacional Autónoma, 1944).

Coahuila, he was the youngest son of a family of modest means. He was educated for the priesthood, receiving the degrees of Licenciado (1807) and Doctor of Canon Law (1808) at the University of Guadalajara. Competing for a vacancy in Canon Law at the Cathedral of Monterrey, he won first place in the competition; but the bishop (as before) refused to appoint him, sending him back to his obscure parish, Real de Bourbón. In 1810, however, the Municipal Council of Saltillo named him deputy to the Cortes called by the rebels against Napoleon in Spain. There he quickly emerged as a leader of the American deputies. He stayed in Spain for eleven years, including twenty months in prison after the restoration of Ferdinand VII. Known as a defender of the Constitution of 1812, he was repeatedly asked while in prison whether sovereignty resided in the king or in the nation. His answer: *"Aqui cerrado no lo puedo saber; dejenme Vstedes salir y ver la sociedad, y volveré al punto a la prisión a contestar."* [39]

Lucas Alamán (1792–1853), the historian of Mexican independence, was one of the best intellectual representatives of traditionalism in early Spanish America. But he also illustrates the difference between the traditionalisms of the Old and the New World. Born in Guanajuato, Mexico, in 1792, he held national offices in the administration of Santa Anna, especially as minister of foreign relations. As the organizer of the Conservative party in Mexico, as in his well-known and excellent history of Mexican independence, Alamán expressed his deep doubts concerning the democratic tendencies of the times. In this respect his thought was comparable to that of the earlier

39. Quoted in Vito Alessio Robles, *Miguel Ramos Arizpe. Discursos, memorias e informes* (México: Universidad Nacional Autónoma de México, 1942), xxxv.

Joseph de Maistre of France (1735–1821) and the contemporary Spanish philosopher Jaime Balmes (1810–1848), for whose traditionalist ideas Alamán expressed admiration in his *History of Mexico*. Alamán believed that independence had brought a decline in Spanish culture in the New World and that only a restoration of monarchy, together with the authority of the Church and of the power of the upper class, could restore Mexican society to its cultural level and socio-economic vigor before independence.

In political economy, however, he was far from the position of European traditionalist Conservatives, tending rather to follow the British school, favoring mining, industrialization, and commerce.[40] As agent for the Cortes family interests in Mexico, he worked for development along these lines, especially through the Compañía Unida de Minas prior to 1830. Later he sought to establish textile factories in Orizaba and Celaya.

LIBERALISM IN CUBA

Féliz Varela (1787–1853) is generally credited with having introduced modern or rational philosophy into Cuba through his classes in the University at Havana. His philosophy was eclectic, influenced especially by the ideas of the French ideologues, as represented in Destutt de Tracy. Basically this eclecticism was the rationalism and sensationalism of Descartes, Locke, and Condillac, combined with the social and economic utilitarianism of the day and including something of the dawning historicism.

Father Varela's ideas and activities so troubled the Spanish authorities, however, that he spent the latter half of his life in

40. See Moisés González Navarro, *El Pensamiento político de Lucas Alamán* (*México: El Colegio de México*, 1952), 14–19, 29ff.; and *Lucas Alamán, Semblanzas e ideario* (México: Universidad Nacional Autónoma, 1939).

exile in the United States. For a while he edited the review
El Habanero. Later, with Antonio Saco, he published in New
York *El Mensajero Semanal*.[41]

41. Varela's *Lecciones de filosofía* has been published in several editions,
the latest (without date) around 1940. José Manuel Mestre, a contemporary,
gives the best comment on Varela's influence in *De la filosofía en la Habana*,
republished by the Ministry of Education (La Habana, 1952) under the editorship of Humberto Piñera Llera. William Rex Crawford refers briefly to Varela
in his *Century of Latin American Thought*, 218. See also Francisco González
del Valle y Ramírez, *El Padre Varela y la independencia de la América hispana*
(La Habana: n.p., 1936) and Antonio Travieso Hernández, *Varela y la reforma
filosófica en Cuba* (La Habana: J. Montero, 1942).

The Era of Positivist
and Evolutionary Thought

Romantic liberalism had reached its apogee in Latin America as in Europe in the revolutionary year 1848. By mid-century it was already being replaced by more scientific and evolutionary tendencies. The aristocratic overtone of altruism and idealism of the earlier decades was giving way to a tone and style more characteristic of the rising urban middle class. Young men of this class in Latin America, and some of their elders, began to absorb the ideas of the European socialist movement, as in the case of Tobías Barreto (1839–1889) of Brazil, whose "Germanism," to use the term of João Cruz Costa, is explained by Gilberto Freyre as an expression of his psychological insecurity as a mulatto. But their ideas usually lacked the working-class labor consciousness of the Europeans. Working-class Marxism found its way to the New World in the late nineteenth century under the leadership and in the press of an incipient labor movement.[1] But the mainstream of social thought in Latin America followed the different, though in some respects related, course of positivism.

Positivism originated in the social science of Auguste Comte (1798–1857). This was a sociological science of "positive" principles underlying social structure and social change and was

---

1. Luis Aguilar (ed.), *Marxism in Latin America* (New York: Alfred A. Knopf, 1968), 4–8. See also Eduardo Nicol, *El problema de la filosofía hispánica* (Madrid: Tecnos, 1961), 44ff. and Leopoldo Zea, *El pensamiento latinoamericano* (México: Pormaca, 1965), I, 62–72 and II, 1–12.

based on a view that history was evolving toward a completely rational and humane stage. It produced prescriptive principles that should guide political action to achieve social progress. Positivism's scientific emphasis opened the way later to theories of social evolution based on Charles Darwin's biological evolution. In this stage the tendency to identify progress with social order and institutions found support in the sociology and social theory of Herbert Spencer. Its humanistic religious emphasis, which not all Latin American positivists accepted, seemed to find more expression in Brazil than in Spanish America. Comte's identification of positivism with the republican form of government in his *System of Positivist Politics* also found notable expression in Brazil. His later defense of the authoritarian republic found echoes in both Brazil and Spanish America.

Orderly progress was the key idea in positivist social thought. In a recent work on the teaching and study of philosophy in the universities of Spanish America, José Echeverría has stated rather clearly the choice confronted by Latin Americans between the colonial past and this policy of progress. Citing Sarmiento's *Facundo* as an expression of the second choice, he writes: "Thus there is posed a sort of choice between a past, characterized by the presence of the Indian, by the Spanish Catholic colonial theology and culture, and by the oscillation between anarchy and despotism on one hand, and on the other a future that is thought of as the triumph of liberty within order, of democracy, of lay education, of science and general welfare, and of the civilized city confronting a retrograde and barbarous countryside." [2]

2. José Echeverría, *La enseñanza de la filosofía en la universidad hispano-americana* (Washington, D.C.: Unión Panamericana, 1965), 35. This author's translation.

PREDOMINANCE OF POSITIVISM

Developing out of the background of the earlier romantic and Liberal eclecticism, positivism retained a revolutionary tone in its earlier stages. But it became more conservative as it came to provide the basic structure of Latin American thought during the last half of the nineteenth century as it was coming to the zenith of its popularity between the years 1880 and 1900.[3] In fact, in no other part of the modern world did positivism as a general pattern of thought achieve a stronger hold on the minds of a dominant elite than it seems to have achieved in Latin America. In Brazil, indeed, as we shall see later in this chapter, positivism became nearly an official philosophy of the Republic. There the *Sociedade Positivista* was founded in 1871 under the influence of Benjamín Constant Botelho de Magalhães. In 1881 Miguel Lemos and Raimundo Teixeira Mendes founded the positivist church, "Templo da Humanidade," which became the most important center of Comtian religious influence and ideas outside France. The "Apostolate" who made up the membership of this *Templo* took little active part in the republican revolution of 1889; but such positivists as Benjamin Constant furnished much of the republican leadership. A Brazilian identification was thus obvious with the Comtian formula of order as the necessary condition of progress, regarded as the objective toward which order was directed. The Brazilian social historian Gilberto Freyre has built his interpretation of late nineteenth century Brazil around this concept.[4]

Comte had set out to systematize the romantic and utopian "socialism" of his day, creating a "science of society" or scien-

3. Eduardo Nicol, *El problema de la filosofía hispánica,* 45–46.
4. See Gilberto Freyre, *Order and Progress,* trans. Rod W. Horton (New York: Alfred A. Knopf, 1970).

tific sociology. He found the basis of this science in a science of history, assuming that social beliefs were the product of historical experience rather than of *a priori* logic and that history revealed certain laws or principles that could be the basis of a social science. Positive liberalism accordingly tended to abandon its earlier natural rights concept of freedom in favor of theories derived from an analysis of experience and finding expression in social structure. This pragmatic concept of freedom was one well suited to the temper of Hispanic American Liberals in an increasingly "scientific" age.

Comte divided the study of society into the two main realms of statics and dynamics. The vital relationship between the two he expressed in the phrase "order and progress" that became the motto of his followers. To some of them this phrase expressed the priority of institutional structure and social order as the necessary basis of social progress. To others social structure was an accompaniment or a consequence of progress, measured in terms of educational freedom. To both groups the phrase also expressed the Comtian pragmatic concept of freedom. Since social progress came inevitably and by evolution, Comtians assumed that it must also come gradually. This progress, whether economic, political, social, intellectual, or spiritual, was measured in terms of "positive" freedom.

Society, said Comte, had evolved through three historical stages: (1) animistic-theological-military, (2) speculative-critical-metaphysical, and (3) rational-scientific-industrial. It is interesting that these three stages suggest in some ways St. Augustine's division of history into three ages — before the Law, the Law, and Grace. Each stage, Comte assumed, had its appropriate institutions. Somewhat paradoxically these three stages were the product as well as the basis of Comte's "scientific" analysis of history, the analysis from which he also deduced "laws of history" that became the basic principles of his new social science. This theoretical analysis led Comte to evolve a hierarchy of the sciences that ranged from mathematics at the base to sociology at the head of the system. Politics, for Comte, was an important branch of sociology, that is, of a single science of society.

Positivism thus provided a "scientific" approach to the pressing problems of the organization of national life that occupied Latin American attention during the nineteenth century. In its later Darwinian and evolutionist phase, this positivist social science characteristically explained political and social instability as a form of illness in society. Alcides Arguedas (1879–1946) of Bolivia, Salvador Mendieta (1882–1958) of Central America, Augustín Alvarez Suárez (1857–1914) and Manuel Ugarte (1878–1951) of Argentina, and César Zumete of Venezuela wrote works of this character.[5] Whatever form it assumed, this popularity of "scientific" positivist thought expressed the preoccupation of Latin Americans with the social basis of their moral, political, educational, and economic problems.

The revolutionary labor-oriented thought that developed in Latin America in the late nineteenth century was in some respects a parallel to positivism, though it was a much less widely accepted current. It had its immediate sources in the French commune, in the Italian Risorgimento, and in the labor-oriented republican movements in Spain. Luis Aguilar contends that the Russian anarchist, Mikhail Aleksandrovich Ba-

5. Alcides Arguedas, *Un pueblo enfermo*, prólogo de Ramiro de Maeztu (Barcelona: Viuda de L. Tasso, 1909. 3rd ed.; Santiago, 1937); Salvador Mendieta, *Le enfermedad de Centro-América* (5 vols.; Barcelona, Spain, 1934); Augustín Alvarez, *Manual de patología política* (Buenos Aires, 1899); César Zumete, *El continente enfermo* (New York, 1899); and Manuel Ugarte, *Enfermedades sociales*, published in 1905. See the excellent Chapter 4, "The Sick Continent and its Diagnosticians," in Martin S. Stabb, *In Quest of Identity* (Chapel Hill: University of North Carolina, 1968).

kunin (1814–1876), called "tender and radiant" by Martí, was on the whole a more influential ideological force than Karl Marx in this "Marxist" current; but other scholars disagree.

In any case, the most important center of this "Marxist" thought in Latin America at the turn of the century was an Argentine group led by Juan B. Justo. Justo read Marx in German and translated some of Marx's works into Spanish. The group that gathered around him included such important figures as Américo Ghioldi, Nicolás Repetto, and Alfredo Palacios. Together, they provided the leadership of the Socialist Party of Argentina, one of the strongest in Latin America and one that continues to this day to play a prominent role in Argentine politics. José Ingenieros was identified briefly with this group, and his *Argentine Sociology*, while basically a positivist analysis, helped to arouse interest in Marxist historical materialism. In Uruguay, Emilio Frugoni (1880–1969) poet and diplomat, founded the Karl Marx Study Center (1904) and the Uruguayan Socialist party. The founder of the Cuban party was Diego Vicente Tejera (1848–1903).[6]

Positivism resembled Marxism in rejecting the earlier utopian socialism in favor of a science of society. Like Marxism it also rejected a metaphysical basis for philosophy in general and for a theory of history in particular. In Comte's scheme of history, as we have noted, society evolved from a metaphysical stage into the rational or positivist stage. For Marx, as for Comte, the basis for the science of society lay in principles evolved from a "scientific" (empirical) analysis of human history, rather than in principles of natural law as previously conceived. Both be-

6. Luis E. Aguilar, *Marxism in Latin America*, 3–8. On Tejera see Max Henríquez Ureña, "Diego Vicente Tejera," *Cuba Contemporánea*, VI (October, 1914), 105–126; and a chapter by Eduardo Tejera in this author's forthcoming *Revolutionaries, Traditionalists, and Dictators in Latin America* (New York: Cooper Square Publishers).

lieved that social progress required the rejection of the religion of the past as superstition. Both saw society progressing in an evolutionary process in which human relations were increasingly guided by reason, and both were interested in understanding history as a means of escaping from control by the past or of rising above it. But there were differences. Positivism emphasized the evolution of social institutions to provide the social "order" needed for progress, while Marxism stressed the importance of a working-class rebellion in one form or another to destroy or radically change existing institutions. Positivism did not embrace this theory of the class struggle as the nexus of the historical dialectic. The "idealism" of positivist thought led to a "religion of Humanity," while Marxism's humanism, because of its atheism, declared that organized religion was unnecessary.

Basic Assumptions of Positivism

Positivism had a distinctive set of assumptions or beliefs concerning the nature of man, society, and social progress. As a sociology, its principles or laws governing the dynamics and statics of society, like those of the earlier romantic Liberalism, assumed man's rationality and his natural sociability. It also assumed a natural tendency for society to evolve in an increasingly structured and stable order. This growth of the institutional structure of society was equated with the rule of law, the triumph of reason over metaphysics, and of a natural moral order over an order based on authority. As positivism took on the organismic concepts of social Darwinism, its followers gave major attention to the question of race, which they came to view as a product of chance variation and natural selection in the struggle for existence. This was the way, for example, Euclydes da Cunha explained the vigor of the *sertanejo* in

backwoods Brazil. Moreover, some positivists, Tobías Barreto of
Recife, Brazil, for example, went on to develop ideas of superior
races along the lines of Gobineau's theory. In Latin America,
however, the superior "race" was often thought of as Portuguese
or Spanish. But even more important than the concept of superior and inferior races was the central importance positivists
attached to race in their analysis of society.

In economics, positivist thought tended to follow the increasingly socialized trends in utilitarianism as it was evolving under
the influence of John Stuart Mill and Herbert Spencer. Positivist politics viewed law, legislation, and political institutions
as products of a social process and as deriving their strength
from social forces and customs. Thus, in the law faculties of
Latin American universities of the late nineteenth century the
study of sociology became in fact the study of political science,
and courses called national sociology were devoted to national
political problems. In its religious aspect, as was noted, positivism was a vaguely Christian humanism. In later years this
positivist religious humanism tended to merge in the Hispanic
world with a neo-Kantian, "spiritual" Krausism and other so-
called spiritual trends. This was a philosophical current which
prevailed in the university of Madrid and spread from there to
the Spanish American universities.

DISTINCTIVE LATIN AMERICAN ASPECTS OF POSITIVISM

Latin American positivism was like that of the Occidental world
in general. But Latin American social and political realities
gave to positivism in the New World special characteristics and
a special importance. One of these realities was the Latin American sense of political inferiority, deriving from the failure to
develop institutions of constitutional democratic government

like the British, French, and North American models. A sense of failure to achieve the economic prosperity promised by independence leaders increased the poignancy of political failure, adding an emotional element to the view of politics as "pathological." Latin Americans found this lag in their economic growth striking enough when they compared it with the progress of Western Europe. But the contrast was even more striking when they compared their economies with that of their thriving North American neighbor.

The Latin American social problem assumed new dimensions as a result of the emancipation of Negro slaves completed by the middle of the century in most of Latin America except Cuba and Brazil,[7] and of the increasing rate of the ethnic assimilation of the Indian peoples in the late nineteenth and early twentieth century. Other social and economic changes also promoted Latin American social and economic mobility. These included a growth in agricultural production for export, development of the mining of nonprecious metals (also largely for export), the construction of railroads, the growth of cities, and greatly increased European immigration. Immigrants came in largest numbers to the countries of southern South America, but also in considerable volume to Cuba. They came to all countries in somewhat larger numbers than before. The dynamic forces released by these social changes undermined the confidence of the governing elite, who in most countries had only recently consolidated their political power after several decades of turbulence. In some instances the traditional oli-

7. José Luis Romero discusses the importance of the abolitionism issue in *El pensamiento político de la derecha latinoamericana,* 59ff. See also Luis Millones, "Gente negra en el Perú: esclavos y conquistadores," *América Indígena,* XXXI (July, 1971), 593–624.

garchy was finding, to its dismay, that new social elements produced by these changes made common cause with the armed forces in striving for political power.

The disinterested observer might see that the increasing social mobility stemming from these changes was lessening the danger of race warfare, which had never been far below the level of consciousness in the colonial mind. But the continuing threat of social and political anarchy made it difficult for the nineteenth century ruling classes to take such a long-range view, with the result that fear of race conflict lurked constantly in the back of men's minds. Under these conditions, the positivist preoccupation with the question of race gave a comforting evolutionary explanation and a rationale of criollo rule even though it offered no real solution to the social and psychological problems arising from the ethnic diversity inherited from colonial days.

The long, drawn-out conflict between Church and state also gave a distinctive character to positivism in Latin America during those years, particularly in Spanish America. Eventally positivism provided a theoretical basis for a *modus vivendi* between Church and state, as in Mexico under Porfirio Díaz. But at first it came as a "scientific" reinforcement for the earlier Liberal demand for a more secular society, especially in the sense of lay education. As such, positivism was embraced by the Liberals and opposed by the traditionalist leadership of the Church, which condemned it as an evil combination of "Liberalism, Marxism, and Masonry." Early nineteenth century Liberalism had dissipated its strength in a not too effective struggle to deprive the Church of its eminent position in society and culture. By mid-century a less revolutionary Liberalism, now moving toward a pattern of positivist scientific gradualism, had achieved notable success in Mexico, Brazil, and elsewhere. In terms of material wealth, the battle over Church-state and Church-society relations had exacted great toll from the Church; it had doubtless caused it to lose something in spiritual qualities as well. But its chief effect had been to force the religious institution of Latin American society into unyielding and often blind opposition to the Liberal movements and philosophy of the age. What positivism challenged most clearly in the late nineteenth century was the political conservatism based on this largely uncritical traditionalism.

CONSERVATIVE POSITIVISTS

Many positivists ultimately became conservatives, though in a different sense. In its earlier stages, positivist thought in Latin America was an expression of Liberal forces intent upon building a strong lay society and state. Reacting to the earlier Liberal defeats in their romantic unrealistic challenges to the forces of traditionalism and surviving colonialism, positivist idealogues sought to bend these forces to their own purposes. Positivists considered education a major mode of social action and a major responsibility of the state. They believed that education must be free of Church influence, because education was the essential means by which man could rid himself of superstition and rise to the rational level of freedom required for the scientific, positive stage of society. To this end, Benito Juárez appointed Gabino Barreda to reorganize the educational program of Mexico along positivist lines after the triumph of the Liberal revolution in that country.[8] Liberal parties gaining

8. See W. H. Calcott, *Liberalism in Mexico, 1857-1929* (Berkeley: University of California Press, 1931); Leopoldo Zea, *El positivismo en México* (México: El Colegio de México, 1943), 45ff.; Justo Sierra, *Evolución política del pueblo mexicano* (México: La Casa de España en México, 1940; published originally by J. Ballesca with other works under the title *México, su evolución social*).

power in other countries likewise tended to reform educational programs along positivist secular lines.[9]

This "scientific" outlook of positivist thought came to have a special value in legitimatizing political systems, making it possible for positivist Liberals and liberal Conservatives to find common ground. In part this was because positivism expressed so well the values implicit in the growing spirit of a nationalism committed to achieving the general welfare. At the same time, it gave to the dominant elite, naturally inclined toward moderation, a well-oriented philosophy of prestige and "scientific" character with which to meet the impatience of the more radical reformers. This political value of positivist theory may be seen in the fact that the leading chairs of philosophy in the universities came to be held by positivists.

The Díaz regime in Mexico is an example of this identification of positivism with a regime emphasizing "scientific progress" and gradual evolution in order to prevent "revolution." As exemplified in the party of the *Científicos,* it is also a good example of the tendency of many positivists to accept Comte's rationale of an authoritarian republic. Justo Sierra was a towering figure in the intellectual life of Porfirian Mexico, at times a critic of Díaz policy. But one may see something of the great significance, not only of Sierra but also of positivism in Mexico, at least as it appeared in the mind of the Mexican José Vasconcelos. A critic of positivism, he called Justo Sierra the "high priest of positivism in the University" and a popularizer of the positivist theory in art and life.[10] That Sierra was a confirmed

9. See, for example, Herbert J. Miller, "Positivism and Educational Reforms in Guatemala," *A Journal of Church and State,* VIII (Spring, 1966), 251–63.

10. See José Vasconcelos, *Ulises Criollo* (México: Botas, 1935), 174, 197. Vasconcelos writes that his studies in the university varied from rigid Comtian thought to Spencerian evolutionism. The sociology of Gustave Le Bon and Ludwig Gumplowicz was just beginning to enter the universities of Vasconcelos's

positivist is apparent in his excellent *Evolución política del pueblo mexicano,* but not all would agree that he was "the high priest of positivism."

Whether the higher degree of political stability achieved in late nineteenth century Spanish America was due in any sense to this positivist ideology and whether positivism was chiefly a force for change or for maintaining the status quo, the reader must decide for himself, partly at least in accordance with his concept of the role of ideas in social action. But, whether or not it was a cause, or whatever direction its influence may have taken, the positivist ideology was at least an expression of the increased political stability that Latin America achieved under Liberal party governments in the late nineteenth century.[11] And it is also clear that positivism provided much of the theory animating the leadership of the political Liberalism of the late nineteenth century. Positivism permeated the thinking of the leaders in the evolution of the party structure that brought political stability in Uruguay, particularly in the Colorado party that shortly thereafter played a progressive role under José Batlle.[12] It may also be seen in the triumph of the Liberal party in Chile, of the *Civilista* party in Peru, and of republicanism in Brazil in 1889.

But positivism, as we have seen, also provided a theory for

---

student days, around the year 1900. Vasconcelos writes that he remained "sumiso a Comte que prohibe las aventuras de la mente y las excluye del período científico que profesamos." The *Evolución política del pueblo mexicano* is available in a 1940 edition by the Casa de España en México and in Volume 12 of the *Obras completas.*

11. See Leopoldo Zea, *El pensamiento social latinoamericano* (México: Pormaca, 1965). The author, while agreeing with Zea's thesis in general, finds it difficult to accept Zea's argument that positivism was an inadequate basis on which to transcend history.

12. Juan Antonio Oddone, *El principismo de Setenta,* Advertencia de Edmundo M. Narancio (Montevideo: Universidad de la República Oriental del Uruguay, 1956), 9–10.

conservative political forces. It is a distortion of the truth to say, as John H. Randall, Jr., has said, that Comte "preached an enlightened despotism of the old order." [13] But certainly, in Latin America, scientific positivism seemed to find some of its most notable expressions as a rationalization of things as they were and were destined to be, rather than of things as they *ought* to be. Sometimes, one may see the theoretical acceptance of Comte's latter-day exposition of the authoritarian republic. As already suggested, this acceptance of positivism by social conservatives is understandable in the sense that the perplexed, faction-ridden ruling elite found security in the positivist concept that institutions must be appropriate to the stages of development and in the doctrine of the inevitable and progressive evolution of institutions. Supporting the cause of President José Balmaceda of Chile in his conflict with the Congress, José Enrique Lagarrigue wrote: "The parliamentary regime was rejected (*desaconsejado*) years ago by the founder of positivism, Auguste Comte." [14]

Because it became nonrevolutionary in general, positivism also became nationalist and was able to concern itself with concrete measures to solve national problems within a national context. Because of this nationalism, it is not surprising that such revolutionaries as the Cuban José Martí, or even the less revolutionary Puerto Rican Eugenio María de Hostos, while adhering to the general patterns of positivism, should revolt against the "inevitability" of positivist thought. In their rebellion they reflected something of the neo-idealism of the twen-

13. John H. Randall, Jr., *The Making of the Modern Mind* (Boston-New York: Houghton Mifflin Co., 1940), 579.

14. José Enrique Lagarrigue, *Dictamen positiva sobre el conflicto entre el Gobierno y el Congreso* (Santiago: Imprenta Cervantes, 1890), quoted in José Echeverría, *La enseñanza de la filosofía en la universidad hispanoamericana* (Washington, D.C.: Unión Panamericana, 1965), 34.

tieth century. The case of José Enrique Rodó of Uruguay as a rebel against the positivism of his day is somewhat different; it is also paradoxical. Rodó was critical of much positivist thought, although in a fundamental sense his ideas were structured within positivist evolutionary historicism and scientism. But his stoical idealism tended to lead him away from positivism. In essence he defended the older aristocratic-democratic values of his intellectual and social class against the "vulgarizing" and "materialist" trends of democracy. But at the same time he appealed to the idealistic sense of *noblesse oblige* of the youth of Uruguay to lead a moral and spiritual revolution in the direction of what he conceived to be a true and less mediocre democracy.

POSITIVISM IN BRAZIL

Silvio Romero has written of the arrival of positivism in Brazil as part of "a wave of new ideas" that came between 1868 and 1878.[15] As a matter of fact, positivism was known earlier. But it was Luis Pereira Barreto (1840–1923) who popularized the ideas in the first volume of his *As tres filosofias,* published in 1874, calling for practical reforms and for intensifying the positive culture of Brazil. Benjamin Constant Botelho de Magalhães (1836–1891) first gave wide currency to the positivist doctrines through his teaching in the Military School of Brazil in the years following 1873. A whole generation of young army officers came under his influence there, including Euclydes da Cunha and some of the leaders of the republican Revolution of 1889.

Both Luis Pereira Barreto and Benjamin Constant saw in

15. Silvío Romero, *Filosofia do Brasil* (1878), quoted in Antón Donoso, "Philosophy in Brazil," *International Philosophical Quarterly,* VI (June, 1966), 286–310, at 295.

positivism a pattern of ideas capable of supplanting the influence of the traditional church-oriented social thought, as well as
that of the earlier vague eclecticism and spiritualism. After
1889, as Minister of Education under the newly established republic, Benjamin Constant had an unsual opportunity, in association with Ruy Barbosa, to apply his theories in the separation
of Church and state, and in a far-reaching reform of the public
educational system, a reform intended to give education a scientific basis and to minimize classical and ecclesiastical (scholastic)
influence.

Miguel Lemos and Raimundo Teixeira Mendes, as previously
noted, emerged as the leaders of religious positivism (humanism) within the broader positivist currents in Brazil. In 1877
these two future "apostles" of Brazilian religious positivism
journeyed to Paris, where Miguel Lemos took up with the ideas
of Comte's disciple, Pierre Lafitte. Returning to Brazil, he and
Teixeira Mendes founded a positivist society which soon became the Positivist Apostolate of Brazil. Their influence (and
that of Lafitte) gave to Brazilian positivism what was probably
a more deeply religious character than it acquired in any other
nation.

Traditional Christian thought continued to oppose positivism
in Brazil in all its forms. But less traditional and more secular
spiritual trends also found expression toward the end of the
century in the Kantian spiritualism of Raimundo de Farias
Brito (1862–1917) of Recife. Farias Brito was a keen critic and
opponent of positivist evolutionary thought in all its forms. His
basic theme is moral regeneration, and in his later years his
thought may well have influenced the emerging Christian socialism of Jackson de Figueiredo. A more accurate comparison
than that with Figueiredo, however, would be with the idealistic
pessimism of Schopenhauer, whom he admired, and with the

stream of Kantian thought that had persisted in Brazil since the days of the flourishing center at Itú,[16] the community established by a mulatto priest, Padre Jesuino do Monte Carmelo, in the early nineteenth century. One of its best-known members was Padre Diogo Antonio Feijó, later Regent of the Empire.

Euclydes da Cunha (1866–1909) was born in Santa Rita de Rio Negro in the province of Rio de Janeiro, the child of Donna Eudoxia Moreira da Cunha and Manuel Rodríguez Pimenta da Cunha. His father was a native of Baía, the province that includes the Canudos of which Euclydes was to write. A poet of the Romantic school, the father imparted to his son his liking for poetry, besides providing him with a good general education.

When Euclydes was ten years old, his father took him to Rio de Janeiro, where at the Colegio Aquino he came under the influence of Benjamin Constant Botelho de Magalhães, then the leading exponent of positivist thought in Brazil. Entering the Escola Militar da Praia Vermelha at the age of 20, he acquired the scientific training that later contributed so much to his work. Under the teaching of Benjamin Constant, he also absorbed the ideas of Auguste Comte, Herbert Spencer, Victor Hugo, the abolitionist poet Castro Alves, James Bryce, Hippolyte Taine, Ernest Renan, Henry Buckle, and Joseph Arthur Gobineau. Gobineau's theory that biological evolution produced superior and inferior races left an indelible mark. Three North Americans also contributed ideas to da Cunha's intellec-

16. On positivism in Brazil see João Cruz Costa, *Contribuição a História das Idéias no Brasil* (Rio de Janeiro, 1956), also in Spanish translation by Jorge López Páez (México: Fondo de Cultura Económica, 1957), and in English translation by Suzette Macedo, *A History of Ideas in Brazil* (Berkeley: University of California Press, 1964). See also his *Panorama of the History of Philosophy in Brazil* (Washington: Pan American Union, 1962), Guillermo Francovich, *Filósofos brasileños*, and João Camilo de Oliveira Torres, *O positivismo no Brasil* (Rio de Janeiro, 1943). See also Gilberto Freyre, *Order and Progress*.

tual development: the geographer Orville Adelbert Derby, the geologist John Casper Brenner, and the geologist-archeologist Charles Frederic Hartt, a Canadian by birth. From them he derived concepts of the influence of geography and climate.

In 1896 da Cunha left the army to take up a career of civil engineering. He was engaged in the construction of public works for the state of São Paulo when the Canudos revolt, led by the strange, half-mad Antonio Maciel, "the Counsellor," took place in 1896. The newspaper *Estado de São Paulo* sent da Cunha to report on the army expedition to suppress this uprising of the *sertanejos,* and his reports dramatically brought to the attention of the Brazilian public the significance of the rebellion of Canudos and the heroic resistance of its inhabitants. Impressed by the isolation and the harsh extremes of climate and the bleak topography of the backlands, da Cunha concluded that these factors were forging a new Brazilian race out of the mixed racial population that his positivist background led him to expect to be inferior hybrids. In the very appearance of Maciel, the back-country Messiah, he now saw a universal cultural phenomenon. The Counsellor and his *sertanejos* were the new race emerging from the mixture of the Indian, the Negro, and the European, under the influence of the harsh backlands geography and climate. Their behavior reflected the still-unformed aspirations derived from the three races and gave dynamic expression to their latent religious feelings. These backlanders, said da Cunha, were "the very base of Brazilian nationality, the bedrock of the Brazilian race." Their shortcomings he attributed to the failure of the more civilized people of the coastal areas to provide education for these men of the backlands. Da Cunha's account of the rebellion at Canudos was acclaimed almost immediately one of the great books of Brazil and of America. He met a tragic death shortly afterwards, but his influence lived on in a school of interpreters who shared his positivist view of the Brazilian backlands and its cultural significance.[17]

Ruy Barbosa (1849–1923) was not a positivist in the strict sense of the term. Although his mind was formed within the scientific sociological pattern of his age, he held firmly to a spiritual view of man and the universe, as did many of his contemporaries who adopted the language of positivism in other respects. Thus, while his ideas are basically naturalistic, a persistent note of moral idealism suggests a resemblance to his contemporary, Woodrow Wilson. Since he does not often write of abstract ideas, it is difficult to define the nature and source of this idealistic inquietude with any precision. Perhaps it was the survival of something in an earlier Brazilian Liberalism, for he came out of an older generation than da Cunha. On the whole his thought, in the ideological sense, was not inconsistent with Brazilian positivism, which embraced all the causes for which Barbosa fought, including his anticlericalism and insistence on the separation of Church and state. His religious thinking was a humanism that suggests the Kantian spiritualism that persisted

17. Euclydes da Cunha's *Os Sertões* has gone through many editions in Brazil. An excellent English translation by Samuel Putnam was published by the University of Chicago in 1943. Other works of da Cunha have been published in various volumes of the *Coleção Documentos Brasileiros* (Livraria José Olympio: Rio de Janeiro). Aside from *Os Sertões*, the most important work of da Cunha is *Canudos: Diario de uma expedição,* edited by Gilberto Freyre (Vol. XVI in the *Coleção*). Among books treating da Cunha are: Gilberto Freyre, *Atualidade de Euclydes da Cunha* (Rio de Janeiro: Casa do Estudante do Brasil, 1941), Eloy Pontes, *A vida dramática de Euclydes da Cunha* (Rio de Janeiro: José Olympio, 1940), Nelson Wernecke Sodré, *Historia da literatura brasileira* (Rio de Janeiro: José Olympio, 1940), 209–12, and João Cruz Costa, *Esbozo de una historia de las ideas en el Brasil* (México: Fondo de Cultura Económica, 1957), 112–13. In English, see William Rex Crawford, *A Century of Latin American Thought,* 193–98; Harold E. Davis, *Latin American Leaders,* 128–33; and Isaac Goldberg, *Brazilian Literature* (New York: Knopf, 1922), 210–21.

in Brazil more than it suggests positivist humanism. After passing through a youthful phase of anticlericalism that led people to call him an atheist, he gave more emphasis in later years to the Christian values of love of God and of man. Yet because he still insisted upon an unorthodox view of man's relationship to his Creator, one suggesting spiritualism or Krausism, something of his earlier reputation for atheism clung to him as long as he lived.

He was born in Baía on November 5, 1849. His father, a physician, was a leader of the Liberal party in Baía and took an active part in the political life of his state. The father's strict adherence to principles in politics left a lasting impression upon his son. During his student days in Baía and São Paulo, Ruy became intimate with a group of young abolitionists, including the poet Castro Alves, and the abolition of Negro slavery became the first of the numerous liberal causes to which his life was to be dedicated. In maturity he became one of Brazil's most renowned jurists and statesmen, and this broader interest led him to espouse such causes as the extension of popular education, religious freedom, federal constitutional government, civilian predominance over the military, the integrity of public officials, the equality of all citizens before the law, and the supremacy of law in both national and international spheres.

As the principal author of the first Constitution (1891) of the Brazilian Republic, and as Minister of Justice in the provisional government, he helped to institute many of the reforms he had been championing. Church and state were separated; freedom of worship was established; marriage, public education, and cemeteries were taken out of the control of the Church. His influence in committing the new republic to an emphasis on public education was especially important. Despite his admiration for British institutions he favored a federal republic for Brazil, and the resemblance of the Brazilian constitution to that of the United States in its federalism is due largely to him.

His *Oração aos moços*, written near the end of his life and delivered by proxy at the Law School of São Paulo in 1921, well sums up his life-long conviction of the importance of man's relation to God, of the need for intelligent citizenship, and of the responsibilities of those in positions of public trust. It shows, particularly, his insistence upon the positivist and evolutionary view of the natural inequality among men and his disagreement with the socialist principle "to each according to his need." But part of the rationale of this speech was nonpositivist. This socialist view, by which Barbosa meant the positivism of his day, erred, he held, in basing values upon human appetites rather than upon man's spiritual nature.[18]

MANUEL GONZÁLEZ PRADA

To Peruvian youth, after the War of the Pacific, Manuel González Prada (1848–1918) was the voice of the Peruvian conscience, leading a liberal intellectual-political revival, while acknowledging guilt for the national errors which had brought the defeat of Peru by Chile in 1879. Jesús Chavarría has recently singled him out as a major intellectual contributor to

18. Other important works of Barbosa include *Os Actos Inconstitucionaes de Congresso e do Executivo, Cartas de Inglaterra, O Papa e o Concilio,* and *O Habeas Corpus.* Extensive excerpts may be found in the volume *Barbosa,* edited by Renato de Mendonça, and published by the Secretaría de Educación, México, in 1944. Mario de Lima Barbosa has published *Rui Barbosa na política e na história* (Rio de Janeiro: F. Briguiet, 1916). In English, see Charles W. Turner, *Ruy Barbosa, Brazilian Crusader for the Essential Freedoms* (Nashville, Tenn.: Abingdon-Cokesbury, 1945) and briefer sketches in William Rex Crawford, *A Century of Latin American Thought,* 190–93, Pedro Henríquez Ureña, *Literary Currents in Hispanic America* (Cambridge: Harvard University Press, 1945), 137–60, and Harold E. Davis, *Latin American Leaders,* 100–108.

what he calls "a group consciousness" of Peruvian nationalism. He is also a major source of the ideology of the Peruvian Popular Alliance for American Revolution (APRA).[19] Born in Lima in the revolutionary year 1848, he was the third son in a wealthy, conservative, and orthodox religious family that had been prominent in Peruvian life since before independence. In the University of San Marcos he absorbed the scientific positivism of the day. There also, to the distress of his pious mother, he learned to admire Francisco Vigil, the controversial freethinking director of the National Library. During a brief sojourn in France he became acquainted with the skepticism of the Church historian, Joseph Ernest Renan (1823–1892), sharpening his pen with the ideas of Renan for later attacks on clericalism and superstition in the Church.

Much of González Prada's thought fits the utilitarian and positivist-evolutionary pattern. He saw the basis of society in morality, as in his defense of the Indian on the grounds of Indian morality. Adopting the theory of Ludwig Gumplowicz in his *Der Rassenkampf,* he analyzed the ethnic conflict in Peru at least partly within the pattern of evolutionary and racist-positivist thought. Ethnic elements, he argued, were competing cultural powers and the Spanish conquest of Indian America was basically a cultural conquest. These ideas appeared in an essay on the Indian in *Horas de lucha (Hours of Struggle),*[20] an interesting forecast of the later emphasis on the Indian question by José Carlos Mariátegui and Víctor Raúl Haya de la Torre.

His followers, including Mariátegui and Haya de la Torre, embraced Marxist thought in differing forms. González Prada

19. See Eugenio Chang-Rodríguez, *La literatura política de González Prada, Mariátegui, y Haya de la Torre* (México: Studium, 1957) and Jesús Chavarría, "The Intellectuals and the Crisis of Modern Peruvian Nationalism: 1870–1919," *Hispanic American Historical Review,* L (May, 1970), 257–78.
20. Manuel González Prada, *Horas de lucha* (Callao, Peru: Tip. Lux), 1924.

seems to have been less affected by Marxist theory, although some Marxist influence may be seen. In *Horas de lucha* he speaks of sociology as "an eminently positive science," as conceived by Auguste Comte, regretting that it had been "converted into a heap of ramblings" by Comte's heirs. The moralist emphasis of positivism prevails in his explanation of the degradation of the Indian as a product of political servitude. The Indians are not presented in classical Marxist terms as a proletariat produced by the economic system, though they are sometimes presented as a social class that may rebel when "the spirit of the oppressed acquires sufficient vigor to chasten their oppressors." González Prada also strikes a Marxist note in taking issue with the positivists in their basic reliance on education. To one who says the *school,* he remarks, one should say "the *school and bread.*" [21]

JUAN MONTALVO (1832–1889)

That Juan Montalvo was Ecuador's greatest intellectual and literary figure is attested by no less authorities than José Enrique Rodó of Uruguay and Miguel Unamuno of Spain. Born in Ambato, Ecuador, April 13, 1832, Montalvo attended the National University in Quito but never finished the course of

21. Numerous editions of individual works of González Prada have appeared, particularly the *Horas de lucha,* the most recent edition of which was published in Buenos Aires by Americalee in 1946. A collection of his works, *Obras completas,* was published in Lima by Editorial P.T.C.M. in four volumes, 1946–1948. Of several anthologies, the most useful is *González Prada: Prólogo de Andrés Henestrosa* (México: Secretaría de Educación Pública, 1943). Luis Alberto Sánchez has written an excellent critical study, *Don Manuel* (2nd ed.; Santiago: Ercilla, 1937). Eugenio Chang-Rodríguez, *La literatura política de González Prada, Mariátegui, y Haya de la Torre,* develops the inter-relationships of the ideas of the three authors and contains an extensive bibliography on González Prada. See the brief sketches in Wiliam Rex Crawford, *A Century of Latin American Thought;* Harold E. Davis, *Makers of Democracy in Latin America,* and his *Latin American Social Thought,* 187–208.

study. He went, instead, to Europe, where his education was completed less formally through contacts with great literary figures of the day, particularly Alphonse Lamartine, the romantic poet and politician.

He has a unique importance in the history of Ecuador because of the intellectual battle he carried on with the mystic-realistic-theocratic-dictatorial president of the nation, Gabriel García Moreno. Some of Montalvo's keenest thrusts, many of them written in exile, were directed against García Moreno. After the dictator's assassination, Montalvo could boast arrogantly and with mordant humor that it was the work of his pen! In passing, it may be noted that the Ecuadorians have deemed it appropriate to commemorate these two men in statues which face each other across one of the plazas of Quito. There, in eternal dialog, they seem to express two diametrically opposite facets of the Ecuadorian national spirit.

Montalvo's rhetoric often breathes the spirit of romantic revolt. But he is saved from banality, as Unamuno says, by his quality of "indignation." [22] Although it is possible to see influences of both romantic idealism and utopian socialist ideas, Montalvo is not so much a romantic in the European sense as a rational idealist who retains much of the earlier American-French Revolutionary and Enlightenment idealism.

The elements of his thought may be summarized as follows. Basically he was a skeptical idealist, influenced by Montaigne. His interest in the American Indian, while idealistic, was too rational and too tempered by skepticism for the romantic concept of the "noble savage." Despite spending much of his life in exile he was the chief of the Liberal movement in Ecuadorian politics in his day. He never accepted the ideology of this party

22. Quoted by Manuel Moreno Sánchez in his *Montalvo* (México: Secretaría de Educación Pública, 1942), xxvi.

completely. Rather, he seems to have joined concepts of the earlier natural rights rationalism with certain liberal Christian ideas similar to the later Christian Socialism. In this trend, as suggested by Frank Spindler, he may well have been influenced by the Liberal Christianity of Lamennais. His moral-idealistic view of society is seen in his *Geometría moral*.

Rodó called him a mixture of Sarmiento and Bello, seeing in him a mixture of the romantic and the classic. His central idea of liberating man from clerical influence is the heart of the Liberal and positivist position, but it is cast within the rational concept of the earlier Liberals rather than in the later positivist evolutionary view. In general he opposed Marxist socialism, rejecting its economic determinism and the materialism he saw in the socialist insistence that liberty was meaningless without economic bases.

Unamuno sensed a spiritual kinship with Montalvo in the latter's reconciliation of a faith in America with the Spanish cultural tradition. But both Montalvo and Unamuno saw the values and concepts of the Spanish tradition developing in new forms in America. Montalvo's concept of love as the social dynamic reaches back over the years to Esteban Echeverría and the romantic idealists. His idea of the power of laughter, best exemplified in his *Capítulos que se le olvidaron a Cervantes*, shows kinship with Montaigne, Voltaire, and above all with Cervantes. One of Montalvo's ideas, vigorously expressed in his vitriolic attacks on García Moreno, is worthy of special note as a link with the sixteenth century Vitoria-Suárez tradition. This is the Suárez natural law concept that regicide is justified under the right circumstances.[23]

23. The collected works of Montalvo are being issued by Ed. José M. Cajica, Jr. S.A. in Puebla, Mexico. There are three anthologies: *Juan Montalvo. Páginas escogidas; selección, prólogo y notas de Arturo Giménez Pastor* (Buenos

AGUSTÍN ENRIQUE ALVAREZ SUÁREZ (1857–1914)

In some respects Agustín Enrique Alvarez Suárez was a late expression of the vigorously realistic and practical idealism that characterized Argentine thought of an earlier generation. More fundamentally, however, he was a late nineteenth century positivist. William Rex Crawford has compared his "secular idealism" with that of Emerson,[24] but the resemblance in this author's judgment is not great, lying chiefly in their religious free-thinking.

Born in Mendoza, on July 15, 1857, Alvarez was educated in that provincial capital and in the law school of Buenos Aires. An orphan who rose to prominence through military service and politics, he was largely self-educated. Among his achievements was that of being the founding vice-president of the University of La Plata. He also became one of its most popular professors. His views on Argentine political life and problems, expressed with vigor, independence, and pragmatism, were published in numerous volumes on social ethics, politics, and edu-

---

Aires: A. Estrada, 1941); *Obras escogidas. Prólogo de Julio E. Moreno* (Quito: Casa de la Cultura Ecuatoriana, 1948); and *Montalvo. Prólogo y selección de Manuel Moreno Sánchez* (México: Secretaría de Educación Pública, 1942). Of the numerous editions of the *Siete Tratados,* difficult to find, the most recent appears to be that of Antonio Acevedo Escobedo (México: Secretaría de Educación Pública, 1947). Other important works include *Geometría moral* (Madrid: Sucesores de Rivadeneyra, 1902), *Catilinarias* (Quito: El Tiempo, 1906), *Capítulos que se le olvidaron a Cervantes* (París: Garnier Hnos., 1921, 1930).

For an excellent study of Montalvo see Gonzalo Zaldumbide, *Montalvo y Rodó* (New York: Instituto de las Españas, 1938). The author is indebted for a number of ideas to the unpublished Ph.D. dissertation of Frank MacDonald Spindler, "The Political Thought of Juan Montalvo," American University, 1966. Max Daireaux gives a good brief comment in his *Littérature hispano-américaine* (Paris: KRA, 1930), 240–44. Rodó's work on Montalvo appeared in his *Hombres de América* (Barcelona, 1920). See also, "García Moreno y Montalvo," in Alvaro Melián Lafinur, *Figuras americanas* (París: Casa Editorial Franco-Ibero-Americana, 1926) and William Rex Crawford, *A Century of Latin American Thought,* 170–73.

24. Crawford, *A Century of Latin American Thought,* 95.

cation. Although the title of one of these books, *La transformación de las razas en América* (1906), suggests a racist outlook, he definitely parts company with such earlier Argentines as Sarmiento and Alberdi who attributed national backwardness to racial factors. To Alvarez the idea of superior and inferior races was merely a popular illusion; yet like other positivists, he discussed the question of race at some length. But the real explanation of Argentina's problems, he believed, was not to be found in race but in customs and institutions; the solutions, he thought, lay in education and in the improvement of national life and institutions.

In his *South America, Natural History of Reason,* Alvarez is the Darwinian-Spencerian-evolutionist. His most significant departure from the older style positivist sociology appears in an emphasis upon psychological explanations of social phenomena. Qualities of Americanism and *Argentinidad* are clearly evident, as is the spirit of moderation and the acceptance of "gradualness." [25]

EUGENIO MARÍA DE HOSTOS (1839–1903)

Hostos is Puerto Rico's greatest writer on social philosophy, and his influence upon Puerto Rican thought has continued into the twentieth century. Born in Mayaguez, Puerto Rico, on

25. Alvarez's *South America, Natural History of Reason,* appeared in Buenos Aires (Folletines de la Tribuna) in 1894, and has been made available in English in a WPA translation (Columbia University, 1938). His *Transformación de las razas en América,* published in Barcelona (F. Granada) in 1906, was reissued in Buenos Aires (Vaccaro, 1918). The most recent edition of the *Manual de patología política* is that of 1916 (Buenos Aires: La Cultura Argentina) with a biography by Evar Méndez. The *Herencia moral de los pueblos hispano-americanos* is available in a 1919 edition (Buenos Aires: Vaccaro) with a prologue by Felix Icasate-Larios. Alfredo Poviña has discussed Alvarez's ideas critically in his *Historia de la sociología en Latinoamérica* (México: Fondo de Cultura Económica, 1940) and William Rex Crawford gives a summary in English in his *Century of Latin American Thought,* 95–103.

November 11, 1839, he was educated there and in Spain. Much
of his later life was spent in the Dominican Republic, Venezuela, Chile, Peru, Brazil, and the United States. Originally a
monarchist, favoring an independent confederation of the West
Indies attached to Spain, he later became the outstanding intellectual leader of the movement for political autonomy in Puerto
Rico. His greatest contribution was not in politics, however, but
in education. Nor was this influence limited to Puerto Rico. He
organized normal schools in Chile, and in the Liceo de Chillán
devised a curriculum to achieve "moral, integral education."
In the Dominican Republic, working with Salomé Ureña de
Henríquez, he initiated higher education for women.

In most respects, Hostos was a typical spokesman of the scientific or "positivist" thought of his day. Following in the path
of Comte and Spencer, and beginning with the principle that
both the individual and society may be analyzed in utilitarian
terms of the satisfaction of necessities, he looked for rational and
essentially moral principles or laws governing social structure
and behavior. His concept of history, which he considered the
basis and origin of the study of society and which he derived
apparently from Vico, was also "scientific." But while he adopted
the utilitarian analysis, Hostos turned away from a Marxist materialism. For him, human necessities were not confined to the
material. The subject of history, he believed, was the *ser humano,* or the human being, and thus history *created* human
ideals. This psychological and existentialist concept of human
history, which he distinguished sharply from biological activity,
and from the Darwinian evolutionary pattern of most contemporary positivism, led him to an idealism that emphasized the
role of free will in society.

Hostos' *Sociology* gives the most comprehensive view of his
thought, although the work does not do justice to the author in

a literary sense, for it consists of student notes on university lectures, never revised by Hostos. The outstanding aspects of his sociological thought are its reliance upon history as the basis of social science, the psychological and existential-organic concept of society, an insistence on the moral essence of social relationships, and a strongly prescriptive tendency.[26]

VALENTÍN LETELIER (1852–1919)

Valentín Letelier was a great intellectual figure in Chile at the end of the nineteenth century. Rector of the National University and leader of the Radical party in the Congress, he believed, with Sarmiento, in the obligation to put ideas to work. Generally speaking, his social concepts were those of positivism, but his positivism was not so much that of Comte as the evolutionism of Herbert Spencer. In some respects, however, his positivism suggested Marxian socialism. This evolutionism and socialism gave to his thought a revolutionary stamp that distinguished him from those positivist contemporaries who defended the status quo.

Born in 1852 in Linares, south of Santiago, Chile, he was the third of eleven children. His father, descended from a French immigrant, was a farmer of modest means; through his mother he could claim descent from the old Basque Madariaga family. After the death of his father, he was brought up by a paternal aunt. Graduating from the Liceo of nearby Talca, he continued his study in the National Institute of Santiago and in the National University. In 1875 he graduated from the Law Faculty.

26. The *Obras completas* of Hostos were published in twenty volumes (Edición conmemorativa del Gobierno de Puerto Rico; La Habana: Cultural S.A. [1939]). Among the works most interesting to the student of Hostos' ideas are the *Tratado de sociología, Hombres e ideas,* and *Tratado de moral.* Juan Bosch has written *Hostos, el sembrador* (La Habana, 1939). For a brief treatment see William Rex Crawford, *A Century of Latin American Thought,* 236–46.

What was to be a lifetime of teaching and writing commenced in the Liceo of Copiapó two years later and with contributions about the same time to the journal *El Atacama*. Shortly thereafter he married Mercedes Beatriz Malta. An election as Deputy to Congress from Copiapó started him on a long congressional career. When he was appointed secretary of the diplomatic mission to Berlin a few years later, he used his stay in Germany to study German education and social development. Returning to Chile in 1885, he gained national fame with two prize-winning essays: *Concerning Political Science in Chile* (*De la ciencia política en Chile y de la necesidad de su enseñanza*) and *Why History Is Being Revised?* (*¿Porqué se rehace la historia?*). The historian, Domingo Amunátegui Solar, had never finished his compilation of the documents for Chilean history to 1845, and Letelier undertook to complete this work that eventually comprised thirty-seven volumes.

The Revolution of 1891 surprised him in the midst of this busy life of teaching, politics, and scholarship. As a member of Congress he signed the act of deposition of President Balmaceda, convinced that the president's "tyranny" was a grave danger. Later, he regretted his opposition to Balmaceda, concluding that the oligarchic control of Congress under the parliamentary system that followed the Revolution was a greater evil than the "tyranny" of Balmaceda. He saw that Balmeceda's significance lay in emphasis upon popular participation in politics.

As rector of the National University from 1906 to 1916, he was the center of much of the intellectual life of his country. Retiring from that post in 1911, he devoted the eight remaining years of gradually failing health until his death to writing two books that were published posthumously.

His ideas developed along three main streams. The first is

well portrayed in the 1957 issue of the *Anales de la Universidad de Chile*[27] devoted to his philosophy of popular education as he had expressed it in his *Filosofía de educación* and *La lucha para la cultura*. Political science was a second major stream. As a positivist, he believed that politics could be a positive science, could establish laws of causation, and determine the relationships of political phenomena. In his early essay, *Estado de la ciencia política en el país,* he argued the need for political education and for professional training of those who assumed government posts. These ideas on political science were developed further in his *Génesis del estado* (1919) and *Génesis del derecho y de las instituciones civiles fundamentales* (1919).

La evolución de la historia (2 vols., 1900), which falls in the third stream, was a further development of the ideas first expressed in his prize essay of 1886. Influenced by the ideas of English historian Henry Thomas Buckle (1821–1862) and the scientific concept of history, he was concerned with ascertaining the "laws" of history by investigating its sources. Although he advocated a scientific or sociological history, he believed that history differs from sociology in dealing with specific facts. Within these phenomena, history tries to discover the nature of the evolutionary process and then to reconstruct the facts on this basis. One is reminded of F. J. Teggert's *Theory of History*.[28]

27. *Anales de la Universidad de Chile,* Año CXV, primer trimestre de 1957, no. 105.

28. F. J. Teggert, *Theory of History* (New Haven: Yale University Press, 1925). Letelier's *La Evolución de la historia* (written for a prize competition in 1886 and originally published as *¿Porqué se rehace la historia?*) was issued in an augmented two volumes in Santiago in 1900. *La lucha por la cultura, miscelánea de artículos políticos i estudios pedagógicos* was published in Santiago in 1895. One volume of *Anales de la Universidad de Chile,* Ano CXV, No. 105 (1957) was given over to a symposium on Letelier, including some of his works. Biographies

RAMÓN ROSA (1848–1893)

Ramón Rosa, an outstanding intellectual of Honduras during these years, may be taken as typical of positivist thought, though with Liberal overtones, in despot-ridden Central America. He was born in Tegucigalpa on July 14, 1848, the illegitimate son of Isidora Rosa and Juan José Soto. Among his ancestors were many distinguished Hondurans. The years in which he grew up and was educated in Honduras were a time of continuous political disorder and anarchy. In Guatemala, where he graduated in law in 1871, Rafael Carrera was governing in a long military dictatorship. The advent to power of Justo Rufino Barrios in 1873 and the Liberal reforms he inaugurated in Guatemala, following the example of Benito Juárez in Mexico, gave new direction to Rosa's life and that of his fellow student Marco Aurelio Soto. In 1876, Soto became president of Honduras and, with the assistance of Rosa as Minister General, carried out Liberal ecclesiastical and educational reforms. Soto and Rosa directed the nation until 1883, when Soto retired and Rosa went briefly to the United States. Political changes soon enabled him to return to Honduras, however. There he devoted the last ten years of his life to study and writing. He died at the age of forty-five, disillusioned and embittered by the return of *caudillismo* to his country.

The *Social Constitution of Honduras,* his major work, was written in 1880 as the turbulence surrounding the introduction of a Liberal church and educational reforms was giving way to more stable and enlightened conditions under the rule of Marco

---

include Leonardo Fuentealba, *Ensayo biográfico de Valentín Letelier* (Santiago: Escuela Nacional de Artes Gráficas, 1956) and Luis Galdames, *Valentín Letelier y su obra* (Santiago, 1947). See also Leopoldo Zea, *Dos etapas del pensamiento en hispanoamérica,* 212–30, and W. R. Crawford, *A Century of Latin American Thought,* 74–78.

Aurelio Soto. In it, while he retains much of the earlier revolutionary Liberalism, Rosa shows clearly the influence of the contemporary social evolutionary and positivist philosophy. Significantly, he introduces the essay with a quotation from Linnaeus to the effect that Nature makes no leaps. The progressive party in Honduras, he wrote, resembles the moderate national parties appearing elsewhere in Latin America.

As a positivist, Rosa relied basically upon science and proclaimed the end of the age of metaphysics, trusting to science to solve all social problems. But he did not follow this scientific tendency to the point of reducing all social action to the evolutionary science of the inevitability of gradualness. Order and progress, the positivist motto, is the *leitmotiv* running through his thought, but a persistent note of idealism also appears. His poetry, for which he is also well known, breathes a romantic spirit.[29]

José Martí (1853–1895)

Most of the short life of the Cuban hero José Martí was spent in exile, much of it in the United States, and was devoted to achieving the independence of Cuba. Cuban independence, he said in Caracas in 1878, would be "the last strophe" of the incomplete "poem of 1810." But he also saw in it something that was more than parochial. He was convinced that the Cuban movement was the beginning of a new and broader revolutionary movement, in the support of which he aspired "to arouse the world." America, he said, must go her own way, but she

29. On Rosa see *Oro de Honduras, Antología.* Prólogo de Rafael Heliodoro Valle, con la colaboración del Lic. Juan Valladares R., Tomo primero (Tegucigalpa, Honduras: Talleres Tipo-Litográficos "Aniston," 1948), 139–50. See also the excerpts from his works, translated by Harold E. Davis in *Latin American Social Thought.*

(with Cuba) must march with Bolívar on one side and Herbert
Spencer on the other.[30] Later, during his fourteen-year stay in
the United States, he absorbed the ideas of Henry George and
other North Americans, including labor leaders sympathetic to
Marxist ideas. Some Cubans have tried to stamp him with the
mark of materialist-socialist doctrine.[31] Fidel Castro has described the Cuban Revolution as "fulfilling the words and fulfilling the doctrine of our Apostle." [32] Others have emphasized
his individualism and devotion to democratic-liberal ideas.[33]
Much of his thought falls into the evolutionary-scientific form
of positivism.

But Martí defies categorization. Even the Cuban Communist Juan Marinello has called him "the poet [who], expressing
reality in an unaccustomed manner, transforms it within himself, makes it a part of his internal tumult, of his spiritual state,
of his dominating emotion." [34] Martí is probably best understood
as expressing these frequently contradictory emotions and anxie-
ties of Cuba and Latin America at the end of the nineteenth century, rather than as the exponent of any particular ideology.
The recurrent emphasis in his speeches and in his writing is a
rejection of determinism, whether Marxist or positivist, and an
insistence upon the possibility of change by revolution. In this
respect he is a precursor of the inquietude of Latin America

30. Jorge Mañach, *Martí, el apóstol* (2nd ed.; Buenos Aires and México:
Espasa-Calpe, 1944), 208. An English translation by Coley Taylor with a preface
by Gabriela Mistral is available (New York: Devin-Adair, 1950).

31. See A. Martínez Bello, *Ideas sociales y económicas de José Martí* (La
Habana: La Verónica, 1941).

32. Fidel Castro, speech of June 7, 1959, in *Guía del pensamiento político-
económico de Fidel* (La Habana: Diario Libre, n.d.), 70.

33. See Emeterio Santovenia y Echaide, *Genio y acción, Sarmiento y Martí*
(La Habana: Trópico, 1938), and *Lincoln en Martí* (La Habana: Trópico, 1948).

34. "Carta de Juan Marinello," in Martínez Bello, *Ideas sociales y económicas
de José Martí,* 216.

that finds expression in many different ways in its twentieth century revolutionary movements.

José Martí grew up during the Ten Years War (1868–1878) for Cuban independence. At the age of thirteen, two years before the war began, he entered the Colegio de San Pablo. There he studied under the revolutionary poet and journalist, Rafael Mendive, until the latter was imprisoned for his revolutionary activities. A visit to his imprisoned teacher left an impression, never to be erased, upon the mind of the thirteen-year-old boy. Later, his first revolutionary poem, "Abdala," was published in *La Patria Libre,* a journal edited by Mendive and Cristobal Madán.

At the age of sixteen Martí was condemned to six years imprisonment at hard labor because of a letter he and a fellow student had written to another student of Mendive, then in the Spanish service, urging him to support the Cuban cause. After two months he was released because of ill health and a wound on his ankle caused by the iron chain he wore as a prisoner — a wound that required repeated surgery. After his release he was sent to the Isle of Pines and later was permitted to go to Spain to continue his studies.

Spain was then undergoing a series of kaleidoscopic political changes following the overthrow of Queen Isabella in 1868, and Martí was soon as much a political agitator as a student. He published a scathing denunciation of Spanish treatment of political prisoners in Cuba, and his poetic ode to the student demonstrators shot on the streets of Havana on November 27, 1871, is said to have had an electric effect on Spanish public opinion. During the historic siege of Zaragoza, he stirred the republican sympathies of that city with his fiery oratory. After the establishment of the Spanish Republic (1873) he again pleaded the

Cuban cause in a pamphlet, *The Spanish Republic Confronting the Cuban Revolution*.

The Spanish Republic was overthrown in 1875, and Martí, as an ardent republican as well as an advocate of the Cuban cause, was forced into exile. He went first to Mexico, where he occupied himself in writing to urge the development of education, literature, thought, and institutions that would be American rather than European. Later, in Guatemala, he lectured in the Normal School and published the *Revista Guatemalteca*.

Returning to Cuba after the end of the Ten Years War, he was soon imprisoned and deported to Spain (1878). Escaping from his Spanish prison, he made his way to Paris, New York, and finally to Caracas, where he vowed to "arouse the world" to the Cuban cause. Because of differences with the Venezuelan dictator-president, he soon left Caracas for New York. There he spent most of the last fourteen years of his life, working constantly to arouse support for the Cuban cause while earning his living as a journalist. His revolutionary agitation culminated in the plans that produced the successful uprising in 1895. It was a severe blow to his plans, however, that United States officials stopped the departure of two vessels equipped at great expense to initiate the invasion of Cuba. Undaunted, Martí and his followers made their way to Cuba to begin hostilities in February, 1895. On May 19, at Dos Rios, José Martí was killed in the first charge of the rebel forces.

Martí became a martyr in the eyes of the Cuban revolutionaries, and his martyrdom made him an idol of the next generation of Latin American youth. At the same time, his poetic and vigorous expression of a new revolutionary philosophy, decrying the notion of Latin American political incapacity derived from the prevalent evolutionary positivist concepts, anticipated the revolutionary trend in twentieth century thought in the

Hispanic countries. Because his life was cut short at the age of forty-two, Martí never wrote the volumes he had planned on such subjects as education and the Negro race. Nor did he have the opportunity to produce a systematic exposition of the new revolutionary philosophy so vigorously expressed in his speeches. The pattern of his thought must therefore be culled from speeches, newspaper and magazine articles, letters, and from the preliminary notes for books never written.

Crawford has called him a practical mystic, utopian yet at the same time realist.[35] But this author sees little of the mystic in Martí, except possibly in the very general sense of a "mystic leap" from skepticism to belief in the humanity of man. This is the sense, of course, in which any strong assertion of belief may be called a mystique. Much of Martí's writing, like that of Rodó, is an eloquent plea for a spiritual revolution, with an ethics based upon love. His admiration for Cecilio Acosta of Venezuela embraced the latter's understanding of the ethical basis of Anglo-American democracy, and his frequent denunciations of the materialism he found in the United States should be interpreted as charges that the United States was forgetting this ethical basis.

He spoke out clearly against racism, defending the cause of the recently emancipated Negroes of Cuba. He urged a program of education for the Indians and Negroes of all of America that would be practical rather than literary. He also urged agrarian reform, by which he meant redistribution of land ownership, and an independence for Cuba that would be economic and cultural as well as political. Such a concept of the social revolution required in America makes him a predecessor of José Mariátegui and Víctor Raúl Haya de la Torre, while his appeal to the

---

35. Crawford, *A Century of Latin American Thought*, 233.

idealism of youth, a constant characteristic of his writing and
speeches, links him with José Rodó, José Ingenieros, and José
Vasconcelos.[36]

36. Manuel Pedro González, *Fuentes para el estudio de José Martí: Ensayo
de bibliografía clasificada* (La Habana: Ministerio de Educación, 1950) is a good
guide to the extensive Martí bibliography. Of the various collected works, the
most convenient is the "Lex" edition in two volumes (La Habana: Edición Lex,
1946). Selected writings are found in *José Martí: Prosas, Selección, prólogo y
notas de Andrés Iduarte* (Washington: Unión Panamericana, 1950) and in *José
Martí: Ideario separatista. Recopilación y prólogo por Félix Lizaso* (La Habana:
Ministerio de Educación, 1947). The excellent biography by Jorge Mañach,
Martí, el apóstol (2nd ed.; Buenos Aires and México: Espasa-Calpe, 1944) is also
available in English: *Martí: Apostle of Freedom,* introduction by Gabriela Mis-
tral (New York: Devin-Adair, 1950). M. Isidro Méndez, *Martí* (La Habana:
F. Fernández y Cía., 1941) is good literary criticism. Manuel Pedro González
has analyzed Martí's writings about the United States in *José Martí: Epic
Chronicler of the United States in the Eighties* (Chapel Hill: University of
North Carolina, 1953), while Martínez Bello, *Ideas sociales y económicas de
José Martí* emphasizes the links with Marxist thought.

End-of-the-Century Traditionalism

CHANGING PATTERNS OF CONSERVATIVE THOUGHT

By the late nineteenth century, the older traditionalism of Balmes, although still an important element in Latin American thought, had ceased to have the significance it enjoyed in the early decades of the century. The most common form of traditionalism had become that of the ideology of the Conservative parties. Oriented basically to the defense of the social position of the Church, it also included a more general defense of the existing social and family structures. In their economics, however, the traditionalists had become scarcely distinguishable from Liberals. They were no longer monarchists in any significant sense, although occasionally they expressed sentimental sympathy with Spanish, Portuguese, or French monarchism. A typical example of this sentimental monarchism appeared in Amado Nervo's *Epitalamio* (1906), a poem expressing the idea that the Spanish American republics were subjects of the Spanish king in spirit. In the main, however, conservatives merely preferred to maintain their traditional values through the Church in a conservative republic.

Andrés Bello's *Filosofía del entendimiento,* published posthumously in 1881 in Chile, expresses a kind of moderate-conservative thought of these years, continuing a development of the earlier decades of the nineteenth century. Bello holds to the Scottish school of natural realism for the most part and also shows the influence of Locke. But he asserts his Christian belief as well and adheres to the view that Providence moves through history — a view of history not unlike that of Giovanni Battista Vico (1668–1744). One critic, García Aponte, has called Bello's thought "realismo espiritualista." [1]

Intellectual traditionalists of the turn of the century were of several varieties. One of these was José Enrique Rodó, who sought the basis of the cultural values he called upon his generation to defend in the combined Christian and Hellenic heritage. Manuel Gálvez of Argentina gave expression to traditionalism in the form of *Argentinidad,* by which Gálvez meant the *criollo* tradition. Fernando Ortiz of Cuba called for a similar search in his *Cubanidad,* and other Latin American writers appealed for nationalism in comparable terms.

Early twentieth century poets like Rubén Darío of Nicaragua and Amado Nervo of Mexico were traditionalists in the cultural and esthetic sense of searching for poetic forms within the Hispanic tradition. Miguel Antonio Caro of Colombia was a traditionalist close to the European pattern in these end-of-the-century years. It is interesting to note that intellectual traditionalists of his type were often the first to take up the Christian socialism of Pope Leo XIII's encyclical *Rerum Novarum.* Juan Zorilla de San Martín of Uruguay, author of the epic poem *Tabaré,* is another example.[2]

In a stimulating little book entitled *El pensamiento político de la derecha latinoamericana (Political Thought of the Latin*

1. García Aponte, cited in Carlos Arturo Caparroso, *Aproximación a Bello* (Bogotá: Edición de la Revista Ximénez de Quesada, 1966), 249.
2. Cf. Martin S. Stabb, *In Quest of Identity,* 185ff.; Carlos Valderrama Andrade, *El pensamiento filosófico de Miguel Antonio Caro* (Bogotá: Instituto Caro y Cuervo, 1961); Guillermo A. Lousteau Heguy and Salvador María Lozada (eds.), *José Enrique Rodó; Juan Zorilla de San Martín* (Buenos Aires: Depalma, 1967).

American Right), the Argentine historian José Luis Romero discusses a number of the turn-of-the-century writers who expressed traditionalist thought and conservative ideologies. The reader may reserve judgment on the special kind of continuity Romero sees in this thought, which is that of the social classes. But Romero's comment on the ideology of the authoritarian Gabriel García Moreno of Ecuador as one of civilization and progress, Catholicism, conservatism, and republicanism is interesting, to say the least. Romero considers traditionalists under three categories: antiliberal rightists, liberal monarchists, and authoritarian republicans. The first and third of these are most prominent at the turn of the century. He also speaks of José Manuel Estrada of Argentina as a defender of traditionalism who saw a necessary choice between "deification of the state by Liberalism . . . or the sovereignty of the Church, integrally confessed." Estrada, and other traditionalists, he writes, defended "the heroic ideals, possession of the land, social inequality, aristocracy of the spirit, and submission of consciences to the Catholic Church."[3]

THE HISTORIANS

Historical writing increased and improved in Latin America during the last half of the nineteenth century, expressing the growing sense of nationalism and a kind of national soul-searching that accompanied the developments of the era. Historical thinking frequently involved elements of traditionalism, often of an American rather than a European character. Mexico produced such historical scholars as Vicente Riva Palacio and Joaquín García Icazbalceta. Peru gave us Manuel de Mendiburu and Pedro Paz Soldán. Chile had an especially outstanding

3. José Luis Romero, *El pensamiento político de la derecha latinoamericana,* Chaps. 3 and 4, especially p. 127.

group, including Diego Barros Arana, Benjamín Vicuña Mackenna, Miguel Luis Amunátegui and José Toribio Medina. Argentina had V. F. López, Bartolomé Mitre, Antonio Zinny, and Vicente G. Quesada. Brazil produced Manoel de Oliveira Lima among others. The history these scholars wrote was nationalistic, reminiscent, and stock taking.

In general, these historians refused to write history within either positivist or Marxist ideology. But there were exceptions. Around the turn of the century the Venezuelan Rufino Blanco Fombona studied the conflict of classes in his *La evolución política y social de Hispano-América*.[4] The "científico" (positivist) Francisco Bulnes of Mexico painted a pessimistic future for Latin America in its relations with the United States in his *El porvenir de las naciones hispano-americanas*.[5] At the end of the century Carlos Octavio Bunge of Argentina gave a similarly pessimistic psychological-social analysis, essentially a positivist interpretation of the mixed racial basis of Latin America, in his *Nuestra América*.[6] The Bolivian Alcides Argüedas wrote historically of the "illness" of the Hispanic nations.[7] Although Justo Sierra, as we shall see, is far from a strict positivist, his *Evolución política del pueblo mexicano*[8] has a generally positivist character and was, in fact, one of the more important historical works written in America within the positivist sociological pat-

4. Rufino Blanco Fombona, *La evolución política y social de Hispano-América* (Madrid: n.p., 1911).

5. Francisco Bulnes, *El porvenir de las naciones hispano-americanas* (México: Pensamiento Vivo de América, 1922).

6. Carlos Octavio Bunge, *Nuestra América* (Barcelona: n.p., 1903). A sixth edition with an introduction by José Ingenieros was published by Vaccaro (Buenos Aires, 1918).

7. Alcides Arguedas, *Pueblo enfermo. Contribución a la psicología de los pueblos hispanoamericanos*, Carta-prólogo de Ramiro de Maeztu (Barcelona: Viuda de L. Tasso, 1909. Third edition, Santiago de Chile: Ercilla, 1937).

8. Justo Sierra, *Evolución política del pueblo mexicano* (México: Casa de España, 1940); original edition, 1910. Also available in English translation.

tern. Francisco Calderón of Peru also wrote in a positivist vein, in this case generally a conservative vein, accepting the Comtian principle of an authoritative republic and interpreting the political development of Hispanic America as an evolution through various stages of dictatorship to a freer and more prosperous society.[9]

Most Latin American historians, in theory if not always in practice, chose rather to follow the historical method of Leopold von Ranke, allowing the documents "to speak for themselves." Like von Ranke, they professed to interpret national development within the framework of the American-French Revolutionary and rational natural law and idealism. They found their pattern of ideas in the independence movements, as modified by the romantic liberalism and historicism of the early nineteenth century. Valentín Letelier, as we have seen, went further in *La evolución de la historia,* attracting wide attention by his positivist, sometimes almost Marxist, emphasis upon ascertaining the scientific laws of history.

JUSTO SIERRA MÉNDEZ (1848–1912)

Justo Sierra Méndez was born in Campeche, Yucatán, on January 26, 1848, the son of the Mexican-Irishman Justo Sierra O'Reilly and Concepción Méndez y Echazarreta. His physician father took an active part in Yucatán politics, particularly in the midcentury move for Yucatecan independence. Among other things, he undertook a mission to the United States, unsuccessful as it turned out, to secure recognition of the short-lived Yucatecan republic. Justo, the son, was educated in Yucatán and, after the death of his father, in Mexico City, where he graduated in law.

9. Francisco Calderón, *Les démocraties latines de l'Amérique* (Paris: Flammarion, 1912).

For a time he was the secretary of the Supreme Court, but his principal career was in education. He taught history in the National Preparatory School, edited various journals, and was elected to the National Congress. Visiting the United States, he learned to admire its regime of freedom, but came to dislike what he called its rule by plutocracy. Because of his support of the "científico" party, at this time considered overly critical of the administration, his election to the Congress in 1892 was blocked by Porfirio Díaz. Later, however, Díaz named him minister of education. In this position he crowned his accomplishments by re-establishing the National University, which had ceased to exist as an integrated body half a century before in the course of the controversy over Church-state relations.

As previously noted, one of the relatively few examples of a positivist-oriented historical work is Sierra's *Evolución política del pueblo mexicano*. Some of the anti-Spanish tone of an earlier era persists in this work, but in a subdued key. Sierra's anticlericalism is that of the rather typically positivist opposition to the superstitious elements that have survived within Christianity, rather than that of the earlier militant Liberalism. Sierra shares the tendency of his times to stress racial factors in the explanation of society and social change. But this positivist preoccupation with race, in his case, does not express racial prejudice against the Indian or the mestizo. Rather, his racial view presages that of later Mexican Revolutionary leaders who saw the mestizo as the dynamic element in Mexican social evolution. His views on education did not differ except in detail from those of his positivist predecessor Gabino Barreda of whose work he had written critically in 1881. Sierra, however, gave more emphasis to historical-cultural factors and to evolutionism. Even more distinctive is the strong spiritual tone of his writing.

"The truth is, my heart is a monastery," he once remarked.[10] This spiritual quality and the generally optimistic spirit permeating his work were portents of the new idealism beginning to challenge the dominant positivism of the end of the century.[11] It should be noted, however, that his reliance upon historical-cultural factors also links him to the traditionalism that managed to survive within a positivist structure of thought.

JOSÉ MANUEL ESTRADA (1842–1894)

The autodidactic Estrada of Argentina, born in Buenos Aires, illustrates the process that a number of Latin American intellectuals went through, as he moved from an earlier Liberalism through a stage of positivism to a new traditionalism in the late decades of the century. Salvador M. Dana Montaño has remarked that Estrada was a dogmatic Liberal in his youth and became an "orthodox Catholic" in maturity. In his *Liberal Policy under the Tyranny of Rosas,* written in 1873, he is still largely the Liberal, studying sympathetically the Generation of 1837 that opposed Rosas, though pointing out their errors. Subsequently he became a critic of both Liberalism and the positivism of his day, moving eventually to a more traditionalist philosophical position. Dana Montaño considers him the founder

10. Justo Sierra Méndez, "El palatino," *El Mundo Ilustrado* (June 14, 1903), quoted by Raúl Carranca y Trujillo, in "Justo Sierra, Maestro de América," *Orbe,* XXX (June 30, 1951), 15.
11. The *Obras completas* of Sierra were published by the National University in fifteen volumes, edited by Augustín Yáñez. Volume XIV, *Epistolario y papeles privados,* is a biography and a study of Sierra's ideas and works (México: Universidad Nacional, 1949). The *Evolución política del pueblo mexicano* is Volume XII, and as previously noted is available in a 1940 edition by the Casa de España en México. There is also an English translation. Selections from other writings are found in *Justo Sierra, Prosas: prólogo y selección de Antonio Caso* (México: Universidad Nacional, 1939). For commentaries in English, see Crawford, *A Century of Latin American Thought,* 137–60, and Pedro Henríquez Ureña, *Literary Currents in Hispanic America* (Cambridge: Harvard University Press, 1945).

of political science in Argentina and calls him the third important Argentine writer on political themes — one who follows
in the footsteps of Juan B. Alberdi, author of the famous *Bases,*
and Florentino González, known for his *Lecciones de derecho
constitucional (Lessons on Constitutional Law).* Dana Montaño's evaluation is based especially on the course on constitutional law inaugurated by Estrada in the Colegio Nacional
in 1877, a course developed around Joseph Story's classic *Commentaries on the Constitution of the United States.*[12]

In one of his major works, *Liberal Policy under the Tyranny
of Rosas,* Estrada criticized the *Dogma socialista* of Echeverría
as doctrinaire, a quality which, he said, explains its failure. In
his later *Catolicismo y la democracia* he defended the Church,
refuting the revolutionary Liberalism of Francisco Bilbao's *La
América en peligro.* He also rejected the positivism of his day
(including that of Spencer), because it culminated in a theory
of sovereignty that leaves unsatisfied the human spirit, a spirit of
individual freedom in the exercise of free will. Positivism, he
said, erred in rejecting a dialectical analysis in favor of a too
simple empiricism. Estrada may have been at least partially
correct insofar as his Argentine positivist peers were concerned,
but he was not correct in saying Comte rejected dialectical
analysis. Comte had his own peculiar dialectic. Estrada also rejected such a simple "historical" explanation as that of Alberdi,
one that merely shows the derivation *(filiación)* of institutions

12. See Salvador M. Dana Montaño, *Las ideas políticas de José Manuel Estrada* (Santa Fe, Argentina: Imprenta de la Universidad, 1944), 23; and José
Manuel Estrada, *La política liberal bajo la tiranía de Rosas* (Buenos Aires: La
Cultura Argentina, 1927), cited in Dana Montaño, *Las ideas políticas de Estrada.*
Estrada's course *(Curso de derecho constitucional)* was published in 1877 from
notes of his students, according to Dana Montaño, *Las ideas políticas de Estrada,*
20 (citing Rodolfo Rivarola, *El maestro José Manuel Estrada en la ciencia política
argentina* [Buenos Aires: Imprenta de Coni Hermanos, 1913], 60).

and does not justify them. The sources of institutions and of constitutional law, as he saw it, were fourfold: (1) written law, (2) tradition, (3) history, and (4) principles, by which he meant principles of natural law. His insistence on "spiritualizing" history, constitutional law, and political science makes him a forerunner of such twentieth century idealist-traditionalists as Manuel Gálvez. Probably the most significant aspect of his thought is the renewed emphasis he brought to the natural law basis of institutions and to the religious aspects of social thought.[13]

MIGUEL ANTONIO CARO (1843–1909)

Colombia is notable among the nations of Hispanic America for her traditionalist writers and philosophers, as well as for the limited success positivist doctrines achieved in her intellectual life. Utilitarianism and its philosophical sensualism gained an early foothold among such Colombian Benthamites as Santander, and anticlerical Liberalism flourished among political leaders advocating federalism until the era of President Rafael Núñez. But positivism made less progress on the whole than in other countries, yielding first place to traditionalist followers of the ideas of de Maistre, Balmes, and Donoso Cortés. Nor were the ideas of Herbert Spencer received with great enthusiasm. One of the notable early Colombian traditionalists was José Joaquín Ortiz (1814–1892), author of *Las sirenas,* a work directed against utilitarianism. The priest Francisco Margallo was

13. This discussion of Estrada is drawn largely from the work of Dana Montaño referred to above, which in turn relies upon Rodolfo Rivarola, *El maestro J. M. Estrada.* Other works treating the thought of Estrada include Rodrigo Octavio, *Noções de direito federal professadas na Universidad de Buenos Ayres por D. José Manuel Estrada* (Río de Janeiro: Livraria de Alves & Co., 1897). Other works of Estrada, in addition to those mentioned, are *La libertad y el liberalismo* (Buenos Aires, 1878) and the earlier two-volume *Lecciones sobre la historia de la República Argentina* (1866–1868). His *Obras completas* were published in four volumes in 1899 by the Librería del Colegio.

another among the first to attack the Bentham ideas in polemic with Vicente Azuero. Ricardo de la Parra (1815–1873) wrote his *Cartas sobre filosofía moral* (1868) to refute the ideas of Ezequiel Rojas (1803–1873), rector of the University and one of the most brilliant Liberal philosophers of Colombia. Rufino Cuervo, candidate for the presidency in Colombia in 1848 and father of the scholar Rufino José Cuervo, was thought by many Colombians to be "the most complete personification of the system that aspired to conserve the present order of things without change."[14] José Eusebio Caro (1817–1853) was originally a follower of Bentham, but turned against utilitarianism, adopting a traditionalist philosophy like that of Donoso Cortés and publishing one of the first outright attacks on the regnant utilitarianism of the then Liberal party.

Miguel Antonio was the son of this José Eusebio Caro. The Caro family had originated in Ocaña, but Miguel Antonio was born in Bogotá, where he grew up and received his education. The Caros were related to prominent families of Colombia that included such literary and political figures as Carlos Holguín and Rafael Núñez, long-time president of the nation (1880–1894). Miguel Caro himself was active in Colombian politics during the last several decades of his life, serving as the vice-president of Colombia under Rafael Núñez from 1892 to 1894 and as president (1894–1898) after the death of Núñez. Also a poet, he was the author of a book of verses entitled *Horas de amor*.

Although many of his published works bear titles indicating a polemic against utilitarianism and positivism, Caro's real importance lies in the vigor with which he expressed a revivified Catholic thought. The Encyclical *Aeternis Patris* of Leo XIII,

14. José Luis Romero, *El pensamiento político de la derecha latinoamericana*, 58–59, quoting Salvador Camacho Roldán.

brilliantly developed in the Colegio Mayor de Nuestra Señora del Rosario, in Antioquia, by Joaquín Gómez Otero, stimulated him in this direction. He was also a pioneer in spreading the ideas of social Christianity expressed in the *Rerum Novarum* of Pope Leo XIII. In 1865, at the age of twenty-two, he began teaching the traditionalist philosophy of Cayetano San Severino in the newly established (Catholic) Colegio of Pius IX. From then until his death he was an active leader of Colombian traditionalist thought. Carlos Valderrama Andrade, who has written the best study of Caro's philosophy, places him among the three greatest philosophers of his country. Valderrama concludes that Caro was more Augustinian than Thomistic, seeing this quality especially in Caro's expression of an "elevated concept of human dignity" with a sense of the "Christian mystery." [15]

Caro's attacks on utilitarianism have a major focus on the atheism, partial or complete, that he finds in its denial of natural and revealed religion and of reason in the Christian sense. It was prompted by a proposal of Ezequiel Rojas, in the Colombian Senate in 1867, to require the teaching of the utilitarianism of Bentham in all public institutions. Caro was expressing a rather general conservative outcry against the proposal. In the history of philosophy, he insists, atheists have usually been utilitarians. Utilitarianism, as he sees it, is fundamentally egoistic and hence Satanic in its origin. The Christian, he urges, finds the basis of morality in metaphysics. "Ethics is a science of which the manifestations are practical, but of which the basis is purely metaphysical." The state has a natural law basis that is also Christian. Hence it is an organ of social cohesion, with

15. Carlos Valderrama Andrade, *El pensamiento filosófico de Miguel Antonio Caro*, 240. See also Enrique Zuleta Alvarez, "La iniciación filosófica de Miguel Antonio Caro" in *Libro de homenaje a Luis Alberto Sánchez en los 40 años de su docencia universitaria* (Lima: Universidad Mayor de San Marcos, 1967), 539–63.

responsibility for social action, and not merely the guardian of individual rights. Caro's thought has an eclectic character. Sometimes he appeals to the logic of the Scottish school, as in his initial attack on utilitarianism. Sometimes he is more Augustinian or Thomistic.[16]

END-OF-THE-CENTURY TRENDS

Positivism was still the most prevalent pattern of thought at the end of the century, but it was finding expression in an increasing variety of forms as it responded to changes in nineteenth century scientific thought and changing attitudes within the Church. A number of such divergent trends have been noted, trends that in many cases pointed toward developments that were to become more notable in the twentieth century. Thus we have seen that Alvarez Suárez spoke with a new accent on naturalistic realism, one that was also finding expression in the novel. Hostos and Rodó, differing as they did in many respects, were alike in being prescriptive moralists, rebelling against the social determinism of much positivist thought, and calling for a kind of moral crusade. The revolutionary emphasis in the thought of Martí and González Prada doubtless owed something to older Liberal revolutionary concepts. But their thought

16. Miguel Antonio Caro, *Ensayo sobre el catolicismo, el liberalismo y el socialismo*, cited in Carlos Valderrama Andrade, *El pensamiento filosófico de Miguel Antonio Caro*, 230. For the background of philosophy in Colombia, Valderrama has relied greatly on Francisco M. Renjifo, "La filosofía en Colombia," *Revista del Colegio Mayor de Nuestra Señora del Rosario*, XXVI (July, 1931), 337–43, and on various writings of the Colombian philosopher Jaime Jaramillo Uribe. The published works of Caro are numerous. His collected *Obras* were published in 1962 by the Instituto Caro y Cuervo, ed. Carlos Valderrama Andrade. In addition to those mentioned, the reader may also find important for Caro's attacks on utilitarianism *Estudio sobre el utilitarismo* (Bogotá: Imp. de Foción Mantilla, 1869) and "Informe sobre los 'Elementos de Ideología' de Tracy," *Anales de la Universidad de los Estados Unidos de Colombia*, IV (September, 1870).

also owed much to positivism and something to Marxism. They were also prescient, anticipating in some respects the twentieth century revolutionary thought that would evolve within the dawning existentialist idealism.

Marxist ideas were widely known to Latin American scholars, although more often in the form in which they were rebutted in papal teaching in the Encyclicals than in terms derived from reading the works of Marx and Engels. But the ideas of Marx or of the Russian anarchists Kropotkin and Bakunin were held by radical leaders of the emerging labor movement and were finding expression in a small labor press.[17]

In the encyclical *Rerum Novarum*, Leo XIII had called upon Catholic philosophers and theologians to examine the traditional patterns of Christian thought with a view to effecting a reconciliation of Christian belief with the new scientific knowledge. A virtual revolution in the scientific explanation of the world and man was taking place at the turn of the century. It was no longer the theories of geological and biological evolution that presented the major challenge to religious beliefs. New theories of energy were challenging the classical Newtonian laws, preparing the way for the Einstein theory of general relativity, while psychologists were revising their science along physiological and behavioral lines, leaving little place for belief in the kind of human reason in which Christians had believed.

Economic and demographic changes were presenting new national and international problems by the turn of the century, and these changes were giving rise to movements of social protest that increasingly sought their ideological basis in forms of thought that challenged the dominant positivism. Sociologists

17. For the labor press see Carlos M. Rama, *Mouvements ouvriers et socialistes (Chronologie et bibliographie) L'Amérique Latine (1492–1936)*, (Paris: Ouvriers, c. 1959).

were giving more attention to empirical psychology by studying social groups and their behavior. Some of the new ideologies had a Marxist base. But non-Marxists found support for a more revolutionary stance in the "creative evolution" and the "élan vital" of Henri Bergson (1859–1941), who insisted on man's creative social role. The neo-idealism of Nietzsche and Renan, and the existentialist concepts of Wilhelm Dilthey (1833–1911), William James (1842–1910), and others, were also beginning to exert their influence as the nineteenth century came to a close. The emerging literary modernism of the poets of Latin America had close links with new Spanish poets of the Generation of 1898, and Spanish American counterparts of the historians and philosophers of this Spanish generation were also raising their heads.

Finally, the spiritualist current should be mentioned as one of importance for the opening years of the new century. It had several forms, including the Spiritualism as known in the United States and Western Europe, the Spiritism of Brazil, and various idealist philosophies, often of Kantian connection, which posited the reality of the spirit. One of the most important forms was the philosophical system known popularly as Krausism. Based on the teaching of the German Karl Christian Krause, this philosophy was early noted by Spanish scholars, including the traditionalist Jaime Balmes. It was introduced into the University of Madrid by Julián Sanz del Río (1814–1869) in the 1860's and soon became the general pattern of Spanish philosophical study, "the first complete expression of the secular spirit of modern philosophy among Spaniards," as Valderrama Andrade has expressed it.[18] From Spain it spread to

18. Carlos Valderrama Andrade, *El pensamiento filosófico de M. A. Caro*, 87. On Krausism see José López Morillas, *El krausismo español* (México: Fondo de Cultura Económica, 1961) and Arturo Andrés Roig, *Los krausistas argentinos* (Puebla, México: José M. Cajica, Jr., 1969).

Spanish America, also producing important repercussions in Portugal and Brazil. Its introduction into the University of Mexico by Telésforo García produced a major intellectual debate. There, as well as in the Iberian peninsula and in other parts of Latin America, the vaguely religious humanism of Krausism was to be the inspiration of a number of philosophers and of several important political leaders.

Five end-of-the-century currents, then, may be pointed out as important for the succeeding period. Positivism was continuing, changed by new concepts derived from scientific developments in psychology, biology, and physics. Krausism was contributing a vaguely mystic and religious, but on the whole secular humanism. The seeds of Marxism and anarchism, so important for the next century, had been planted. A revival of Christian, Thomistic thought was occurring. Finally, and in some respects this current was the most important of all, the philosophical basis was being laid for the remarkable growth of twentieth century existentialist idealism by contact with the new idealist trends of thought in Western Europe and the United States.

Revolutionary and Traditional Twentieth Century Thought

As the nineteenth century drew to a close, the flame of revolutionary ideas, so characteristic of Latin American thought, had been virtually smothered if not extinguished in a dominant pattern of positivism, scientism, and evolutionism. The revolutionary flame was to reappear, with new fire and brilliance, in the twentieth century. But for the time being the forms of this new social thought would conform in the main to those generally prevailing in Western culture. Yet new dynamic concepts appeared in connection with revolutionary movements, reacting with traditional attitudes and ideas to give distinctive character to the thought currents of the new world.

Certain themes run through all these various expressions of the twentieth century: the nature of man, the nature of being, the nature and possibility of social change, the nature of law and of institutions in general, the nature or theory of revolutions and, above all, the nature and meaning of history.

THE OLD AND THE NEW

As the new century began, old patterns of thought were still strongly embedded, continuing to exist alongside the new forces and trends well into the century. The predominant intellectual atmosphere was that of scientific positivism. The Argentine Carlos Octavio Bunge (1875–1918) was diagnosing his *Nuestra*

América (1903) as a sick continent in the scientific, organicist, racial terms of Gustav Le Bon. Alcides Arguedas, as we have seen, analyzed Bolivia in similar vein in his *Pueblo enfermo* (1909), discussing the Indian and the mestizo in racial terms as the source of Bolivia's *enfermedad*. Francisco García Calderón of Peru was somewhat less addicted to the psychology of racism in his analysis, perhaps showing the influence of Rodó. But he was willing to ask, in his history of Latin America (*Les demo-craties latines de L'Amèrique*), whether miscegenation might not explain the inability of Latin America to achieve political stability and hence its need for caudillo dictators.[1] This positivist thought was often Liberal, sometimes escaped racism, and was sometimes tinged with Marxism, as in the notable case of José Ingenieros whose writings appealed so strikingly to the youthful leaders of the university student movements. It was usually anticlerical, sometimes freethinking, but more often liberal Christian. But it could also be socially conservative, as among the defenders of the Díaz regime in Mexico.

As suggested in the previous chapter, old trends of thought that continued into the new century included ideas of Marxism, anarchism, and syndicalism that circulated among leaders of the emerging labor movement and to some extent among radical university youth leaders. Traditionalist thought, usually with a religious emphasis, as distinct from the social conservatism often expressed in positivist sociological terms, still found major spokesmen. One of the most interesting carryovers from the nineteenth century — interesting especially as it merged with twentieth century trends — was the spiritualist and vaguely humanist trend, also noted in the previous chapter.

1. Cf. Martin S. Stabb, *In Quest of Identity,* Chap. 2. The work of García Calderón was first published in Paris in 1912.

KRAUSISM

Krausism requires special mention not only because of the social and humanist, vaguely religious, motivation it provided in Spanish America and in Spain; but also because of its links with other "spiritual" or spiritist philosophical and religious trends of the times. As we have seen, Krausism was popularized in Spain through the teaching of Julián Sanz del Río and was passed to Spanish America in the late nineteenth century. The introduction of Krausism into Mexico centered around the question of adopting the philosophy textbook of the Belgian Krausist Tiberghien. Its Mexican advocate, Telésforo García, emphasized the ideals of "God, *patria,* and liberty" in attacks upon the "conservatism" of positivist social thought. Beginning with ideas of Hegel and Kant, Karl Christian Krause (1781–1832) had evolved an idealist philosophy in which God was equated with conscience. God, man, and the universe were merged in a kind of pantheism, while man and society were assumed to develop in the image of God. Thus, as society became more closely integrated, man became more a part of God. The influence of this religious humanism may be seen in many young writers and political leaders of the early years of this century, both in Spain and in Spanish America, giving a religious idealism to their social consciousness.[2]

Such Krausist ideas animated the minds of many of the younger followers of Francisco Madero in the Revolution of 1910. In Argentina, this "spiritualist" philosophy had a pro-

2. Leopoldo Zea, *Apogeo y decadencia del positivismo en México* (México: El Colegio de México, 1944, 112–36; Francisco Larroyo, *La filosofía americana* (México: Universidad Autónoma de México, 1958), 99–101; Gerhard Masur, "Miguel Unamuno," *The Americas,* XII (October, 1955), 139–56; José López Morillas, *El krausismo español* (México: Fondo de Cultura Económica, 1961); and Arturo Andrés Roig, *Los krausistas argentinos* (Puebla, México: Ed. José M. Cajica, Jr., 1969).

found influence upon the leader of the Radical party, President Hipólito Irigoyen.[3] In Uruguay it helped to form the idealism initiated with the writings of Rodó,[4] and indirectly influenced the development of José Batlle. In Peru, Alejandro Deústua acknowledged his debt to Krausism, especially for the concept that "liberty is the essence of grace."

Alejandro Deústua (1849–1945) spanned almost a century in his life. He was born in Huancayo, Peru, in 1849 and died in Lima in 1945. His education was acquired in Lima, culminating in graduation from the University of San Marcos. Almost immediately after graduation he became a professor in the university and held this position for most of his life. In the course of time he became dean of the faculty of letters and rector of the university. He also served as director of the National Library.

Deústua's career in the university began as the new "spiritual" current of Krausism was making itself felt in Spain and Spanish America as a "spiritual" trend against the dominant evolutionary positivism. Deústua soon became one of the ablest spokesmen of the new philosophy. The structure of his thought shows a continuing positivist influence, however, as appears in his essay "The Ideas of Order and Liberty in the History of Human Thought," [5] in which he still holds to a positivist concept of the evolution of thought. But the distinguishing characteristic of Deústua's philosophy is Krausism. He found that in Krause, as previously noted, "liberty is the essence of grace." He

3. Manuel Gálvez, *Vida de Hipólito Irigoyen* (2nd ed.; Buenos Aires: the author, 1939). Also, see passing references in A. A. Roig, *Los krausistas argentinos.*

4. Arturo Ardao, *La filosofía en el Uruguay en el siglo xx* (México: Fondo de Cultura Económica, 1956), 144.

5. Alejandro Deústua, "Las ideas de orden y libertad en la historia del pensamiento humano," *Revista Universitaria* (Lima, primer semestre, 1922), 147–59.

also found in Krause the principle of harmony or balance that led him to postulate an esthetic based upon liberty and to formulate a concept of creative liberty based upon esthetics, making esthetics rather than ethics the basis of a social philosophy. The influence of Bergson may perhaps be seen in Deústua's insistence upon the relation of thought to action. But when one sees his creative liberty tied to the idea of a moral imperative one realizes that the basic influence is the Krausist neo-Kantianism.

The external world, wrote Deústua, works to suppress man's intellectual activity, the basis of all action. But order, as the essence of science, spurs speculative thought, counteracting the negative influence of the world. What one must seek, therefore, is a kind of Hellenic balance. Roman civilization achieved a balance of ideals in which the collective liberty was reduced to exterior action as expressed in law; its symbol was the infinite power of imperialism. Later sensual excesses in the Roman world led to concentration on the mystic and a surrender to divine power. A new (Medieval) order then arose on the basis of this mysticism. Individual conscience lost its spontaneity and freedom of action; humans dissipated their activity in seeking perfection and affirming tradition. Thus the only form of freedom remaining was moral, a kind of freedom that satisfied a practical need for reinforcing authority. Creative liberty, lacking an objective, virtually disappeared.

The Renaissance and Reformation did not change the situation in any fundamental way, according to Deústua. The freedom of thought which it brought did not alter the deterministic concept of the universe; liberty continued to have merely practical objectives — social, economic, and political. The Renaissance opened the way for new kinds of speculative thought, but the science that followed in later years, says Deústua, excluded speculation in accordance with its principle of order, as it still excludes everything except the cognitive, wishing to explain what should be by what is. Thus, the powerful artistic movement of the Renaissance era had little or no influence upon this science that continued to receive its ideas from the classic spirit of order — intellectualism. An intellectualism was bred that converted what should have been a means (order) into an end. On the basis of this concept of order intellectualism created the various classifications that are the basis of all scientific knowledge, but "pure liberty, psychic liberty, remained untouched, because its disinterested character excluded it from these forms."

Rejecting other concepts of liberty as "causal," Deústua concluded that the only sense in which man is really free is in that of a "will governed by moral purposes." Yet, as he saw, this concept is still causal in the psychological sense; only in the realm of esthetics is genuine creative liberty to be found. Hence, the problem of philosophy in the future, he writes, is to found a philosophy on esthetics. In this philosophy the old Aristotelian problem of the opposition of the theoretical and the practical will be solved by the more radical concept of the relation of order to liberty, science, and art — the esthetic basis of liberty. At this point one is struck by a resemblance of this aspect of the thought of Deústua to the thought of José Vasconcelos, with whom Deústua engaged in a major debate over esthetics.

"Creation, liberty, art, imaginative activity, expressions of the same idea and opposed to those of repetition, order, science, and logical activity, will be the new elements of philosophical criteria in the future, against which the objective man will always fight — the utilitarian man, who aspires to confound himself with nature to gain the advantage of her laws, as the mystic renounces interior expansion in order to be absorbed by divinity and find there absolute repose." The task of philosophy,

Deústua insisted, is to rise above the utilitarian to the realm of the disinterested and the universal. In this connection, he posed the problem of how to achieve the inner life without falling into mysticism. This problem, so perplexing to twentieth century existentialism, he left unanswered.[6]

ANTIPOSITIVISM AND POSITIVIST SOCIAL SCIENCE

Latin Americans responded in many different ways to the challenge of the changes and revolutionary movements of the twentieth century. But on one point the various patterns of reaction tended to converge. This point of convergence, as has been suggested, was a rejection of positivist sociological thought, at least in its nineteenth century forms. Somewhat less clearly, and on the whole slowly, the new trends also converged in seeking their basic orientation within the evolving relativist and existentialist thought of the age. This latter characteristic ultimately came to influence most of the widely different currents of thought — Marxist, neo-positivist, traditionalist, and Christian.

In Mexico, for example, Antonio Caso and the group of young intellectuals who made up the *Ateneo de Juventud* led

6. The author is indebted to Aníbal Sánchez Reulet for much of the foregoing analysis. See his *La filosofía latinoamericana contemporánea* (Washington, D.C.: Unión Panamericana, 1949). See also Manfredo Kempff Mercado, *Historia de la filosofía en Latino-América* (Santiago, Chile: Zig-Zag, 1958), 140–45, 176, 192; Francisco Larroyo, *La filosofía americana*, 120, 121, 122, 123; and Risieri Frondizi, "Tendencies in Contemporary Latin-American Philosophy," *Inter-American Intellectual Cultural Exchange* (Austin, Texas: Institute of Latin American Studies, 1943), 35–48. *Bibliografía de las obras del dr. dn. Alejandro O. Deústua* (Lima: Gil, 1939), prepared and published by Deústua's students at the Universidad de San Marcos, Semenario de filosofía, on his ninetieth birthday, gives the best listing of Deústua's works. In addition to the essay discussed and quoted above, the scholar should consult *Estética general* (Lima: Imprenta E. Ravago, 1923), *La cultura superior en Italia; informe elevado al supremo gobierno del Perú* (Lima: Librería Francesa Científica, 1912), *Estética aplicada; lo bello en el arte; la arquitectura* (Lima: Cía de Impresiones y Publicidad, 1932); and *La estética de José Vasconcelos* (Lima: P. Barrantes C., 1939).

an attack on the philosophy of positivism in the national university. The significance of their convergence on antipositivism becomes clearer when it is noted how differently the members of this group attained later prominence in Mexican intellectual life. Some of them developed ideas along Marxist lines in a general sense, but with Mexican modifications — Jesús Silva Herzog and Diego Rivera. Some, like Caso, were more traditionalist, but in a twentieth century sense that assimilated much of the new existentialist antirationalism. Most, however, developed along lines related more closely to the new idealist trends of thought in Europe, especially in Germany, as they were being expressed in Spain and America by José Ortega y Gasset, or to the special Kierkegaardian trend of thought expressed by Unamuno.

In the twentieth century, positivist ideas were modified by the new scientific concepts of the century, notably those of behavioral psychology and relativist physics. Within this new scientific context, positivism often continued to hold a place of prominence in the thought of social scientists, even though rejected by neo-idealist philosophers. The major changes that may be seen in the ideas of such twentieth century sociologists as Raúl Orgaz of Argentina and Fernando Azevedo of Brazil stem in considerable measure from the psychologism of Gabriel Tarde and the syncretic sociology of Emile Durkheim. Tarde's concepts of social determinism and imitation came to be widely accepted, while Durkheim's emphasis upon the religious roots of culture, upon accretion and coalescence in social evolution, and upon the social restraints imposed on the individual by the group, appear in much of the social theory taught in the schools.

Another source of reinforcement for positivist thought is the anthropological theory of Franz Boas as, for example, in the Brazilian Gilberto Freyre. Quite generally in Brazil, and occasionally among such Spanish American philosophers as Enrique Molina of Chile, it is also possible to see an influence of the less clearly positivist pluralism and pragmatism of William James and John Dewey. The Dewey influence is particularly evident in educational philosophy. By mid-century, the trend in social theory was generally toward some kind of relativism, as shown by the popularity of Karl Mannheim's sociology of knowledge. These trends of psychologism and social relativism, as elements of the new positivism, have tended to supplant the earlier historical and evolutionary explanations of the past with an analysis which concentrates more upon forces of the present.

Scholarly and scientific study by Latin Americans of their society, people, and geography has increased notably but unevenly in the decades since World War I, some but not all of it in the neo-positivist vein. Perspectives have been broadened by archaeological research which has opened up new vistas in indigenous history, while anthropological studies have widened acquaintance with the traits of native cultures and with the processes of cultural change among mestizo and Afro-American peoples. Most of this study is an extension of scientific activity within previously established principles, raising few questions concerning its theoretical or philosophical premises. Often, however, it reveals a trend away from the older nineteenth century positivist premises of racial and cultural determinism and of progress based on an evolving institutional system of order. Some writers have gone further along the lines of empirical anthropological and historical philosophy in an effort to find a philosophical-theoretical basis for cultural pluralism, a departure from rationalistic positivism. Among these a number have looked for elements which presumably distinguish thought and art in America or give to American historical experience a meaning distinctly its own. The resulting trends in thought, based upon aspects of American experience or existence, sometimes lay claim to being American philosophies. Usually they are pluralistic, empirical, and naturalistic; frequently, as in the case of Gilberto Freyre of Brazil, they reveal the influence of the cultural relativism and psychoanalysis of North American anthropological thought, particularly that of the Franz Boas school. Occasionally, however, this Americanist quest is couched in the neo-idealistic terms of a search for norms of some universality derived from historical experience. Sometimes it has a tinge of Unamuno's personalism and existentialism. Sometimes it becomes revolutionary.

THE SCHWARTZMANN CONCEPT OF MAN IN AMERICA

The Chilean philosopher, Felix Schwartzmann, has propounded the existence of a distinct concept of man, or of the human, in America. Deriving this idea from experiences peculiar to American existence, which he analyzes in a comprehensive survey of the writings of Americans, North and South, he concludes that the American concept of man provides the key to the interpretation of American cultural history. His most general conclusion in respect to the concept of man, as revealed in the thought of American writers, is that it is more optimistic than that expressed by their contemporaries in Europe.[7] The phases of the trajectory of a history expressing this view of man, he claims, should determine the epochs of American historiography.

JOSÉ INGENIEROS (1877–1925)

The *Mediocre Man* of Ingenieros expresses in some respects the literary trends of the turn of the century better than it expresses

7. Felix Schwartzmann, *El sentido de lo humano en América* (Santiago, Chile: Universidad de Chile, 1950).

the character of Ingenieros' social thought. Yet it deserves special attention in the history of Latin American ideas as his most
widely read book and as a work that influenced the thought of a
whole generation. Ingenieros was already well known as a physician and scholar when his failure to receive what he and his
student followers considered a well-deserved university appoint-
ment caused him to leave Argentina for a period of self-imposed
exile in Switzerland. *Mediocre Man* was a product of this period.[8]

Basically, Ingenieros expresses the evolutionary social thought
of Herbert Spencer. But Ingenieros' social thought also shows
considerable influence from the psychologism of Tarde. It has a
strongly moralistic basis and contains more than a little Marxism derived from his early association with the Argentine Socialist party and its leaders, such as Alfredo L. Palacios and Juan B.
Justo. Occasional tones of a stoical idealism like that of Rodó
also appear.[9]

Although differing from Rodó's *Ariel* in its premises and development, the *Mediocre Man* of Ingenieros made an appeal to
the idealism of university youth of the day comparable to that
of the Uruguayan classic. This book made Ingenieros one of
the outstanding intellectual forces shaping the mentality of the
rising student generation in Argentina. Thus, he was one of the
professors for whom the students of the University of Córdoba,
Argentina, went on strike in 1918, and Haya de la Torre ranks
him with José Vasconcelos as one of the two greatest influences
in the Latin American student movement for university re-

8. First published in 1920, José Ingenieros' *Mediocre Man* went through
numerous editions. The most recent is in Vol. X of the twenty volume *Obras
completas* (Buenos Aires: Elmer, 1956).

9. Francisco Larroyo, *La filosofía americana*, 117–19; José Luis Romero,
Las ideas políticas en Argentina (México: Fondo de Cultura Económica, 1946),
215.

form. Sergio Bagú of Argentina has called Ingenieros "the most solid, enthusiastic and influential" of the inspirers of university reform in Argentina.[10]

Omnivorous reading led Ingenieros into most of the new philosophical and sociological trends of his day. For years he edited a philosophical journal that enjoyed wide circulation. In it one finds Ingenieros accepting something like the concept of being or existence emanating from German thought of the day as well as contemporary Italian ideas. Occasionally the influence of Anglo-American empiricism may also be seen. The most notable influence, however, stems from the psychological and psychiatric training that led him to modify his social evolutionism by introducing concepts of imitation, simulation, and pretense, as when he explained race conflicts in somewhat Marxist terms as fictions invented to cover up the real conflicts of economic interests. His *Simulation in the Struggle for Existence* expresses many of these ideas; they also run through his *Argentine Sociology.*

Ingenieros imbibed Marxist socialism from his father, Salvador Ingenieros, an Italian immigrant labor leader and journalist. But, after a brief youthful phase of political agitation, as his biographer has noted,[11] he ceased to be an orthodox Marxist, ending up, rather, as a broadly scientific positivist.

He was born in Buenos Aires on April 24, 1877, and was educated in the Colegio Nacional and in the University of Buenos Aires, studying first law and then medicine. It was the positivist physician Dr. José María Ramos Mejía who turned Ingenieros toward medicine, becoming in other ways, as well, a major in-

10. Haya de la Torre, *¿A dónde va Indoamérica?* (3rd ed.; Santiago, Chile: Biblioteca América, 1936). According to Bagú, Haya's statement was made ten years before he published it in this book in 1936. See Sergio Bagú, *Vida ejemplar de José Ingenieros* (Buenos Aires: Claridad [1936]), 184.

11. Sergio Bagú, *Vida ejemplar de José Ingenieros*, 51–52.

fluence on his intellectual orientation. Although he died in 1925, at the early age of forty-seven, Ingenieros had already produced a bibliography of over five-hundred items.[12]

INDIGENISMO

Studies of the indigenous peoples and their cultures have profound roots in the revolutionary movements of the twentieth century. Their social importance is reflected in the kind of support they have received. Archaeological and anthropological studies have received official support through UNESCO, the Inter-American Indian Institute, and various national institutes and museums. They have had private support as well from North American foundations and universities. The French *Societé des Americanistes,* which has long enlisted the collaboration of Latin Americans, has also played a significant role in the development of such studies. *Indigenismo* has found expression in the literature and programs of the Mexican Revolution, in the Peruvian APRA, in the Guatemalan Revolution under José Arévalo, in the Bolivian Revolutionary Party (MNR), and to a lesser extent in comparable movements elsewhere.

In some respects this *indigenismo* is a more profound reasser-

12. The complete works of Ingenieros were published in 23 volumes (Buenos Aires: L. J. Rosso, 1904–1940). A new edition in 20 volumes was published in 1956 at Buenos Aires. His most important works from the standpoint of social thought are *Argentine Sociology, Simulation of Madness* and *Simulation in the Struggle for Existence* (published together), *Principles of Biological Psychology, Toward a Morality Without Dogma. The Evolution of Argentine Thought* (2 vols.), and *Mediocre Man.* All went through numerous editions. *Mediocre Man* is conveniently available in a Chilean edition (Santiago: Ercilla, 1937), or in Volume X of the 1956 edition of the *Obras completas.* Biographical studies besides that of Sergio Bagú include Gregorio Bermann, *José Ingenieros* (Buenos Aires: Gleizer, 1926); and Ricardo Riaño Juama, *Ingenieros y su obra literaria* (Habana: Arellano, 1933). W. R. Crawford, *A Century of Latin American Thought,* 116–42, and H. E. Davis, *Latin American Leaders,* 147–52, provide brief treatments in English.

tation of the concept earlier expressed by certain independence leaders that the cultural history of America is significantly continuous with that of the pre-Conquest civilization.[13] Such a theory makes of indigenous cultures and their influence much more than a question for the sociologist or anthropologist because it introduces cultural value concepts to condition the very science which seeks to analyze and ameliorate these twentieth century problems.

The influence of *indigenismo* upon the study of history may be seen in Mexico, where a national history based upon indigenous origins has been considered essential in the cultural assimilation of the native peoples.[14] The Mexican concept of the continuity of Indian history through the period of European domination has resulted in a distinctly new historical perspective, producing efforts to establish the significant epochs or decisive historical moments from this standpoint.[15] As we saw in Chapter 2, students of the pre–Conquest cultures have also begun to give us new insights into the religious, legal, and social thought of these cultures.

A philosophy which takes the form of a mystique of the land has developed among a group of Bolivian writers, finding par-

13. See Alejandro Lipschutz, *Indoamericanismo y la raza india* (Santiago, Chile: Nascimento, 1937) and his *Indoamericanismo y el problema racial de las Américas* (Santiago, Chile: Nascimento, 1944); Juan Comas, *Ensayos sobre indigenismo*; the excellent introduction to Aida Cometta Manzoni, *El indio en la poesía de América española* (Buenos Aires: Joaquín Torres, 1939); and Luis Villoro, *Los grandes momentos del indigenismo en México* (México: El Colegio de México, 1950).

14. See Rafael Ramírez *et al*, *La enseñanza de historia en México* (México: Instituto Panamericano de Geografía e Historia, 1948).

15. See particularly Juan Comas, *Ensayos sobre indigenismo,* and Luis Villoro, *Los grandes momentos del indigenismo en México*. Also the work of the Swedish scholar, Sverker Arnoldson, *Los momentos históricos de América* (Madrid: Insula, 1956) and Pedro Armillas, *La América indigena* (2 vols., mimeograph; México: Pan American Institute of Geography and History, 1956).

ticular expression in the journal *Kollasuyo*. Franz Tamayo, Roberto Prudencio, Humberto Plaza, and Fernando Diez de Medina are some of the writers who ascribe to the Bolivian landscape the source of a spirit that is communicated in some mystic way to the subconscious in man, giving form and substance to American culture and American thought. This mystic element of Bolivian thought may well owe a debt to the survival of some aspects of indigenous nature worship and other pre-Conquest ideas. The late Fernando Ortiz expressed a similar idea in his studies of the Indian background of Cuba, though avoiding the mysticism of the Bolivians. Fernando Ortiz found in the spiral form of the hurricane, for example, a cultural symbol whose highest expression was the generalized deification of the plumed serpent. The Mexican philosopher Francisco Larroyo has commented on this Bolivian tendency to create a mystique of the land, calling it a "philosophical school of Bolivia." [16]

AFRO-AMERICANISM

Afro-Americanism, like *indigenismo*, has directed attention to non-European cultural influences which also appear among the results of American experiences. But its effect upon social thought seems, on the whole, to have been less profound. The racism and geographic determinism of da Cunha, noted in the previous chapter, continued for many years to influence a group of writers, one of the most notable of whom is Arthur Ramos,[17] and to inspire regional novels with Afro-American overtones. The Brazilian social historian Gilberto Freyre reflects the an-

16. Fernando Ortiz, *El huracán* (México: Fondo de Cultura Económica, 1947); Francisco Larroyo, *Filosofía americana*, 48.

17. Arthur Ramos, *A aculturação negra no Brasil*, trans. Richard Pattee as *The Negro in Brazil* (Washington: Associated Publishers, 1939).

thropological theories of Franz Boas in his treatment of racist themes. His *Masters and Slaves (Casa grande e senzala)* portrays the Negro outlook from within a changing culture, with special emphasis upon the cultural and psychological effects of slavery, as distinct from those of race. Freyre avoids mechanical determinism, both that of culture and of geography. He asserts a cultural regionalism, yet, in the *Masters and Slaves,* as in subsequent volumes of his history, he sees many attitudes and cultural values in the Brazilian areas of former plantation-slave economy that have universal significance in the sense that they are similar to those in the former plantation areas of North America and elsewhere.[18] Fernando Ortiz of Cuba, in his sociological studies of the effects of tobacco and sugar production, also points to Afro-American influences.[19] In the French Caribbean, Aimé Césaire of Martinique has evolved a theory of negritude that has been exploited by the late President Duvalier of Haiti as a political ideology linking Haiti to Africa.[20] A similar ideology accompanies the movement for black power in Trinidad and Jamaica.

Sometimes this pursuit of an American element in culture has led to the quest for an American aesthetic combining values of European and American origin, as in Ricardo Rojas's *Eurindia,*[21] or Luis Alberto Sánchez's *Vida y pasión en la América.*[22]

18. In addition to Gilberto Freyre's *The Masters and the Slaves* are *The Mansions and the Shanties (Casa Grande, Subrados e Mucambos)*, trans. Harriet de Onís (New York: Alfred A. Knopf, 1963); and *Order and Progress (Ordem e Progreso)*, trans. Rod W. Horton (New York: Alfred A. Knopf, 1970).

19. Fernando Ortiz Fernández, *Contrapunteo cubano del tobaco y el azúcar.* Introd. de Bronislaw Malinowski (La Habana: Consejo Nacional de Cultura, 1963; original edition, 1940).

20. Aimé Césaire, *Return to My Native Land,* trans. Emil Snyders (Paris: Présence africaine, 1968; original French edition, 1956).

21. Ricardo Rojas, *Eurindia,* in *Obras completas* (Buenos Aires: J. Roldán y Cía, 1924), V.

22. Alberto Sánchez, *Vida y pasión en la América* (Santiago, Chile: Biblioteca

Pedro Henríquez Ureña, in his *Historia de la cultura en la América hispánica,* has also traced the development of a literature of an autonomously American character in Hispanic America.[23] In his last published (posthumously) work, a series of lectures on philosophical anthropology given at the University of Mexico, the late José Gaos, a Spanish philosopher long domiciled in Mexico, devoted two chapters to delineating the significance of the useful (*útiles*) and the fine (*bellas*) arts in a philosophy of man and human values.[24]

José Vasconcelos, as we shall note, believed he saw the emergence in America of a "cosmic race," a "new cultural being" that combined Indian, African, and European elements.[25] The philosopher Eduardo Nicol, however, points out the contradiction or paradox in both *indigenismo* and negritude — that they search for ideality on the basis of race, while seeking at the same time to eliminate racial distinctions in the society and culture.[26]

PHILOSOPHY OF HISTORY

The argument over the philosophy of history has been particularly keen in the twentieth century. It may not be the most important contemporary debate on the subject, but it has certainly been one of the liveliest and has had marks of greatness. In the

América, 1936); and his *Los fundamentos de la historia americana* (Buenos Aires: Américalee, 1943).

23. Pedro Henríquez Ureña, *Historia de la cultura en la América hispánica* (México: Fondo de Cultura Económica, 1947). Also in English version.

24. José Gaos, *Del hombre* (México: Fondo de Cultura Económica and Univ. Nac. Autonóma de México, 1970), Chaps. 39 and 40.

25. Jorrín and Martz, *Latin American Political Thought and Ideology,* 216, citing *La raza cósmica* and the *Indología* of Vasconcelos.

26. Eduardo Nicol, *El problema de la filosofía hispánica,* 77.

attention it has received it is rivaled in Latin America only by the discussions of the philosophy of man or anthropology.

The debate on history is broad in scope and comes from a variety of sources. It has been spurred by the work of a new generation of historians in Spain, Portugal, and Hispanic America. One thinks immediately of Rafael Altamira of Spain and his monumental studies of the Laws of the Indies. One also thinks of such advocates of the new history as Enrique de Gandía of Argentina and of the works of Ricardo Levene and his disciples in Argentina, reinterpreting the legal and institutional history of their country in order to bring out the element of Americanism. Archaeologists such as Luis Valcárcel of Peru and Alfonso Caso of Mexico have also contributed to the debate, as have Marxist historians of the Indian such as Luis Chávez Orozco of Mexico and the intellectual historians with whom we have already been concerned.

Finally, there has been a hemisphere-wide group of historical scholars working under the direction of Silvio Zavala of Mexico in a program sponsored by the Pan American Institute of Geography and History to synthesize and interpret the history of the American hemisphere. This program has also embraced the history of historiography, the teaching of history, the history of ideas, technical aspects of archivology, and historical methodology.

Philosophers have also entered the fray, often stimulated by the historical concerns of Ortega and Unamuno. The Spanish emigré José Gaos was an important catalyst in stimulating the interest in philosophy of history among a group of Mexican philosophers. Also in this group of younger Mexican scholars who shared his interest in the philosophy of history was Edmundo O'Gorman who, while rejecting the concept of a unique history

of America, found meaning in the American experience of applying natural laws to the creation of a better society.[27] Retain-
ing an essentially Hegelian concept of history, O'Gorman is led
by an examination of the nature of historical knowledge, after
the manner of Heidegger, to the existentialist concept that historical knowledge is authentic only "when the reality examined
is raised to the level of personal revelation." [28]

Leopoldo Zea, another of this group, has already been referred to several times in this book. Zea has made notable studies
of the history of thought in nineteenth century Mexico and
Spanish America.[29] His neo-Hegelian interpretation of history,
as previously noted, emphasizes the paradox that Latin American thought began with an outright repudiation of the authority
of the European historical tradition, but has sought to create a
history of its own, building on the Occidental tradition. In the
manner of Ortega, Zea sees that a people acquires freedom to act
by first experiencing the full meaning of its history and then, in
a sense, putting it aside or transcending it.

Víctor Raúl Haya de la Torre, mentioned above as the organizer and leader of the Aprista party in Peru for more than a
quarter of a century and as a Marxist theoretician of originality,
has also contributed to the discussion of the philosophy of
history. His concept of historical time-space must be noted here,
as one considered by some scholars to be an original American
contribution to historical theory. His general relativism and
pluralism led him to accept the idea of many histories, thus

27. Edmundo O'Gorman, *Fundamentos de la historia de América* (México:
Imprenta Universitaria, 1942), 131–32.
28. Edmundo O'Gorman, *Crisis y porvenir de la ciencia histórica* (México:
Imprenta Universitaria, 1947), 308–309, and *The Invention of America.*
29. See especially Leopoldo Zea, *Dos etapas del pensamiento hispano-americano,* his *Latin American Mind,* his 2-volume *El pensamiento latinoamericano,*
and his *El positivismo en México* (México: Fondo de Cultura Económica, 1943).

finding a theoretical basis for an American socialism distinct from that of Europe.[30]

Gilberto Freyre of Brazil approaches history in a way fundamentally different from that of Haya, yet resembles Haya in making a pluralistic approach to the history of cultures. Following Franz Boas in interpreting the psychology of a culture from within, Freyre arrives at a regional concept of culture and history, a concept of regions defined by elements in American cultural experiences as well as by geographic factors. In passing, it may be noted that I. R. Grig, in an article on Latin American historians in the Soviet historical journal *Voprosy Istorii,* has called Freyre a "vulgar sociologist . . . under the baneful influence of various North American subjectivist schools." Grig does not even mention Haya de la Torre! [31]

The literary historian Pedro Henríquez Ureña of the Dominican Republic and Mexico has traced the outline of American cultural history through its literature, finding in Hispanic America distinctive traits which justify speaking of it as a historical unity within the more complex scope of universal culture. The Mexican philosopher Antonio Caso saw America as a place that provides the greatest opportunity for culture to develop, hence an area of ecumenical importance. The *ser* or "being" of America, he urged in existentialist terms, also involved the Indian, who must be redeemed. In a somewhat neo-Kantian sense he saw the Bolivarian concept of the unity of America as "a categorical imperative of the international Latin American conscience." Edmundo O'Gorman, on the other hand, considers America to be the extension in European culture of

30. Víctor Raúl Haya de la Torre, *¿Y después de la guerra, qué?* (Lima: PTCM, 1946). The essay first appeared in the magazine *Hoy* (August, 1942).

31. I. R. Grig, "Notes on the Status of the Science of History in Latin America," *Voprosy Istorii,* No. 10 (October, 1955). Translation furnished by Hispanic Foundation, Library of Congress.

the ecumenical image of the world to all the earth and of universal history to all humanity. America, he writes, is the ecumenical process in history.[32]

Some other historians who have produced work that is significant for its theoretical basis are: Jesús Silva Herzog and Alfonso Teja Zabre of Mexico, Francisco Encina and Guillermo Feliú Cruz of Chile, José Honorio Rodrígues and Pedro Calmón of Brazil, Dantés Bellegarde of Haiti, and Augusto Mijares and Mariano Picón Salas of Venezuela.

In the broadest sense, this historical argument has been a search for a meaningful history of the Americas. As Leopoldo Zea has written, "America can not escape such a preoccupation in this stage of its culture which it has been defining through its concern with identity (*preocupación ontológica*)." [33] At its worst, it has become a prostitution of history and philosophy to Machiavellian politics or a surrender to an uncritical Marxist dialectical interpretation.

This pursuit of Americanism in a theory of history is at least as old as the era of independence, as we have already noted. Postindependence writers rejected their historical past sharply under the influence of romantic idealism and the historical philosophy of law, coupled with the movement for *desespañolización*. In the late nineteenth century most historians continued to write within these earlier idealist patterns, rejecting the doctrines of evolutionary sociological and economic determinism then developing in European thought.[34] Even though they continued to accept the idea of a natural and inevitable progress, nineteenth century Latin American historians wrote national

32. Francisco Larroyo, *La filosofía americana* (México: U.N.A.M., 1958), 255–65. See also Edmundo O'Gorman, *The Invention of America*.

33. Leopoldo Zea, *El pensamiento latinoamericano* (2 vols.; México: Pormaca, 1965), I, 2.

34. *Ibid.*, 53–54.

history within the framework of the revolutionary natural rights rationalism, as modified by the early nineteenth century idealist historicism and historical philosophy of law. Generally they were more preoccupied with national political history than with the evolving internationalism of the century.

Twentieth century thought rudely challenged this inherited belief in an American meaning to be derived from building a new civilization upon the ruins of the old, as well as the view that America's historical destiny was to be an example to the world. The challenge came with the neo-Hegelian idealism of Benedetto Croce, Oswald Spengler's idealist and cyclical treatment of the decline of civilization, the Christian ecumenicalism of Arnold Toynbee, Miguel Unamuno's tragic existentialist view that history is the source of personal and cultural values, and the neo-idealist existentialism of German origin expressed in the Spanish-speaking world by José Ortega y Gasset and others. Such philosophers of history have not lacked twentieth century Latin American spokesmen.

HISTORY AND REVOLUTION

This historical disillusionment also happened to coincide with a period of revolutionary social and political change that included the Mexican Revolution, *Batllismo* in Uruguay, *Aprismo* in Peru, the MNR in Bolivia, the July 26 Cuban Revolution, and similar movements elsewhere that called for social philosophies of action. The literature of the Mexican Revolution and that of *Aprismo* in Peru reveal a special prominence accorded to the discussion of the meaning and philosophy of history; the Cuban Revolution, as we shall see in the next chapter, introduced a somewhat more novel revolutionary theory.

An extensive and often vindictive argument over the nature and philosophy of the Mexican Revolution was initiated in 1935 with the publication of José Vasconcelos' controversial and widely read autobiography.[35] Then, and for several years thereafter, the rapid pace of agrarian and labor reform under President Lázaro Cárdenas was arousing increased resistance in certain Mexican quarters, while the Spanish Civil War was sharpening the division in public opinion over socialist measures in Mexico as elsewhere in Latin America. This mounting feeling gave a special pungency to the charges exchanged at this time between the partisans of Madero, Carranza, Obregón, and Cárdenas in the form of published reminiscences and polemics. The argument failed to give a definitive expression to the social philosophy of the Revolution, but it brought divergent views more clearly into focus and stimulated the interest in an interpretation of Mexican history that has since become so striking a characteristic of the Mexican intellectual scene.[36]

As in the past, twentieth century Latin Americans have seemed to reject the more pessimistic and fatalistic views of history, finding in Ortega, Croce, or Unamuno, and in their Latin American peers, an at least relatively freewill philosophy that permitted historical decision making, assigned a significant role to leadership, and accepted the possibility of change by revolu-

---

35. José Vasconcelos, *Ulises Criollo* (1935), *La tormenta* (1936), *El desastre* (1938), *El proconsulado* (1939), all published by Botas in Mexico.

36. Among the many books which constitute this discussion of the Mexican Revolution, the following may be mentioned: José Vasconcelos, *¿Qué es la revolución?* (1937), Blas Urrea (Luis Cabrera) *Veinte años después* (1938), J. M. Puig Casauranc, *El sentido social del proceso histórico de México* (1936), Manuel Gamio, *Hacia un México nuevo* (México, 1935), Alfonso Teja Zabre, *Panorama histórico de la revolución mexicana* (1939), Moisés Sáenz, *México íntegro* (Lima, 1939), and Miguel Alessio Robles, *Historia política de la revolución* (1938). Also Jesús Silva Herzog, *El agrarismo mexicano y la reforma agraria* and Victor Alba, *Las ideas sociales contemporáneas en México* (México: Fondo de Cultura Económica, 1960). The fiftieth anniversary of the Revolution in 1960 produced numerous historical works, of which the excellent collaborative *México: cincuenta años de revolución* (4 vols.; México, 1960–1962) is one of the best.

tion. In some respects the most radical expression of this view appears in the writing of the late Ernesto "Che" Guevara. An increased interest in history brought new defenders of Bolívar, not only in Venezuela, but elsewhere as well. San Martín's glory was revived upon the centenary of his death (1950), and even Agustín Iturbide began to receive more attention in the history of Mexico. At the same time, the exploitation of history for political purposes by Mussolini and Hitler stimulated the already notable tendency of Latin American historians and popular writers to magnify the historical importance of such "strong men" as Diego Portales of Chile, Juan M. Rosas and Justo José Urquiza of Argentina, Antonio Guzmán Blanco of Venezuela, Dr. Francia of Paraguay, and Porfirio Díaz of Mexico.

The historical and theoretical analysis of revolutions has interested Latin Americans since the days of national independence, beginning with José M. Mora's *Mexico and Her Revolutions*. Early in the twentieth century, Enrique José Varona criticized the revolutions of his day as sterile, predicting that the time would come, however, in which the forces of socialism and Caesarism would "come like hurricanes." [37] In the early 1930's three Argentines, Alfredo Poviña, Antonio Grompone, and Alfredo Colmo, published studies of revolution, suggesting the importance they assigned to the interruption of their constitutional system in 1930.[38] Luis Alberto Sánchez of Peru has also sought the meaning and popular basis of revolutionary change. The years since World War II, and especially since the triumph

37. Enrique José Varona, quoted by D. Agramonte in Medardo Vitier, *José Varona* (Habana: n.p., 1937), 253–54.
38. Alfredo Poviña, *Sociología de la revolución* (Argentina: Universidad de Córdoba, 1933); and *El pueblo en la revolución americana* (Buenos Aires: Américalee, 1942); Antonio Grompone, *Filosofía de las revoluciones sociales* (Montevideo: Peña Hnos., 1932); and Alfredo Colmo, *La revolución en la América Latina* (Buenos Aires: M. Gleizer, 1932).

of the Castro revolution in Cuba, have produced a much more extensive literature on revolutionary theory, generally Marxist in character. The outstanding example is the book of Ernesto "Che" Guevara, *Guerrilla Warfare: A Method.*[39]

By way of contrast, the Colombian Alvaro Gómez Hurtado has written that he sees no meaning or historical significance in what he calls the "climate of the permanent revolution" in which America has existed. Revolution in America is irrational, he argues; it is "a tendency toward bestiality or, at least, toward primitivism." The reason, he believes, is that American revolutionism lacks the four essential conditions for the institutional basis of historical continuity: (1) the desire for security, (2) the recognition of hierarchy, (3) a sentiment of solidarity, and (4) a moral criterion which presumes a minimum base of religiosity. It is not hard to see in this position of Gómez Hurtado a twentieth century version of nineteenth century traditionalism, minus its monarchism and ultramontanism. It is equally significant that Gómez Hurtado sees no real originality in Latin American thought and no historical basis for such originality. "America," he writes, "is born in history five millennia too late." He rejects as inadequate and untrue the three bases for originality most commonly advanced: *indigenismo,* ethnic assimilation or *mestizaje,* and "the hope for cultural redemption on a telluric basis." [40]

THE NEW TRADITIONALISM

Closely connected with the debate over history is the rise of a new traditionalism, philosophical and political. The traditional-

39. See Jay Mallin (ed.), *"Che" Guevara on Revolution* (Coral Gables, Florida: University of Miami Press, 1969), especially chapter 4.

40. Alvaro Gómez Hurtado, *La revolución en América* (Barcelona: AHR, 1958), II, 163.

ism of the early nineteenth century, as we have seen, had been modified by its transfer to America, by scientific evolutionary positivism and, after the turn of the century, by the new social Christianity. In this modified form the older traditionalism continued to animate the Conservative parties in Latin America, but it was no longer a philosophy of great vigor. It took on renewed vigor, however, in a kind of metamorphosis, in the more vigorous and idealistic form of *Hispanidad* and in nationalist thought such as *Argentinidad, Mexicanidad,* and *Peruanidad.* In these forms it achieved a kind of symbiosis with the secular rationalism of contemporary European fascist theory, finding expression in such various ideological forms as Brazilian *integralismo,* Argentine *peronismo, falangismo* in Bolivia and elsewhere, Mexican *sinarquismo,* and in the political movement in El Salvador headed by José María Lemus. From the standpoint of the Marxists these ideologies were counterrevolutionary, and from the democratic standpoint they were ideologies of authoritarian dictatorships. Yet in many respects they were reform movements in which traditionalists sometimes joined forces with revolutionists.

Manuel Gálvez (1882–1962). One of the most brilliant of these new traditionalists was the Argentine literary critic and novelist, Manuel Gálvez. Another was Carlos Ibarguren, author of a laudatory biography of Juan Manuel Rosas. Gálvez, who has been chosen for discussion here, was more brilliant than profound; he pled for an idealistic Argentine literature. When he applied the techniques of his literary craft to social and cultural questions, he often involved himself in philosophical contradictions or paradoxes. Thus, while his early writing, beginning in 1910, was in a romantic-idealist vein of Argentinism and Hispanicism, during the following quarter century his works in-

creasingly assumed a tone of what might be called intellectual
and moral fascism. He became authoritarian, anticommunist,
antimaterialist, Catholic, mildly anti-Semitic, admittedly reactionary, and generally antidemocratic. He condemned the university youth movement of his day and extolled the virtues of
Mussolini, Hitler, and such Latin American "strong men" as
Juan Manuel Rosas and Gabriel García Moreno.

His career presents one interesting parallel with that of the
Mexican Marxist Vicente Lombardo Toledano — both wrote
university theses on the white slave traffic. Vice and pornog-
raphy continued to be recurring themes in the writing of Gálvez.
However, his first literary work to receive serious attention, *El
diario de Gabriel Quiroga* (an imaginary figure), was a passion-
ate nationalistic appeal to restore the Argentine spirit, which he
believed still lived in the provinces but had been submerged in
urban cosmopolitanism, materialism, and anti-intellectualism.
In *El solar de la raza,* published a few years later, the dominant
themes are the restoration of traditional Spanish spiritual ideals
as preserved in the provinces and of Christianity as the most per-
fect expression of these ideals. This book may be noted as one
of the literary expressions of the Hispanicism stimulated by the
Generation of 1898 in Spain and America.

El espíritu de aristocracia, published in 1924, echoed Rodó
in its reconciliation of the principles of aristocracy and democracy. In this work Gálvez reveals his own struggle with the
twentieth century existentialist problem — that of understanding the nature of being, or the problem of identity. It is in this
work, also, that Gálvez makes the aphoristic and paradoxical
statement that if he had to choose between art and life he would
choose life, though realizing that only works of imagination
last, while those of "social science" perish.[41]

41. Cited in W. R. Crawford, *A Century of Latin American Thought,* 156.

By the mid nineteen-thirties, Gálvez was prepared to go much further in rejecting universal suffrage and parliamentarism as "lies" and politics as evil. *Este pueblo necesita,* published in 1934, was later to furnish more than a little of the Peronista ideological background. In this latter book Gálvez listed ten Argentine needs: youth, patriotism, a heroic sense of life, moral reform, idealism, order and discipline, a sense of social hierarchy (only General Uriburu, he felt, had such a sense of the role of a social elite!), state action rather than politics (democracy, he wrote, has been a "stupendous failure"), social justice, and political authority to carry out the program. His concept of social justice — by which he meant solution of the social problem by state authority without resort to the class struggle or party politics — may well have been the inspiration of Juan Perón's later ideology of *justicialismo.*[42]

José Enrique Rodó (1871–1917). Rodó was one of the least American and one of the most universal of modern Latin Americans. Keenly sensitive to the problems and conflicts involved in the rapid development of American life and culture, he did not reject the value of the American scene and its amorphous democracy, as exemplified in his own Uruguay. Yet neither did he find the basis of his thought in the American soil or American ex-

42. Gálvez' novels, such as *La tragedia de un hombre fuerte* (Buenos Aires, 1922) and his biographies of Juan Manuel Rosas, Hipólito Irigoyen, and Gabriel García Moreno best express his social ideas. There are several editions of *Solar de la raza* (Buenos Aires: La Facultad, 1930; Madrid: Saturnino Calleja, 1920, and others). Other important works include *El Diario de Gabriel Quiroga* (Buenos Aires: A. Moen & Hno., 1910), *El espíritu de aristocracia y otros ensayos* (Agencia Gen. de Librerías, 1924), *Este pueblo necesita* (Buenos Aires: A. García Santos, 1934), and *La Argentina en nuestros libros* (Santiago, Chile: Ercilla, 1935). For critical comments see Max Daireaux, *Litterature hispano-americaine,* 196–200; Otis H. Green, "Manuel Gálvez, 'Gabriel Quiroga,' and *La maestra normal,*" *Hispanic Review* (July, 1943), and W. R. Crawford, *A Century of Latin American Thought,* 149–64.

periences; he found it, rather, in a combination of Hellenic and Christian sources.

Born and educated in Montevideo, Rodó inevitably reflected in his thought something of the sensitiveness of the Uruguayan upper classes to the social challenge presented by the overwhelming wave of European immigration and the social changes it was bringing in his country. He did not leave Uruguay until the time of the First World War, when a journalistic excursion to Italy ended in illness and an early death. Twice a member of the national congress and briefly a professor of literature, he was ill-adapted for success in either calling. Wearing thick glasses to correct his nearsightedness, he was coldly shy and ill at ease in social gatherings. In some ways, no doubt, the detached Olympian tone of his writing compensated psychologically for this timidity. At all events, his pen spoke with assurance and evoked the social and political optimism for which Latin American youth yearned in order to rise above the failures of their democracy and to face the problems presented by the rapid tempo of social and economic changes in which they were caught up.

The basis of his thought was an idealistic revolt against the growing materialism of his times. In this tendency he reflects influences from such sources as Joseph Renan (the most important), Hippolyte Taine, Alexis de Tocqueville, Thomas Carlyle, Ralph W. Emerson, Gustave Flaubert, Henrik Ibsen, Friedrich W. Nietzsche, Domingo F. Sarmiento, José Martí, and Juan Montalvo. In some respects he also presaged the later popularity of the ideas of Wilhelm Dilthey and Henri Bergson in Latin America. He speaks with approval of the new German idealism, and his views sometimes suggest an influence from Ortega. Christianity, he wrote, provided one of the two basic historical impulses that gave modern civilization its essential characteristics: the sentiment of equality. But Christian equality, he felt, was vitiated by its ascetic tendency to deprecate spiritual and cultural selectivity. Classical civilization provided a second and counterbalancing impulse in its sense of order and hierarchy, coupled with religious respect for genius. This classic impulse, too, had its weak side, that of "aristocratic disdain" for the humble and the weak. As expressed in Nietzsche's idea of the elite, it became "monstrous." For democracy to succeed, said Rodó, it must combine these two elements, synthesizing Judaic Christianity with Hellenism, both being essential elements of freedom.

To symbolize this synthesis, Rodó chose Ariel, the blithe spirit of freedom in Shakespeare's *The Tempest*. In his volume of that title he speaks in a quiet, serene tone, expressing a stoic spiritual purpose and enunciating the values to be achieved within a democratic American setting. The scene is the study of the revered master, bidding farewell to his students gathered around a bronze statue of Ariel. In aphoristic, oracular language the master speaks of the most serious problems of the spirit.

With Renan, the master in *Ariel* believed that democracy tended toward mediocrity. But he refused to follow Renan in condemning democratic equality of rights. "The spirit of democracy is . . . for our civilization, a principle of life against which it is useless to rebel." Yet, democracy also required a spiritual elite to lead it up and away from mediocrity. While both philosophy and science testify to the need for a "sense of the select," art provides its most natural medium. It is in art that "with deep resonance, the notes which acknowledge the sentiment . . . of the spirit vibrate." But art should not lead to a "delicate and sickly Parnassianism." Youth should avoid "aristocratic disdain for the present" and should renew its ideals and hopes by dedication to the spirit of Ariel.[43]

José de la Riva Agüero (1885–1944). The strong strain of traditionalism inherent in Peruvian culture found intellectual expression in the writing of José de la Riva Agüero on the history of Peruvian literature and Peruvian historiography. His pioneering work on this latter subject, *La historia en el Perú*, published in 1910, treated historiography as a branch of literature, using it to discover "a philosophy of history which may be the very history itself," as Jorge Basadre has written in a prologue.[44]

Riva Agüero began his history with an optimistic view of pre-Conquest Peru derived from study of the writing of the Inca Garcilaso de la Vega. He then moved on to a much more critical and balanced view, one that retained the Incaic tradition but also rejected the black legend of Spanish rule. In this way he found positive historical values deriving from the Spanish conquest, the colonial system, and the Christian bases of the tradition. If Riva Agüero is to be considered a traditionalist, it is in the sense that he considered Peruvian history the existential

43. The complete works of Rodó are available in two separate editions: *Obras completas* (Montevideo: Casa A. Barreiro y Ramos, 1945) and *Obras completas* (Buenos Aires: A. Zamora, 1948). *Ariel, El Mirador de Próspero, Motivos de Próteo,* and *Los últimos Motivos de Próteo* are available in various editions. An English translation of *Ariel* has been made by F. J. Stimson (Boston: Houghton Mifflin, 1922) and of *Motivos de Próteo* by Angel Flores (New York: Brentano's, 1928). Emilio Oribe provides a critical commentary and convenient anthology in his *El pensamiento vivo de Rodó* (Buenos Aires: Losada, 1944). Among works on Rodó are Max Henríquez Ureña, *Rodó y Rubén Darío* (La Habana: Sociedad Editorial Cuba Contemporánea, 1918), Gonzalo Zaldumbide, *Montalvo y Rodó* (New York: Instituto de las Españas, 1938). See also Alberto Zum Felde, *Proceso Intelectual del Uruguay* (Montevideo: Claridad, 1941), 223–50. In English see W. R. Crawford, *A Century of Latin American Thought,* 79–90 and H. E. Davis, *Latin American Leaders,* 141–46.

44. Basadre's comment appears on page xvii of Volume IV of the Riva Agüero *Obras completas* (Lima: Pontífica Universidad Católica del Perú, 1962).

reality of the nation, and that historical studies were the essential basis for the regeneration of Peru. Frederick B. Pike, identifying him with the traditionalism of the Arielists, whose ideas were akin to Rodó's, points out that Riva Agüero's Christianity was accompanied by a desire to see the Indian and his cultural values incorporated into Peruvian life.[45]

Jesús Chavarría has commented that after Riva Agüero left behind him his earlier positivism and reforming zeal, he committed himself to "a militant aristocratic-religious conservatism." Yet Chavarría seems to suggest, correctly in this author's judgment, that Riva Agüero's nationalism and a religious traditionalism that embraced the social Christianity of *Rerum Novarum* kept him at least not too far from a kind of group consensus emerging among Peruvian intellectuals at the turn of the century.[46]

45. "The Old and the New APRA in Peru: Myth and Reality," *Inter-American Economic Affairs*, XVIII (Autumn, 1964), 6–11. The idea is further developed in Pike's *Modern History of Peru* (New York: Praeger, 1967). See also Jorrín and Martz, *Latin American Political Thought and Ideology*, 328–29.

46. Jesús Chavarría, "The Intellectuals and the Crisis of Modern Peruvian Nationalism: 1870–1919."

CHAPTER 8

Twentieth Century Marxist Thought

Marxist thought entered Latin America in the nineteenth century, as noted earlier. By the beginning of the twentieth century, it was finding expression in a small labor press and in a number of socialist parties. During the first quarter of the century it acquired a number of spokesmen, such as Juan B. Justo and Alfredo Palacios of Argentina, Diego Vicente Tejera and Carlos Baliño of Cuba, Santiago Iglesias of Puerto Rico, Emilio Frugoni of Uruguay and Ricardo Flores Magón (who eventually became an anarchosyndicalist) and his brothers of Mexico.[1] In these early years of the century the line of separation between Marxist thinkers and evolutionary positivists was not always clear. Marxism challenged few of the basic positivist theoretical concepts, except in its insistence on the centrality of the class struggle in history, its appeal to lower-class consciousness, and its tendency to reduce social philosophies and religion to the secondary role of ideologies expressing the interests of the class controlling the structure of economic production. Thus, the thought of many such writers as José Ingenieros of Argentina could be considered a combination of Marxism and positivism; the difference between the two patterns of thought frequently

1. Brief excerpts from the writings of Justo, Tejera, Iglesias, and Frugoni are found in Luis Aguilar (ed.), *Marxism in Latin America* (New York: Alfred A. Knopf, 1968), 70–85. On Ricardo Flores Magón and his brothers see James D. Cockcroft, *Intellectual Precursors of the Mexican Revolution, 1900–1913* (Austin: University of Texas Press, 1968).

escaped the attention of an increasingly materialist generation then growing up.

EARLY TWENTIETH CENTURY MARXISM

When Leninist Communism came to America, principally in the 1920's, it divided the existing stream of Marxist revolutionary thought (omitting anarchism) into Socialists and Communists. After the rift between Stalin and Trotsky, a Trotskyite stream also appeared. The advent of Leninist Communism soon sharpened a split within the *Aprista* movement in Peru between Haya de la Torre and José Carlos Mariátegui. The latter, author of the Peruvian classic *Seven Essays on Peruvian Reality*, embraced Communism; Haya, the philosopher-theoretician of *Aprismo*, elaborated an American socialism based upon concepts of cultural and philosophical pluralism, on being as change, and on the relativity of historical reality to its position in time and space. Moreover, as twentieth century neo-positivism lessened its emphasis on the historical basis of social science, another aspect of Marxism in all its varieties stood out more clearly. This was its insistence upon a concept of historical development that moves toward rational ends through a dialectical process that is presumed to yield rational meaning and that can be the basis of a science of society.

Marxist thought of some sort has been prominent in several of the political movements in the twentieth century: in *Batllismo* in Uruguay, in the Mexican Revolution, in Peruvian *Aprismo,* and in related movements in Bolivia, Venezuela, Cuba, Guatemala, and elsewhere. This socialism has not always been the classic Marxism; but Marxist ideas, particularly economic theory, seem to have found broader and more explicit acceptance in these movements than in political movements in the United States. By mid-twentieth century, Marxism had penetrated the liberal and reforming social thought of the Latin American reform movements much as positivism had penetrated the Liberalism of the nineteenth century. Marxism slowly found acceptance in the intellectual middle class, in university circles, as in the student movement for university reform in the 1920's, and among immigrant and native labor leaders, appearing in an emerging labor press. Limited to a small minority among the professional classes in the early years of the century, it came to be the most common pattern among professionals by the 1960's.[2]

Both the Mexican Revolution and the Uruguayan (*Batllismo*), led by José Batlle y Ordóñez, had Marxist spokesmen, but neither movement produced one who was able to reconcile its inner theoretical contradictions. Batlle and his brilliant disciple, the later president Baltazar Brum, were the best spokesmen of the Uruguayan movement. But while on the concrete level their thought is socialist, neither was really a Marxist; rather, they merely expressed socialist principles widely accepted among liberal political leaders in the early years of the century. If one looks in *Batllismo* for a philosophical basis it appears to be largely that of positivism or Krausism, combined with a high degree of nationalism. Indeed, according to his biographer, Milton Vanger, Batlle was directly influenced by the Krausism and "spiritual" philosophy prevalent in the University of Montevideo.[3]

The nationalist preoccupation of socialist thought in general, together with a lack of well-defined social theory, appears

2. See Alvaro Mendoza Díez, *La revolución de los profesionales e intelectuales in Latinoamérica* (México: Universidad Nacional Autónoma, 1962), 44–52, and Carlos M. Rama, *Mouvements ouvriers et socialistes (Chronologie et bibliographie): L'Amérique Latine (1492–1936)* (Paris: Les Editions Ouvriers, 1959), Chaps. 4, 5.

3. Milton Vanger, *José Batlle y Ordóñez of Uruguay: The Creator of His Times, 1902–1907* (Cambridge: Harvard University Press, 1963), 21–22.

clearly, in Chile, in the socialistic expressions of Arturo Alessandri and in those of such leaders of the Radical party as Pedro Aguirre Cerda. The Chilean labor leader Luis Emilio Recabarren (1876–1924), founder of the Socialist party, and later of the Communist party in Chile, is an exception in some respects to this nationalist emphasis. The agrarianism of the Mexican Revolution, as developed by Andrés Molina Enríquez and Jesús Silva Herzog, as well as the Peruvian *Aprismo* of Haya de la Torre, add the most distinctively American note to socialist thought. Linking *indigenismo* with an analysis of the social or labor movement, these movements produced a doctrine that admits its debt to Marx but is distinct from the philosophy of the European labor movement in its emphasis on the land and peasants, and on the "redemption" of the Indians.[4] Alfredo Palacios, of the earlier generation of Marxists in Argentina, was still one of a number of spokesmen of pre-Lenin socialism as late as the 1960's.

Many, perhaps most, of these early twentieth century Marxists had only superficial acquaintance with the writings and theories of Marx and Engels. Luis Aguilar concludes that in this respect the most serious Marxists were the Argentines surrounding Juan B. Justo, including Alfredo Palacios, Americo Ghioldi, and Nicolás Repetto. Justo studied Marx's writings and undertook to translate parts of *Das Kapital* into Spanish.[5]

AMERICAN MARXISM:
VÍCTOR RAÚL HAYA DE LA TORRE (1895–) AND APRA

As we have seen, the anarchism of Proudhon, Bakunin, and Kropotkin, and the syndicalism and theory of violence of Sorel,

4. Andrés Molina Enríquez, *La revolución agraria de México* (México: Museo Nacional, 1934). Jesús Silva Herzog, *El agrarismo mexicano y la reforma*.
5. Luis Aguilar, *Marxism in Latin America*, 6. See also Luis Pau, *Justo y Marx* (Buenos Aires: Monserrat, 1964).

made more appeal to Latin American intellectuals and early labor leaders in the early years of the century than did Marx and Engels. In this respect they were like the Spanish, Portuguese, and Italian leaders of labor and of revolutionary activities. Two notable examples of this anarchist influence, both of whom have already been mentioned, are Ricardo Flores Magón of Mexico and Emilio Recabarren of Chile.[6]

Even more significant than this syndicalism and anarchism was the stream of American Marxist thought that achieved special importance in Peru and was then copied in other parts of America in the inter-war years. In Peru, Víctor Raúl Haya de la Torre and his APRA (Popular Alliance for American Revolution) rejected the universalism and the labor-class consciousness of European socialism in favor of concepts derived from American historical experience. Aprismo, wrote Haya, "bases the examination of the objective conditions of the social reality of Indo-America and the interpretation of its historical future" on a relativist concept of history.[7]

Haya came from a prominent family of Trujillo, in northern Peru. His father, who was the editor of a Liberal paper, *La Industria,* instilled Liberal ideas in his son's mind by setting him to read Tolstoy, Darwin, Kropotkin, Marx, Kant, Hegel, Einstein, and Harold Laski. He later studied under the last of these in the London School of Economics.

As a university student in Peru, Haya identified himself with the student movement for university and social reform. Forced into exile in 1923 because of his opposition to the dictatorial regime of President Augusto B. Leguía, he traveled and studied

6. On Recabarren see chapter 8 of the author's forthcoming *Revolutionaries, Traditionalists and Dictators in Latin America* (Cooper Square Publishers).

7. Víctor Raúl Haya de la Torre, *¿Y despues de la guerra, que?* (Lima: PTCM, 1946), 176ff.

in Switzerland, the Soviet Union, France, England, the United States, and Mexico. He is said to have formulated in Paris, in May, 1924, the five basic principles of what was to become the doctrine of the APRA party he subsequently formed (Popular Alliance for American Revolution). These principles were anti-imperialism, Latin American unity, nationalization of land and industry, internationalization of land and industry, internationalization of the Panama Canal, and solidarity with all oppressed peoples and classes in the world.[8]

After the fall of Leguía in 1930, Haya returned to Peru to run for the presidency, as the *Aprista* candidate, against Colonel Miguel Sánchez Cerro, leader of the uprising that had overthrown Leguía. The Apristas charged that the victory of Sánchez Cerro in this election was fraudulent, and the assassination of the president shortly thereafter was accordingly blamed on them. The party was then suppressed until the election of 1945, when its legalization resulted in the election of José Luis Bustamante with *Aprista* support. Bustamante was not an *Aprista*, although he owed his election to *Aprista* votes; Haya was the power behind the presidential throne. When the coalition behind the president fell apart and he was driven from power by General (later President) Manuel Odría, Haya was forced to take refuge in the Colombian Embassy. There he remained for several years, studying and writing on the historical concepts of Arnold Toynbee, while a dispute between Colombia and Peru over his right of asylum was carried to the World Court.

Haya uses the term "Indoamerica" to indicate the basic importance of the Indian cultural element and the Indian problem to America. "Hispanic Americanism," wrote Haya, "belongs

8. These principles are stated in Víctor Raúl Haya de la Torre, "¿Que es el Apra?" *Acción femenina* (enero-feb., 1937), 18.

to the colonial epoch; Latin Americanism to the republican; while Pan Americanism is a Yankee imperialistic expression. [Haya later reversed this anti-United States stand.] Indo-Americanism is the expression of the new revolutionary conception of America which, having passed through the period of the Iberian and Saxon conquests, will evolve into a definite economico-political and social organization on the national basis of its labor forces." [9] But Aprismo, he insisted, also appeals to all "manual and intellectual laborers" who are urged to unite in a "common program of political action." [10] It may be added that APRA and similar parties in other countries had considerable success in organizing the political support of labor syndicates.

In his essay on "Aprismo, Marxism, and Historical Time-Space," Haya brilliantly developed a relativistic and existentialist theory of history that enabled him to see in Indo-America the basis for a socialist policy and science of society with Marxist characteristics, but distinct from the Marxism of Europe. In simple terms, his theory was that historical truth is four-dimensional, a function of both time and space. Hence, he argues, one cannot assume that Marx's interpretation of European social and economic history is valid for America, since America may not pass through the same revolutionary stages as Europe in its progress toward socialism.[11]

9. Víctor Raúl Haya de la Torre, ¿A dónde va Indoamérica? (3rd ed.; Santiago, Chile: Biblioteca América, 1936), 23. The author's translation.
10. Haya de la Torre, "¿Que es el Apra?"
11. Three books by Haya de la Torre are of fundamental importance: ¿Y despues de la guerra que? (Lima: PTCM, 1946), El plan del Aprismo: programa de gobierno del Partido Aprista Peruano (Lima: Libertad, 1933), and ¿A dónde va Indoamérica? Other works include: Por la emancipación de América Latina. Artículos, mensajes, discursos, 1923–27 (Buenos Aires: M. Gleizer, 1927), El anti-imperialismo y el Apra (Santiago, Chile: Ercilla, 1936), and Toynbee frente a los panoramas de la historia (Buenos Aires: Cía. Ed. del Plata, 1957). For comments on Haya, see Felipe Cossio del Pomar, Haya de la Torre, el indoamericano

José Carlos Mariátegui (1895–1930)
and Leninist Marxism

The conversion to Communism of the brilliant young liberal Peruvian journalist, Mariátegui, was a great triumph for Leninist Marxism in Latin America. He was one of a small band of intellectuals who embraced Communism in the years immediately following World War I, a group that included the much older Carlos Baliño (1848–1925), one of the founders of the Cuban Communist party, and Luis Emilio Recabarren, previously mentioned as the leader in the formation of the Chilean party.

It is one of the surprising anomalies of conservative Peru that it should have produced this "dean" of Latin American Communism and author of *Seven Essays of Interpretation of Peruvian Reality,* one of the great Latin American books of the twentieth century. Mariátegui grew up in poverty in Lima. His formal schooling ended at the age of twelve when he entered a printing shop to work as a copyboy. Beginning to write at an early age, he had become one of Peru's well-known journalists by the age of eighteen. An injury to his knee then made him a cripple, and this injury later developed into a cancerous condition, causing his early death. During these early years he was associated with a group of young writers who opposed the "Futurism" and "Arielism" of the critic Riva Agüero, insisting that the major attention of writers should be given instead to social

(México: América, 1939); Luis Alberto Sánchez, *Raúl Haya de la Torre, o el político* (Santiago, Chile: Ercilla, 1934); Harry Kantor, *The Ideology and Program of the Peruvian Aprista Movement* (Berkeley, Calif.: University of California, 1953); Luis Alberto Sánchez, "Aprista Bibliography," *Hispanic American Historical Review,* XXIII (August, 1943), 555–85; Thibaldo González, *Haya de la Torre: Trayectoria de una ideología* (Caracas: Tipografía Garrido, 1958); and Eugenio Chang-Rodríguez, *La literatura política de González Prada, Mariátegui, y Haya de la Torre* (México: Andrea, 1957).

and political questions. This group supported a popular movement in 1918 for the election of Augusto Leguía, the later
president-dictator.

Because of his journalistic support of Leguía in the election,
Mariátegui received a grant for study and travel in Europe.
There, examining and comparing the careers of Lloyd George
and Lenin, Mariátegui developed a somewhat Marxist theory of
political leadership. From his study of the agrarian aspects of the
Russian Revolutionary program he derived another important
element in his concept of the problem of Peruvian social renovation. A turning point in his life came in Italy, when he joined
the Communist party.

Back home in Peru, he founded the journal *Amauta,* a title
taken from the Quechua word for wise man or teacher. Much
of his subsequent writing appeared in this journal. At this time
he also collaborated with Haya in supporting the student movement for university reform, helping to channel it toward co-
operation with labor groups and into a program of social reform with special emphasis on the redemption of the Indian.
His *Seven Essays,* published in 1926, soon became a kind of
bible of the rising political opposition to the then dictatorial
regime of Leguía. It also provided much of the ideological basis
for the new APRA that Haya de la Torre forged out of that
opposition.

Although Marxist in its historical determinism, Mariátegui's
thought differs from orthodox Marxism. He argues, for example, that Spanish colonialism did not bring capitalism to the
New World, but merely interrupted the pre-Conquest indigenous economic development. This effect of the Conquest was
the source, he insisted, of Peru's later troubles, and the only
remedy was to renew the lines of pre-Conquest economic and
political development. This was much more a revolutionary and

neo-positivist theory of *indigenismo* than was classical Marxism.
It is ironical, of course, that while Mariátegui himself embraced international Communism, his *Seven Essays* provided this Indianist element in the ideology of APRA's anti-Communist nationalism and American revolutionary socialism. Another classical Marxist concept, that the class struggle was the product of a certain historical stage, is also obscured in Mariátegui's work by this racial preoccupation with the Indian. The primacy of economic causation appears clearly enough, but it too is lost sight of in the explanation of the Conquest, which is presented as "more of a military and ecclesiastical . . . than of a political and economic enterprise." On the other hand, independence, for Mariátegui, appears to have been brought about by "the necessities of the development of . . . capitalist civilization." [12]

RÓMULO BETANCOURT (1908–) AND THE VENEZUELAN AD

Rómulo Betancourt of Venezuela is another of the young intellectuals who, like Mariátegui, joined the newly forming Communist parties during the inter-war years. While a student in the University, he became involved in opposition to the gov-

12. José Carlos Mariátegui, *Siete ensayos* (Santiago: Universitaria, 1955), 5–21. Two other books deserve note: *La Escena contemporánea* (Lima: Minerva, 1925) and *Defensa de marxismo: la emoción de nuestro tiempo y otros temas* (Santiago, Chile: Ediciones Nacionales y Extranjeras, 1934). Significant excerpts of Mariátegui's writing are found conveniently in *José Carlos Mariátegui: Notas de Manuel Moreno Sánchez* (México: Universidad Nacional, 1937).

On his ideas, see Eugenio Chang-Rodríguez, *La literatura política de González Prada, Mariátegui y Haya de la Torre*; Armando Bazán, *José Carlos Mariátegui* (Santiago: Zig-Zag, 1939); the prólogo by Guillermo Rouillón to the 1955 edition of the *Siete ensayos*; and, for a Marxist criticism, V. Miroshevsky, "El populismo en el Perú: papel de Mariátegui en la historia del pensamiento social latinoamericano." *Dialéctica* (La Habana), Año I, No. 1 (mayo-junio, 1942), 41–59. In English see W. R. Crawford, *A Century of Latin American Thought*, 182–89, and Jorrín and Martz, *Latin American Political Thought and Ideology*, 277–80.

ernment of the president-dictator Vicente Gómez. In 1928 he was imprisoned for his political activities and the following year was exiled. His subsequent wanderings took him to the Dominican Republic, Colombia, Peru, and Costa Rica. There he seems to have joined the Communist party in 1930. He subsequently left the party, probably expelled because of his independent ideas.

After the death of President Gómez, Betancourt returned to Venezuela in 1936, founding a newspaper to express his views and those of his followers. Again ordered into exile the following year, he went underground instead, managing for two years to hide from the police while secretly organizing the Partido Democrático Nacional. He was finally deported in 1939 and lived thereafter in Chile, Mexico, and the United States until 1941. In that year he returned to Venezuela to work for the Izquierda Democrática group of parties in support of the presidential candidacy of the novelist Rómulo Gallegos. After the defeat of Gallegos in the election, Betancourt became the secretary of the newly formed Acción Democrática de Venezuela, much like an *Aprista* party, founded by Betancourt and a group of Marxist intellectuals.[13]

In October, 1945, with the support of a group of younger army officers, Acción Democrática effected a revolution in the midst of preparations for the next presidential election. Betancourt became president of the ruling junta. Later he was made provisional president by action of a Constitutional Assembly that met in December, 1946. He held this position for over a year, until Rómulo Gallegos was elected and duly inaugurated as president on February 15, 1948. When a military *golpe de estado* overthrew the Gallegos regime a few months later (No-

13. Mario Monteforte Toledo, *Partidos políticos de Iberoamérica* (México: Universidad Nacional Autónoma, 1961), 75.

vember 24, 1948), Betancourt went into exile again, continuing his opposition to the regime of Marcos Pérez Jiménez from the United States, Costa Rica, and other parts of America to which he traveled. After the overthrow of Pérez Jiménez he returned to Venezuela and was elected president in 1958.

Like Haya, Betancourt rejected both the classical Marxist concept that a nation must pass through the capitalist stage before the socialist revolution was possible, on the one hand, and the Leninist theory of revolution, on the other. Consistent in his anti-Communism, he turned against the Cuban Revolution (after first giving Castro a rousing reception in early 1959) when the Cuban leader abandoned the earlier nearly *Aprista* position (of the July 16 movement) for a more Leninist position.

Betancourt's thought offers little that is original or innovative on the theoretical level. His importance lies rather on the practical level of policy. Here his most notable contribution has been the concept of "sowing petroleum" — using the royalties and taxes from the thriving petroleum industry to capitalize new industries and social development. His theory of a political power structure was to combine student, professional, labor and peasant organizations in support of the Democratic Action party (A.D.) that supported him.[14]

14. The author is indebted to Professor Harry Kantor for basic data on Betancourt. The principal works of Betancourt include: *¿Con quién estamos y contra quién estamos?* (Barranquilla, 1932); *Dos meses en las cárceles de Gómez* (Barranquilla, 1928); *En las huellas de la pezuña*. Panfleto por R. Betancourt y Miguel Otero Silva. Prólogo de José Rafael Pocaterra, colofón de Magda Portal (Santo Domingo: 1929); *Problemas venezolanos* (Santiago, Chile: "Futuro," 1940); *Rómulo Betancourt: Pensamiento y Acción*. Recopilado y editado por miembros de Acción Democrática en el exilio (México: 1951); *Trayectoria democrática de una revolución* (Caracas: Imprenta Nacional, 1948); *Una república en venta* (Caracas, 1938); *Venezuela, factoría petrolera* (México, 1954) and *Venezuela: política y petróleo* (Caracas: Senderos, 1967; original ed., México: Fondo de Cultura Económica, 1956). Betancourt's works have been published as *La revolución democrática en Venezuela, 1959–1964* (4 vols.; Caracas, 1968). See also John D. Martz, *Acción democrática* (Princeton University Press, 1966).

LATER MARXIST THOUGHT

Radical Marxist thought of the second quarter of the century appears in two quite distinct forms: the unimaginative "party line" writing, on the one hand, and the more innovative writing of such intellectuals as Juan Marinello of Cuba, Julio Cesar Jobet and Luis Emilio Recabarren of Chile, Vicente Lombardo Toledano and José Revueltas of Mexico, Rodney Arismendi of Uruguay, Leoncio Basbaum of Brazil, José Manuel Fortuny of Guatemala, and Ernesto "Che" Guevara of Argentina and Cuba. Most, but not all of the latter group, have been members of the Communist party. Artists like Diego Rivera of Mexico and poets like Nicolás Guillén of Cuba and Pablo Neruda of Chile seem to have made membership in the Communist party chiefly an expression of a social revolutionary protest that they have felt was an esthetic necessity.[15]

VICENTE LOMBARDO TOLEDANO (1894–1969)

Vicente Lombardo Toledano is best described as an aberrant Marxist-Leninist. He was the grandson of a mid nineteenth-century Italian immigrant who founded the village of Gutiérrez Zamora in Vera Cruz and became wealthy by developing a copper mine. His father was a prosperous merchant and later treas-

---

15. On Communism in Latin America see Robert J. Alexander, *Communism in Latin America* (New Brunswick, New Jersey: Rutgers University Press, 1957); Luis Aguilar, *Marxism in Latin America*; Rollie Poppino, *International Communism in Latin America* (Glencoe, Ill.: Free Press of Glencoe, 1964); and Dorothy Dillon, *International Communism in Latin America* (Gainesville, Florida: University of Florida Press, 1962). For a Russian Communist comment on social interpretations by Latin Americans, see I. R. Grig, "Notes on the Status of the Science of History in Latin America," *Voprosy Istorii*, No. 10 (October, 1955). Ideas of Recabarren, Jobet, Guevara, Fortuny, and Revueltas may be found in L. Aguilar (above). A good critical summary of recent Marxist trends appears in Jorrín and Martz, *Latin American Political Thought and Ideology*, Chap. 9, especially 302ff.

urer of Mexico City. Vicente was born and attended school in the small town of Teziutlán, Puebla, until he was taken to Mexico City at the age of 15 to study, first in the National Preparatory School, and later in the National University. In the university he came under the influence of the emerging intellectual "Generation of 1910," notably Antonio Caso. His thesis for graduation from the law faculty was entitled "Public Law and the New Philosophical Currents." [16] In it he sought a balance between individual rights and social needs, criticizing provisions of the new Mexican Constitution of 1917 that provided for land and labor reform as presenting obstacles "to the free play of the material and moral activities of man."

In the years immediately following, he moved from this position to the more Marxist stance, with traces of anarcho-syndicalism, that characterized his later thought. Several factors contributed to this change. The most important were his employment in the government of the Federal District, which led him to participate in land distribution to peasant villages, his association with the Popular (workers') University after 1936, and his long association with the labor movement that made him the major leader of Mexican labor during the presidency of Lázaro Cárdenas (1934–1940). Thereafter he was a figure of political-ideological prominence until his death in 1969, guiding the actions of the Mexican Left through his tactical ideas, which were often those of the Leninist anti-imperialist strategy. Robert Paul Millon writes that Lombardo told him he had not studied Marxism prior to a visit to the United States in 1925 when he purchased Marxist works in English because "first class Spanish translations were still scarce." As Millon points out, however, it

16. Vicente Lombardo Toledano, *El derecho público y las nuevas corrientes filosóficas* (México, 1919).

was not really true that Spanish translations of Marxist works were lacking.

There is no questioning the intellectual brilliance of Lombardo or his major contributions on the positive and concrete level to the ideology of the growing leftist opposition in Mexico after the Cárdenas presidency. But it is hard to see that he contributed much on the theoretical or philosophical level. This judgment is confirmed by the fact that he himself always insisted that the basis of his theory lay in the Mexican Revolution.[17]

LEONCIO BASBAUM

Leoncio Basbaum of São Paulo, Brazil, is a typical academic Marxist in that he is a professor of economic history. But he is atypical in his deviation from orthodox historical materialism in his historical theory when he seeks to restate the nature of the historical process in humanistic terms somewhat suggestive of the existential idealism (neo-Marxism) of Jean Paul Sartre. Basically, like all Marxists, he sees that history opens "the road to the discovery of the laws that govern the development of human societies." It is not limited, as some Soviet historians have often insisted, he says, to the history of labor and the workers.

17. The best work on Lombardo is that of Robert Paul Millon, *Mexican Marxist: Vicente Lombardo Toledano* (Chapel Hill: University of North Carolina Press, 1966). The quotation appears on page 21. See also Víctor Alba, *Esquema histórico del movimiento obrero en América Latina* (México: B. Costa-Amic, n.d.), 102ff.; and the same author's *Las ideas sociales contemporáneas en México* (México: Fondo de Cultura Económica, 1960). Lombardo's published works are numerous. A few of the more important, in addition to *El derecho público y las nuevas corrientes filosóficas*, are: *Las corrientes filosóficas en la vida de México* (1963), *Escritos filosóficos* (1937), *La evolución de México durante la primera mitad del siglo XX* (1956), *La filosofía y el proletariado* (1962), *La izquierda en la historia de México* (1963), and *Teoría y práctica del movimiento sindical mexicano* (1961; original edition, 1921). All were published in Mexico.

Rather it is the history of all of society, or as Marx wrote, "the true natural history of man."

Basbaum, who seems to rejoice in being a deviationist, tries in his book, *The Evolutionary Process of History,* to rid contemporary Marxism of its dogmatic rationalistic heritage and to give it greater relevance to present-day world problems. The book ends with an especially revealing chapter on "Alienation and the Meaning of History" that suggests a kinship with the thought of Sartre and Herbert Marcuse.[18] True to his basic historical materialism, Basbaum writes that it is nonsensical to search for meaning in history in the sense of "an end, reason or objective." Rather, what is to be found in history is a dialectical process in which liberty (thesis) becomes the slavery of man to the products he has created (antithesis) which in turn produces liberty in another form (synthesis). The new form, of course, is socialism. The cue to understanding modern alienation Basbaum finds in Marx, who saw alienation as part of the historical process. For Marx it was a conflict between what is and what ought to be, between conscience and consciousness of self, between the subjective and the objective. Contemporary alienation, says Basbaum, is the reaction against the capitalist system, and the solution to the problem lies in understanding the relationship of this alienation to the historical process. To escape from the slavery to the machine which produces alienation, man must find a new consciousness of producing things of social value and of controlling their use.

ERNESTO "CHE" GUEVARA (1928–1967)

Because of the circumstances of his death in Bolivia, "Che" Guevara is destined to be more important to Latin Americans

18. Leoncio Basbaum, "O sentido da história e a alienação," in *O proceso evolutivo da história* (São Paulo: Obilisco Ltda., 1963), 14, 20, 281–95.

as a martyr than in any other respect. Yet he may well be the revolutionist of his generation who has best expressed the frustrated aspirations of the Latin American masses, impatient for the better life they hope for. It is ironical, however, that he may better express the frustrations of the urban masses than those of the *campesinos* he presumed to fight for and to represent. On the whole, Guevara expresses a kind of Maoist doctrine of revolution, asserting that rigorous guerrilla action can create the subjective conditions for revolution and positing a strategy of revolution based on guerrilla warfare with campesino support.

Born and educated in Buenos Aires, young Guevara and a friend left Argentina in 1952 on a transcontinental journey, first by motorcycle, then by hitchhiking, which took them through Chile, Peru, and Colombia to Miami, Florida. Later in the year he returned to Buenos Aires to receive his medical degree, but left again the same year. Going first to Bolivia, at that time in revolution under the MNR, he went on from there to Peru, Ecuador, Panama, Costa Rica, and finally to Guatemala. There, under President Jacobo Arbenz, he obtained a position in the agrarian reform program. One of his closest friends in Guatemala was Hilda Gadea, an exiled *Aprista* from Peru, whom he married in 1955 but later divorced. When Arbenz confronted the uprising that drove him from office in 1954, Guevara volunteered for active participation in the defense of the capital. When the regime fell before the forces of the rebellion under Castillo Armas, Guevara took refuge in the Argentine embassy and, when allowed to leave, went to Mexico with others who had received asylum.

There, through Hilda Gadea, he made the acquaintance of Fidel Castro and the group of Cuban emigrés with whom his career was to be linked for the next decade. Guevara was a member of the little band that accompanied Castro on the

Granma; he was one of the few who escaped death upon landing in Cuba, surviving to initiate the guerrilla campaign in the Sierra Maestra. "Che" proved to be a daring and successful guerrilla leader, commanding one of the major divisions of the Castro forces. But at least equally important was his role as an intellectual leader of the movement. While still in Mexico, he impressed upon the Cubans the importance of disciplined adherence to a revolutionary program. After the triumph of the July 26 movement at the end of 1958, he became a literary voice of the movement, interpreting through his writings the history of the successful guerrilla campaign and expressing the strategic and tactical principles employed as well as his theory of the social revolution to be achieved.

His *Guerra de guerrillas* is a kind of textbook on guerrilla warfare that has been compared favorably with the writings of Mao Tse-tung and General Vo Nguyen Giap of Vietnam. Its most revolutionary doctrine, derived from the Cuban experience, is that guerrillas can defeat a regular army without having to go through the stage of developing a regularly organized revolutionary army of their own.

His *Socialism and Man,* published in Montevideo in 1966 just as he was about to launch his ill-fated campaign in Bolivia, though bearing marks of haste in composition, is the most mature and thoughtful of his writings. In it he looked back on nearly a decade of struggle and success in Cuba and stated his view of the role of youth in leading revolutions. "The basic clay of our work is youth," he wrote. The party, to which he assigned a vital role, he saw as a vanguard organization, to become a mass party only when the masses have achieved the level of development of the vanguard — that is, he meant, when they were educated for communism. This concept of party and its relation to the masses appears to differ little from that of orthodox

Leninism in its view of the role of the lumpen proletariat. The chief difference is that Guevara is speaking more particularly of rural masses, while the Bolsheviki were thinking of urban workers. Guevara's view of the dictatorship of the party is also that of Lenin: ". . . it is the dictatorship of the proletariat being exercised not only over the defeated class but also, individually, over the conquering class." [19]

OTHER NEO-MARXISTS

Many of the older generation of Marxist intellectuals continued through the 1960's to hold to early Leninist or Trotskyist views. Thus in Cuba Juan Marinello and Blas Roca have expressed little change in their thought despite their collaboration with Fidelismo. José Manuel Fortuny, the Guatemalan leader, rejects the adventurism represented in trying to follow the Cuban model, as he also rejects anything suggestive of Trotsky.[20] Julio César Jobet, the economic historian of Chile, still pleads for Marxist studies of Chilean history along rather orthodox lines.[21]

Silvio Romero of Argentina, on the other hand, rejects not

19. Ernesto "Che" Guevara, *El socialismo y el hombre* (Montevideo: Nativa Libros, 1966), 13. *Guerra de guerrillas,* published in Cuba in 1960, is probably his most important book, but his *Pasajes de la guerra revolucionaria* brings together a series of articles in which he told the story of much of the Cuban war. His Bolivian diary was published in 1968 in Cuba, the United States, and elsewhere. Among the numerous works on "Che" may be mentioned Richard Harris, *Death of a Revolutionary* (New York: Norton, 1970) and Luis J. González and Gustavo A. Sánchez Salazar, *The Great Rebel,* trans. Helen R. Lane (New York: Grove Press, 1969). Jay Mallin (ed.), *"Che" Guevara on Revolution* (Coral Gables, Fla.: University of Miami Press, 1969), brings together for the English reader an interesting and representative collection of excerpts from Guevara's writing. See also the bio-bibliography in the *Latin American Research Review,* V (Summer, 1970).

20. See the excerpt from José Manuel Fortuny, "Has the Revolution Become More Difficult in Latin America?" *World Marxist Review,* VIII (August, 1965), 38–45, in L. Aguilar, *Marxism in Latin America,* 204–206.

21. Julio César Jobet, "Notas sobre la historiografía Chilena," in *Historiografía Chilena* (Santiago: Nascimento, 1949), 345–77.

only the old evolutionary socialism, but both Leninism and Trotskyism in favor of a new revolutionary Marxist left. "The dilemma of the hour is very clear," he writes, "either socialism or bourgeois dictatorship." [22] Similar radical departures are also to be seen among leaders of revolutionary Christian thought.

22. Excerpt from Silvio Romero, *Las izquierdas en el proceso político argentino* (Buenos Aires: Palestra, 1959), in Aguilar, *Ibid.,* 164–67.

Existentialist Idealism
and Spiritualism

In the early years of the twentieth century, Latin American intellectual life displayed a spiritual restlessness, amounting in some places to a renewed spirit of revolution. This restlessness took different forms. It was Krausist, Spiritualist, neo-Kantian, Bergsonian, Leninist-Marxist, and anarchist in the pattern of Sorel. Increasingly, as the century advanced, it was existentialist and relativist. In the science of physics, the quantum theory, the Einstein theory of relativity, and other theoretical concepts seemed to erase the distinction between matter and energy, while the growing science of psychology shattered the rationalistic basis of nineteenth century thought. Even theology could not escape the revolutionary impact of these changes, and Pope Pius X found it necessary to issue a stern warning against the agnosticism and theories of vital immanence advanced by modernist theologians in the Encyclical *Pascendi Dominici Gregis* (1907). Philosophers, sociologists, and students of law tended to turn away from formalism in philosophy and to seek an understanding of the reality of man, God, and the universe in being or existence, rather than in the duality of matter and idea (or the Hegelian immanent idea) as Cartesian rationalism had required.

Existentialist and relativist thought was becoming the mode in Western intellectual circles, and the thought of Latin American intellectuals was to be no exception. While Latin American political, social, and even artistic ideologies were increasingly autonomous, distilling the effects of American historical experience, the underlying philosophies were even more than in the past a part of the universal pattern. One of the central characteristics of the new trend has been the agonizing search for norms within a pattern of thinking that seems to have no place for universals of any kind. This search, closely linked with the quest for identity and escape from alienation, is indeed a distinguishable trend, especially insofar as it is a search for a "scientific" or naturalistic philosophy. But it also permeates Marxist thought, as we have seen, and Christian thought, as we shall see, in addition to being central to this humanistic idealism.

Eduardo Nicol has expressed the opinion that the Hispanic American concept of philosophy in the nineteenth century was that of an "instrument for the formation of the national conscience" and that what he calls "the power of the word" continues to be a Greek and Hispanic trait of the Hispanic American form of life. Although the search for national identity was basically a nineteenth century problem, the effect of the search is still apparent in the twentieth century, not only in the national sense but in a more universal sense as well. One aspect of this effect may be the preoccupation of Latin American philosophers with ontological inquiry.[1]

SPANISH INFLUENCES

The external influences on twentieth century Latin American thought have come from various sources, but notably from Spanish writers who, once again in the twentieth century, have assumed a role suggestive of Spaniards of an earlier age. The literary and philosophical renaissance that accompanied Spain's

1. Eduardo Nicol, *El problema de la filosofía hispánica,* 34–35 and *passim.*

loss of the vestiges of her empire in the New World and the Far East in 1898 became a major stimulus to Spanish influence in Spanish American intellectual activity. Once again Spain has produced poets of the first order, such as Antonio Machado and Juan Ramón Jiménez, historians like Rafael Altamira, and such philosophers of world renown as Miguel Unamuno and José Ortega y Gasset.

The ideas of Unamuno and Ortega have had special influence in Latin America. Ortega popularized existentialist views derived from Wilhelm Dilthey and other Germanic sources, while Unamuno brought from Sören Kierkegaard a dramatic emphasis on the tragic sense of life, tragedy and suffering in Christianity, together with a quest for meaning in Spanish history. Unamuno also gave a special emphasis on personalism in his philosophy.

Unamuno's appeal to Spanish America was greatly strengthened by his interest in Spanish American literature and history. Like Henri Bergson of France, he believed there was a kind of historical thinking distinct from that of science. His philosophy, like that of Ortega, made history a sequence of states of belief. But Unamuno went further than Ortega in equating history with faith, thus making freedom a product of belief. Both Unamuno and Ortega, as we shall see, influenced the thinking of Antonio Caso, who, through the ideas of Henri Bergson, influenced the early thinking of Vicente Lombardo Toledano.

Ortega appealed to class conscious Latin American liberals with his fundamental belief, like that of Rodó, in the necessity of an intellectual elite to guide the masses, whose inevitable growth degraded everything. The influence of his *Revista del Occidente* and his reputation among Spanish Americans as a spiritual father of the Spanish Republic, gave Ortega great influence upon the liberal historical, sociological, and legal thought of Spanish America.[2]

HISPANIDAD AND YANKEEPHOBIA

The Spanish literary revival also contributed a note of Hispanidad to the growing current of Yankeephobia in Spanish America. José Enrique Rodó's *Ariel,* as Unamuno pointed out, was directed most sharply against the materialism which was destroying the traditional Graeco-Christian values in modern life. But Rodó's examples of materialism were frequently drawn from the United States. Rubén Darío, who was also a traditionalist in the sense of leading a return to older and more thoroughly Spanish forms of poetry, produced one of the bitterest pieces of anti-Yankee writing, his *Ode to Theodore Roosevelt.* The Argentine Manuel Ugarte, another idealist-traditionalist, argued along somewhat more Marxist lines of economic determinism in his *Destiny of a Continent* against the imperialism of the United States as a threat to Latin American independence.[3]

EXISTENTIALIST TRENDS

The most significant new directions, however, are what may be termed, in a broad sense, existentialist. They have roots in the irrationalism, intuitionism, and "creative evolution" of

2. Gerhard Masur, "Miguel de Unamuno," *The Americas,* XII (October, 1955), 139–56; Leopoldo Zea, *Dos etapas del pensamiento en Hispanoamérica,* 16–17. On the influence of Ortega in Mexico see José Gaos, *Sobre Ortega y Gasset* (México: Imprenta Universitaria, 1957), and Patrick Romanell, "Ortega in Mexico: A Tribute to Samuel Ramos," *Journal of the History of Ideas,* XXI (October, 1960), 600–608. See also Eduardo Nicol, *El problema de la filosofía hispánica,* 113–51, and Rafael Olivar Bertrand, "Los tiempos que le tocó vivir a Unamuno," *Cuadernos Americanos,* No. 5 (Nov.–Dic., 1964), 177–200.

3. Manuel Ugarte, *The Destiny of a Continent,* ed., with introduction and bibliography, J. Fred Rippy; trans. Catherine A. Phillips (New York: Alfred A. Knopf, 1925).

Nietzsche and Henri Bergson. But they derive more particularly from the existentialism of the Danish Sören Kierkegaard (by way of Unamuno) and from such German existentialists as Wilhelm Dilthey, Edmund Husserl, and Martin Heidegger; from such writers of the Marburg school as Hermann Cohen and Ernst Cassirer; from the Austrian Hans Kelsen, with his theories of a pure science of law; and from such neo-idealists as Max Scheler, Max Weber, and Heinrich Rickert. These sources represent a wide span in thought, joined chiefly by their common acceptance of being or existence as reality, their concern with its nature, and their general rejection of evolutionary determinism, both Marxist and Comtian. Since many of these German philosophers first became known in Latin America through the pages of Ortega's *Revista del Occidente,* not a little of Ortega's influence rubbed off in the process of their introduction to Latin American readers. William James, John Dewey, and Franz Boas brought somewhat comparable influences from the United States.

Accepting existence as reality, these Latin American "existentialists" rejected the Cartesian dichotomy of matter and idea, subject and object. Their rejection of deterministic and evolutionary views tended to give them a renewed interest in history, while the relativism of this twentieth century thought, expressing a profound skepticism and a pluralism, made it impossible for them to conceive of universal truths. Yet, paradoxically, this profound skepticism, as in Unamuno's classic *Tragic Sense of Life,* seemed to require the affirmation of belief in the philosophical possibility of values and principles, an affirmation that inspired revolutionary thought and made it possible to consider a large role for freedom of choice and decision in the historical process. Thus, a lively argument over philosophy of history is one of the outstanding characteristics of the contemporary scene.

PERSONALIST HUMANISM AND SPIRITUALISM

Antonio Caso and Samuel Ramos, two outstanding Mexican philosophers, provide examples of what may be termed personalist humanist thought. Behind their thinking one may see a vaguely Krausist or "spiritual" influence, though neither may be categorized as Krausist. Ideas derived from Bergson and William James are more important, while a kinship with Nietzsche, Ortega, and Unamuno is also apparent. The personalist emphasis in Caso may possibly be a direct influence of Unamuno. The thought of both Caso and Ramos is personalist in that it stresses the freedom of the individual from social determinism; it is humanist in regarding man as more than animal, though less than God, and in making philosophy neither basically theological nor rationalistic. While the personalism of Caso has rather obvious roots in Nietzsche and Miguel Unamuno, that of Samuel Ramos derives more definitely from Kant. Sometimes this personalism of both writers tends toward the stoic idealism earlier expressed by Rodó, manifesting ties with Renan. In a more general sense, because of its stress on individual freedom within the limits of the cultural tradition, their personalist thinking has tended to be conservative in its social outlook. Both philosophers have been critical of reforms emanating from the socialist labor movement. Caso, in fact, left the University in the 1930's in protest against the required teaching of Marxist socialism. Frequently both philosophers have found support in the literary and sometimes political *Hispanidad* stemming from the Generation of 1898 in Spain.

Spiritual and Neo-Kantian Trends

A number of twentieth century philosophers continued the stream of nineteenth century spiritualism and turn-of-the-century Krausism. This was particularly true of a group of philosophers who added to an older influence from Kant something of the idealist-existentialism of the new century.

Alejandro Korn (1860–1936) of Argentina, although of an older generation, was one of the more important voices of this kind. Like Ingenieros, as a student in the medical faculty he became interested in the Lombrosian abnormal psychology. Later, as a physician, he directed a hospital for the insane. In 1906, he began to lecture in the Faculty of Philosophy and Letters of the University of Buenos Aires; thereafter his interests centered in philosophy. From his university days he carried the influence of the spiritual or Krausist philosophy then being taught, as well as the positivism of José María Ramos Mejía. His enthusiasm for the writings of Schopenhauer gave him a further idealist bent, reinforced by an interest in Plotinus and in the German and Spanish mystics. But the most profound influence on his thought came from Kant, and Korn's students came to constitute an important, if not the most important, nucleus of neo-Kantian thought in the Spanish-speaking world.

One of the major characteristics of Korn's thought is his insistence upon the fundamental distinction between the subjective and the objective (*la conciencia y mi conciencia*), a distinction that led to the late nineteenth century German neo-idealism. His heritage of positivism may partly explain this refusal to accept the more complete subjectivity of many existentialists. But fundamentally it was his insistence upon an objective world outside the *yo* but not outside consciousness that led to his rejection of Heidegger's kind of intuitionism.

Korn retained the concept of causality in his thinking about the physical world, but as a Kantian he saw that in human society the free will of the individual has its basis in the moral law. Thus liberty is a creative process in history through which man has developed all that is best in his culture, and liberty also furnishes the impulse to this creative process. While science seeks a quantitative interpretation of reality, philosophy is a theory of knowledge and a theory of values or axiology.[4]

Francisco Romero (1891–1962) was a friend and student of Alejandro Korn and his successor in the professorship of philosophy in the University of Buenos Aires. His thought resembles that of Korn in many ways, particularly in its neo-Kantianism. But Romero goes further than Korn, following such idealist and existentialist German philosophers as Max Scheler and Nicolai Hartmann in rejecting the formalistic remnants of positivist scientism. He was born in Seville, Spain, but came to Argentina while still a child with his immigrant parents. Educated in Argentina, he came under the influence of the older Korn in his university days. Romero's first career was the Army, but he soon abandoned the military life to devote himself to writing and teaching.

The personalist emphasis of Romero's thought immediately suggests Unamuno, but Romero presents a less agonizing, less skeptical, more serene — in short, a more spiritual and Kantian — version of personalism. For him, the physical, the living, the

4. Korn's thought is best expressed in his *La libertad creadora* and in his *Axiología,* both of which are found in his *Obras completas,* edited by Francisco Romero (La Plata, Argentina, 1938). For critical comments see Aníbal Sánchez Reulet, *La filosofía latinoamericana contemporánea* (Washington, D.C.: Pan American Union, 1949), 83–85; and William J. Kilgore, "Una evaluación de la obra filosófica de Alejandro Korn," in *Estudios sobre Alejandro Korn* (La Plata: Universidad Nacional de la Plata, 1963), 52–75.

psychic and the spiritual are four levels of being through which one rises from the stage of immanence, transcending the subjective, to achieve a reality and a meaning which is total. "To be is to transcend." From this transcendence comes a realization or understanding of values. For Romero, "the assimilation of ethical value to transcendence is a common and universal datum (*dato*) of human experience." [5]

Francisco Larroyo, a professor of philosophy and former Director of the Faculty of Philosophy of the National University of Mexico, is another outstanding example of the neo-Kantian tendency. He acknowledges a special debt to the Argentine Alejandro Korn, but also owes something (as do so many of his generation in Mexico) to José Vasconcelos. His neo-Kantianism focuses on the philosophy of man (*antropología filosófica*). Of the philosophy of history, he writes, "As doctrine of the essence, factors, and meaning of history, this branch of philosophy embraces and evaluates the life of each era and place for the purpose of measuring its product (*rendimiento*) (be it positive or negative) within the universal current of human culture." His philosophical anthropology is stated succinctly: "Philosophical anthropology, the theory of man, thus constitutes the essential instrument for constructing, on the philosophical scale, the historical-cultural types." [6]

Alfredo Poviña, long associated with sociology in the University of Córdoba, Argentina, has done his most important work as a historian of sociology. His own sociological theory is essentially that of a historical sociologist and as such belongs to the school of Ortega's historical vitalism. This concept of

5. Francisco Romero, quoted in Aníbal Sánchez Reulet, *La filosofía latino-americana,* 327, 335. Translation by the author.
6. Francisco Larroyo, *La filosofía americana,* 253–55.

Ortega's permeates Poviña's textbook on sociology as well as his *History of Sociology in Latin America*.[7] His thought is recognizably antipositivist and idealist. In general, he seems to have adopted Georg Simmel's concept of sociology, in respect to (1) a theory of knowledge and (2) social metaphysics. But as a historical sociologist he is less than sympathetic to Simmel's "formalizing sociology as a discipline distinct from history."

One of his major concerns is the sociology of revolution. His view that revolution is the abnormal process of social change is not startling, but the theory behind it is quite interesting. His theory is that normal evolution is in the realm of being (*el dominio del ser*). It is the fulfillment of the life of the group. Thus he seems to think of *being* as *becoming*, parting company with the classic, Eleatic concept of unchanging *being*. Revolution, on the other hand, combines the realm of the *ser* (being-becoming) with that of the *más allá* (the ideal objective). Revolution aims at either a simple change in the power group or a more complex change in social structure. Revolutions, he says, pass through three stages: (1) prerevolutionary ferment and formation of revolutionary spirit; (2) the crisis in which the revolution is exteriorized, emerging in the streets — the stage in which armed forces play a decisive role; 3) the postrevolutionary phase, beginning in anarchy and followed by dictatorship. The reorganization of society "closes the circle." [8]

Alberto de Seixas Martins Torres (born in 1865) is a somewhat neglected figure in twentieth century spiritual idealism in Brazil, as the historian Cruz Costa has pointed out. An abolitionist in his youth, Alberto Torres later became a spiritualist

7. Alfredo Poviña, *Sociología* (5th ed.; Córdoba: Assandri, 1966); *Historia de la Sociología en Latinoamérica* (México: Fondo de Cultura Económica, 1940).
8. Alfredo Poviña, *Sociología de la revolución* (Argentina: Universidad de Córdoba, 1933), 302–303, 306–307.

philosopher with an interest in political thought. His *O problema nacional brasileiro,* according to Cruz Costa, may have given
the *Estado Nôvo* of Getulio Vargas some of its ideology.[9]

Raimundo de Farías Brito was an important turn-of-the-century neo-Kantian philosopher in Brazil. Some Brazilians consider him their greatest philosopher. His *Mundo Interior* (1914)
and his somewhat later *Finalide do Mundo* are said to have influenced the thought of the neo-Thomist Jackson de Figuereido.[10]

LEGAL PHILOSOPHY

Legal thought has always had a prominent place in Spanish
America, ever since the great debate on law and policy insti-
gated by the missionary-historian, Bartolomé de las Casas. Concern for the peoples of America, as we have seen earlier, was an
important element in the thinking of Francisco de Vitoria that
led to his formulation of international law.[11] Much careful
thought went into the formulation of the Spanish Laws of the
Indies, and, by an interesting coincidence, the first major codi-
fication of these laws, in the seventeenth century, was completed
by Antonio de León Pinelo, who also prepared the first comprehensive bibliography on the New World.[12] Study of the Laws of

9. João Cruz Costa, *Esbozo de una historia de las ideas en el Brasil* (México:
Fondo de Cultura Económica, 1957), 131–36.

10. *Ibid.,* 128–31.

11. See Francisco de Vitoria, *Las Relecciones de Indis y De Jure Belli de Fray
Francisco de Vitoria, O.P. Fundador del Derecho Internacional* (Washington,
D.C.: Unión Panamericana, 1963).

12. Antonio de León Pinelo, *El Epítome de Pinelo, primera bibliografía del
Nuevo Mundo,* Estudio preliminar de Agustín Millares Carlo (Washington, D.C.:
Unión Panamericana, 1958), and *Discurso sobre la importancia, forma, y dispo-
sición de la Recopilación de Leyes de la Indias Occidentales que . . . presenta
el Licenciado Antonio de León, 1623,* Estudios biobibliográficos de José Toribio
Medina. Prólogo de Aniceto Almeyda (Santiago: Fondo Histórico y Bibliográfico
José Toribio Medina, 1956).

the Indies in the universities in the eighteenth century, as we have seen, was one source of the thinking of independence leaders.

In the nineteenth century, Juan B. Alberdi adopted the historical theory of law, following the theories of Count Volney (1757–1820) and Friedrich Karl von Savigny (1779–1861), applying the philosophy in the whole realm of social thought. His contemporary, Manuel J. Quiroga Rosas, in a book entitled *Sobre la naturaleza filosófica del derecho* (1837), called for a more idealist but still historical basis in accord with the then current eclectic philosophical ideas. The influence of the historical jurisprudence of both these writers continued in later years. In the twentieth century, the late Ricardo Levene (1885–1959) continued and deepened this tradition of an historical theory of law through his extensive writing on Argentine legal history and through the Instituto de Historia del Derecho Argentino that he founded in the University of Buenos Aires and which now bears his name. The purpose of this Institute, "to cultivate the national juridical tradition, which is not a web of illusions and reminiscences, but a defensive and progressive moral force," is strikingly akin to the "institutional" history concept of Rafael Altamira, the noted Spanish historian. Levene insisted that Argentine legal institutions derived from a combination of American and European sources.[13] Ricardo Zorraquín Becú and Carlos Mouchet, two of Levene's disciples, have continued the Levene tradition, but with significant differences

13. See the review by Osvaldo Vinitsky of two books by Levene in *Revista del Instituto de Historia de Derecho*, Núm. 9 (1958), 164; also Levene on Quiroga Rosas, Núm. 6 (1954), 11–12. The history of the Institute has been written by Sigfrido Radaelli, *El Instituto de Historia del Derecho Argentino y Americano* (Buenos Aires: Coni, 1947). Levene's dedication to the concept of a history of the Americas appears in the multivolume hemispheric history which he edited.

that reflect contemporary social thought, particularly an effort to strengthen the concept of universality in judicial norms.[14]

Two Mexican scholars, Luis Recaséns Siches (of Spanish origin) and Eduardo García Máynez, have made notable contributions to the contemporary discussion of legal philosophy. Both reflect current sociological theory and existentialist philosophical concepts in their concern for the theoretical basis and nature of the juridical norm. García Máynez's interest in Hans Kelsen's (1881–) pure theory of law is shown in the fact that García translated two of the Viennese scholar's works. He also reveals the influence of Max Scheler and Nicolai Hartmann in seeking the philosophical basis for an axiological system, and his legal logic follows the Husserl phenomenology in thinking of philosophy as a rigorous science in which the thinking ego is a given. The intuition by which these norms are reached is an intellectual process, not emotional as in Heidegger.

García Máynez has tried to establish a natural law concept of justice within contemporary relativist sociological principles. His philosophy is existentialist in being formulated within a philosophy of life or being and phenomenological in the method of its search for juridical norms. Thus he avoids both the pure cultural relativism into which much contemporary thought falls and the subjectivism of psychologically oriented theory.[15]

Luis Recaséns Siches, a Spaniard born in Guatemala but educated in Spain and domiciled in Mexico since the days of the

14. See Ricardo Zorraquín Becú and Carlos Mouchet, *Introducción al derecho* (Buenos Aires: Depalma, 1943, and subsequent editions).

15. See García Máynez, "The Philosophical-Juridical Problem," in Joseph L. Kunz (ed.), *Latin American Legal Philosophy* (Cambridge, Mass.: Harvard University, 1948), and Máynez's "Libertad como derecho y como poder," with English translation by Cornelius Kruse and commentary by William Ernest Hocking, in *Philosophy and Phenomenological Research*, IV (December, 1943), 144–66; also his *Introducción al estudio del derecho* (México: Porrúa, 1953).

Spanish Civil War, was a student of Ortega; he continues the Ortega tradition in legal philosophy, though with numerous elements of originality. He has described his views himself as "shaped mainly under the influence of the great Spanish philosopher José Ortega y Gasset, along the line of the so-called 'metaphysics of vital reason' . . . a sort of existentialism." In his *Philosophy of Law* he identifies four historical elements and a fifth nonhistorical element as the sources of juridical ideals. The four historical elements are diversity and change in social conditions, the changing concrete needs of each historical moment and the means adopted to meet them, the lessons of practical experience, and the scale of priority of the various needs in a given historical moment. The nonhistorical element is the multiplicity of values in law, some, but not all, of which have a certain historical character in that they arise in different times and places. In this way, Recaséns believes, he has found an objective (natural law) basis for values in the historical moment. He goes beyond Max Scheler, who called attention to the need for study of the relationship between values and phenomenological reality, to make the study which Scheler did not himself make. Through the Ortegan "historical metaphysic" which Recaséns elaborates, he had added an axiology to the Kelsen theory — an axiology that Kelsen pointed out the need for but did not develop. Among numerous other provocative ideas in the thought of Recaséns that indicate the course and interpretation of Mexican legal philosophy is his view that the history of modern legal thought has a generally revolutionary character.[16]

García Máynez, in attacking the theory of natural liberty in the First Inter-American Congress on Philosophy, asserted the

16. Luis Recaséns Siches, *Filosofía del derecho* (2nd ed.; México: Porrúa, 1961), 66–68, 386, 462–77; "Juridical Axiology in Iber-America," *Natural Law Forum*, III (1958), 135–69; see also his *Sociología* (México: Porrúa, 1961).

principle of heteronomy, or interdependence, in which juridical
norms with intrinsic validity also have objectivity. This view had
been earlier expressed in a general sense by José Vasconcelos,
as he recounts in the first volume of his autobiography, *Ulises
Criollo*. As a law student in the years immediately preceding
the Mexican Revolution, he writes, he came to define his legal
philosophy as one that would analyze laws, legal actions, and
legal process as part of the dynamics of society. Thus, he was
stating a kind of existentialist sociological theory, what he called
"a dynamic causal relationship to explain social functions and
especially the conflicts of natural desires which establish the
need for law." [17]

This Latin American preoccupation with the nature of juridical norms, usually with the idea that these norms have reality
as law even when not fully coactive, has deep roots in the tradition of the Civil Law and its natural law basis. The preoccupation has been accentuated by the past century and a half
of striving, often against seemingly overwhelming odds, for political stability and the rule of law in national political life.
In the twentieth century, it has been necessary to seek a new
rationale for legal norms in neo-idealist, existentialist, or neo-
Kantian thought. Thus, the Argentine Sebastián Soler has defined the juridical norm as "an idea endowed with power . . .
[which] subsists even when what it desires does not occur; events
do not destroy it, but merely give occasion for it to achieve or
not the desired result. Only another norm destroys the norm." [18]
José Salvador Guandique of El Salvador has discussed the
juridical norm in somewhat similar idealistic terms: "Thus the

17. José Vasconcelos, *Ulises Criollo* (México: Botas, 1935), 266–69. An English
translation by William Rex Crawford, *A Mexican Ulysses*, was published by the
University of Indiana Press, 1963. The quotation is from the translation in
H. E. Davis, *Latin American Social Thought*, 386–89.
18. Sebastián Soler, *Ley, historia y libertad* (Buenos Aires: Losada, 1943).

susceptibility to violation (*violabilidad*) of a juridical norm indicates nothing against its intrinsic validity, since we find ourselves in the realm of the *ought to be* (*deber ser*), even when in fact the latter does not come to pass." [19] José Manuel Delgado Ocando has defined philosophy of law as a branch of axiology (concerned with values) and has applied the intuitive theory of knowledge of Husserl's phenomenology in presenting the study of law to students in Venezuela.[20]

International law has long held an important place in Latin American intellectual life. Hence it is not surprising to find a group of international lawyers, including among others J. M. Yepes and Edgardo Manotas Wilches of Colombia, Pedro Baptista Martins (1896–1951) and Jorge Americano (1891–1951) of Brazil, Francisco Cuevas Cancino of Mexico, José L. Bustamante of Peru, and most notably, Alejandro Alvarez (1868–1960), Chilean member of the World Court, all advocating what they call a "new" and, in the case of Alvarez, an "American" international law. For Alvarez, the essence of international law is psychological, derived from a study of "the life of peoples, in their full extent and in all their profundity." [21] His controversial concept of an American international law rests basically on the view "that due to social, psychological, and geographical circumstances, the Americas have consistently entertained a peculiarly intense sentiment of solidarity." [22]

19. José Salvador Guandique, "Problemas en torno a la norma jurídica," *Proyecciones* (San Salvador, El Salvador: Ministerio de Cultura, 1957), 111–25 at p. 119. First published in *Jus* (Mexico), March, 1942.

20. José Manuel Delgado Ocando, *Lecciones de filosofía del derecho* (Maracaibo, Venezuela: Universidad Nacional del Zula, 1957), 185–91.

21. Alejandro Alvarez, *Despúes de la guerra*, 123, quoted in H. B. Jacobini, *A Study of the Philosophy of International Law as Seen in Works of Latin American Writers* (The Hague: Martinus Nijhoff, 1954), 106.

22. Jacobini, *The Philosophy of International Law in Latin American Writers*, 126, crediting Alvarez, *Le droit international américain*, 17–21.

As the century wears on, this idealist-existentialist quest for a philosophical basis for a value system, as in juridical norms, and for a theoretical basis for dealing with the growing alienation in urban society assumes an increasingly defensive attitude against more radical doctrines advanced by the rising generations. These new doctrines are not only the neo-Marxist varieties already discussed. They are also new varieties of anarchism and new forms of theological radicalism.

Neo-Christian Thought

The twentieth century revival of Christian thought, coupled with a notable growth of Christian social consciousness in Latin America, has a major source in papal encyclicals such as the *Rerum Novarum* of Leo XIII (1891), the *Quadragesimo Anno* of Pius XI (1931), and the *Mater et Magistra* of John XXIII (1961). But in some respects it also has older roots in the nineteenth century traditionalism of Joseph de Maistre, Jaime Balmes and Juan Donoso Cortés. One result of this traditionalist element has been that the new Christian thought often had a conservative social and political orientation, at least in the early twentieth century, and its spokesmen often appeared in Conservative parties and in the youth and lay organizations they sponsored. Usually they were avowedly anti-Marxist.

By mid-twentieth century, stimulated by the development of one or more Catholic universities in many countries, this neo-Christian movement had experienced a remarkably rapid growth in scope and influence. It had also begun to move in a more liberal political direction within the Christian Democratic parties. Lay Christian leaders had assumed increasing importance in politics, in business, in labor unions, in the armed services, and in university circles. Many of these leaders continued to be politically conservative, even while accepting the new theological, philosophical, and social concepts. Some, however, like Eduardo Frei Montalva of Chile, had adopted the language of revolution. Still militantly anti-Communist, leaders like Frei seemed to achieve a left-of-center amalgam of Marxism with the papal teachings. An increasing number of the clergy, including several bishops, moved in this direction, and Christian student groups increasingly proclaimed such ideologies. Some carried their radicalism to the point of reconciling Christian teachings with Leninist social doctrine.

NEO-THOMISM

In the early years of this century, the French philosopher Jacques Maritain launched an attack on the secularism and "anti-Christian" tendencies of the Bergonian philosophy of intuitionism and creative evolution to which he had previously subscribed and to which he probably owed much of the voluntarism in his philosophy. His ideas found a favorable reception in Catholic Latin America, especially in the newly flourishing Catholic universities. In part this was because these ideas were a response to Pope Leo XIII's call to philosophers to re-examine Christian thought in the context of the new science. Thus the Maritain ideas also came at a time, as we have seen, when Latin Americans were ready to re-examine their commitment to "scientific" positivist evolutionism. The major impetus to the acceptance of this new Christian thought came, however, from the establishment of the Communist parties in America in the 1920's after Pope Pius XI restated Catholic social doctrine in the *Quadragesimo Anno* (1931) and especially after the Spanish Civil War in the 1930's aroused political passions to a high level. The growth and spread of the religious organization *Opus Dei* from Spain to the New World also gave lay support to the spread of Christian thought and doctrine, along rather conservative social lines.[1]

1. Jacques Maritain, *Bergsonian Philosophy and Thomism* (New York: Philosophical Library, 1955). For the encyclicals see Anne Freemantle, *The Papal*

Several Latin American philosophers have dedicated them-selves to what may be called in very general terms a reinterpreta-tion of the philosophy of Aquinas, attempting to do for the twentieth century, confused and bewildered over the nature of being and knowledge, what Aquinas did for the thirteenth. Like Aquinas, these philosophers have sought universals within the new scientific knowledge in biology, psychology, and physics. This has been an especially frustrating, anguished search within a relativist physics and a psychology that rejects the validity of Aristotelian logic and often questions the very possibility of objective knowledge. Whether these neo-Thomists and neo-Aristotelians have really restored God and theology to the heart of philosophy as they claim, or whether they have merely cre-ated an illusion to that effect, their influence upon contempo-rary thought has been great. It has been especially important in emphasizing voluntarism, both social and individual, and in consistently opposing the materialism of Leninist-Marxism. In-sofar as they share Saint Thomas' preoccupation with the nature of being, these neo-Christians tend to find a common ground with other existentialists, though holding a different concept of being. Many Christian philosophers, accordingly, assert a kind of troubled Christian existentialism. Others have taken on a neo-Kantian character, sometimes embracing some of the Jan-senist concepts of Blaise Pascal.

JACKSON DE FIGUEIREDO (1891–1928)

Jackson de Figueiredo is generally credited with being the first Brazilian, and one of the first Latin Americans, to give effective expression to twentieth century neo-Thomism and Christian

---

Encyclicals in Their Historical Context (New York: The New American Library, 1956), 166–95 and 228–35. A useful view of *Opus Dei* is found in *Conversations with Mgr. Escrivá de Balaguer* (Dublin: Scepter Books, 1968).

social thought. He was born in Aracajú, Sergipe, Brazil, receiving his early education there and in Baía, where he graduated in law. In his early years he had some contact with a Protestant missionary school conducted by W. E. Finley, and as a youth he was radically anticlerical. At the age of nineteen he took part in the stoning of a group of Portuguese priests expelled from Portugal in 1910, when they arrived in Baía. Eight years later he experienced a religious conversion which brought him back into the fold of the Church and made him what João Cruz Costa has called "the instigator — and the energetic champion — of the intellectual and political renovation of Catholicism in contemporary Brazil." [2]

As we have seen, the neo-Kantian spiritualism of Raimundo de Farías Brito was a major influence on the formation of Figueiredo's thought — an influence reflected in the fact that he wrote two books on this Brazilian philosopher. In the Jansenism of Blaise Pascal, he discovered a skeptical inquietude, a seeking for faith, that struck a sympathetic chord; he admired particularly the manner in which Pascal had submerged his rationalism and individualism in religious faith. Maritain, of course, was a major inspiration, but Figueiredo's near mysticism and his anguished doubt and tragic sense of life suggest an almost equal influence from both Sören Kierkegaard and Miguel Unamuno.[3]

2. João Cruz Costa, *Panorama of the History of Philosophy in Brazil* (Washington, D.C.: Pan American Union, 1962), 95–96.
3. Figueiredo's principal works are *Algunas Reflexões sôbre a Filosofia de Farias Brito* (Rio de Janeiro, 1916), *A Questão Social na Filosofia de Farias Brito* (1919), *Pascal e a Inquietação Moderna* (1922), and the posthumous *Correspondência* (1944). In addition to Cruz Costa's work cited in note 2 above, see his *Esbozo de una historia de las ideas en el Brasil* (México: Fondo de Cultura Económica, 1957), 150ff.; see also Aníbal Sánchez Reulet, *La filosofía latinoamericana contemporánea*, 301–303; and Manfredo Kempff Mercado, *Historia de la filosofía en Latinoamérica* (Santiago: Zig Zag, 1958), 165–69.

ALCEU AMOROSO LIMA

Alceu Amoroso Lima has been well known in Brazil under the pen name Tristâo de Ataide, as a literary critic writing in *O Journal* of Rio de Janeiro. He has also been a popular professor of philosophy in the Catholic University of Rio de Janeiro. During 1951 to 1952, he was the dynamic director of the department of cultural affairs of the Pan American Union. His writing upon a wide range of subjects is voluminous. Since his youth he has been a spokesman for Christian Social Action, dedicated to the social Christian objectives of the *Rerum Novarum*. He was a founder of the Catholic student movement in Brazil and has participated in the Christian Socialist party of his country. Born in Rio de Janeiro on December 11, 1893, he was educated in Rio de Janeiro and in France. In addition to literature, philosophy, and teaching, his career has embraced law, government service, and politics.

The general character of his thought is Thomistic and Aristotelian, and he frequently cites Aquinas. But he also expresses a neo-idealist philosophy of history suggestive of Croce. For his neo-Thomism, he acknowledges a debt to Jackson de Figueiredo, the original innovator of such ideas in Brazil. Like Jacques Maritain, whose influence is obvious, Lima admits an element of pluralism,[4] some suggestions of which may be seen in his discussion of method. Here and there, too, something of the seemingly inescapable positivism of Brazilian thought appears, perhaps more in the structure of the logic than in the substance of the ideas.

Among his numerous published works, one of the most typical and challenging is *The Problem of Labor*. Labor, he writes

---

4. See his "Silvio Romero and the Evolution of Literary Criticism in Brazil," *The Americas* (Academy of American Franciscan History), X (January, 1954), 277–88.

in this book, is "the biggest problem of our time." Fear, indifference, and conventionalism prevent Christians from seeing this reality and from understanding that the destiny of all contemporary societies revolves around labor. Following Aristotle and Aquinas, he sees that labor "is at the same time of the speculative order and of the practical order." Labor as "the force of life" is the most general expression of human life and of the human spirit. Hence it "is indissolubly linked to the human personality." For the Christian, freedom of labor is inseparable from essential liberty.[5]

EDUARDO FREI MONTALVA (1911–)

Eduardo Frei Montalva was born in Santiago, Chile, the son of Eduardo Frei and Victoria Montalva. Educated in the Instituto de Humanidades, he went on to study law in the Catholic University of Santiago, where he won an honor prize, despite the fact that he was working part-time. While in the university he took an active part in student organizations, and by 1932 he had become President of the Chilean Association of Catholic Students. In 1939 he was chosen secretary of the Congress of American Catholic Students held in Rome.

In Iquique, in northern Chile, he practised law and edited a newspaper. Soon he was active in politics there within the Conservative party. In 1938, with a group of other young men, he left the Conservative party to found the Falange Nacional, later

5. The *Obras completas de Alceu Amoroso Lima* (including works published originally under the pen name Tristão de Ataide) have been published in Rio de Janeiro by Livraria AGIR, at various dates. The statements cited above are from *O problema do trabalho,* 19–49, which appeared in 1947 as volume XX. Other important works include volume XII, *Preparação a sociologia* (originally published 1931); volume XXII, *Politica* (originally 1932); volume XIII, *Problema da burguesia* (originally 1932); volume VI, *A estética literaria* (originally 1945); volume XVII, *Meditação sobre o mundo moderno* (originally 1942); and volume XIV, *Pela reforma social* (originally 1935).

to become the Christian Democratic Party of Chile. Meanwhile, he had published his first book, *Chile desconocido* (1937). Other volumes followed, expressing the reform demands of Chilean Christian youth. But success of the Falange in politics was difficult to achieve, partly no doubt because its religious traditionalism ran counter to the anticlericalism and Marxism of northern Chile. Frei was defeated as a candidate for deputy from Iquique in 1937 and later suffered a similar defeat in Santiago.

Invited into the cabinet of President Juan Antonio Ríos (1942–1946), Frei served briefly as minister of public works. Then in 1949 he was elected to the Senate from the northern provinces of Atacama and Coquimbo. Re-elected to the Senate in 1957, he was nominated for the presidency by his party the following year. His vigorous campaign in all parts of the country made him and his party a serious contender in this election, giving him the third largest vote in a field of five major candidates.

After 1939 he was a professor of labor law in the Catholic University, and his teaching, writing, and speaking made his word heard on all major questions of national policy. His books consist chiefly of his speeches and newspaper articles, but some have a more philosophical character. They all show the influence of Jacques Maritain and other neo-Thomist philosophers. He may also have been influenced by the ideas of his brilliant but tragically short-lived compatriot, Clarence Finlayson.

Frei insists upon the revolutionary character of Christian ideals and beliefs when applied to the social problems of today. Christian democracy has "an inflexible democratic will." But its "stand with the poor," suggesting the Marxist class struggle even while finding its ideological basis in the papal encyclicals, calls for an antiestablishment "transformation of the structures." Politics must have an ethical basis, Frei insists, but he gives little attention to the anguishing philosophical problem of finding the basis for a normative ethics within the relativist and existentialist contemporary philosophy. The most revolutionary aspect of Frei's thought is his explicit rejection of the nineteenth century ideologies of Liberalism. But he stops far short of any identification with the Christian radical activists who advocate the violent overthrow of the whole structure of Western society.[6]

THE MEXICANS: PRECIADO AND BASAVE

In Mexico, Christian thought has encountered some peculiar difficulties because of its political implications in the Mexican Revolution. Yet Mexico has produced some important spokesmen of the neo-Christian thought. Hernán Preciado was one of the first Mexicans to expound the new Christian social doctrine. Shortly afterward, Oswaldo Robles emerged during his all-too-short life as a brilliant interpreter of neo-Thomism in the Faculty of Philosophy of the National University.[7] The indefinable José Vasconcelos, despite his addiction to a kind of neo-Kantianism, stimulated a return to Christian oriented thought. One of his disciples, Agustín Basave Fernández del Valle, has produced a challenging Christian political philosophy. A professor of Philosophy in the University of Nuevo León, Mexico,

6. Frei's published works include: *Chile desconocido* (Santiago: Ercilla, 1937); *La política y el espíritu* (2nd ed.; Santiago: Pacífico, 1946); *Aún es tiempo* (Santiago: Talleres Gráf. "El Chileno," 1942); *Sentido y forma de una política* (Santiago: Pacífico, 1951); and *Pensamiento y Acción* (Santiago: Pacífico, 1956). Citations are from "El Camino a Seguir," in *Una Tercera Posición* (Lima: Universitaria, 1960), 99–106, Frei's closing speech at the Fifth Congress of Latin American Christian Democrats, Lima, October 27, 1959.

7. See Oswaldo Robles, *The Main Problems of Philosophy*, trans. Kurt F. Reinhardt (Milwaukee: The Bruce Publishing Co., 1946).

Fernández del Valle has become almost a neo-Kantian, though he still retains marks of Thomism; he tries to reconcile his thought with that of Aquinas and with such neo-Kantians as Kelsen and Herman Heller. He agrees, for example, with the latter's theory of the necessity of the concept of sovereignty in the theory of the state.

Basave's philosophy achieves a kind of Christian existentialism combined with an element of neo-Kantian transcendentalism. In addition to the various European, and particularly German, sources he has drawn upon, the ideas of Ortega and Unamuno seem to have provided some of his inspiration. His concept of life as feeling, anguish, and misery, combined with the anticipation or hope based on religious faith, suggests Unamuno at once. Either from his teacher Vasconcelos, or from the current philosophical atmosphere in Mexico, he may have derived certain of his less Thomistic trends that are suggestive of neo-Kantian idealism. From such influences, however they may have influenced his thought in various and somewhat diverse ways, he emerges advocating a natural law based on laws of God which can be known by human reason and are consistent with man's nature and his free will.

When he writes that man by nature had a political vocation, because as an individual he is conscious of his insufficiency, Basave is expressing an idea of vocation based on a Christian concept of the nature of man. He cites Saint Thomas Aquinas to the effect that man's social nature has its basis in the fact that his ultimate end is to become one with God. Hence it is that man needs the aid of other men, both in knowledge and in love. Basave thus finds the basis of natural law in a metaphysics rooted in Christian belief concerning the nature of man and his relation to his fellowmen through God. Politics, a task of human life, is a struggle to achieve a "living together" (*convivencia*), and to this end "we create, we develop, and we exercise power." [8]

CARLOS ALBERTO SIRI

Carlos Alberto Siri of El Salvador has provided an excellent recent statement of neo-Catholic social thought. In his *Preeminence of the Civitas and the Insufficiency of the Polis* he has presented a neo-Thomistic position, with an emphasis on humanism like that of Maritain. He also states the case for Christian rejection of the Marxist-Leninist ideology and the classical Christian view of the inadequacy of the state to provide for all human needs. Communism, writes Siri, "violates natural law, according to which law is based upon the universal exigencies of human life." Its weakness in the spiritual realm lies in its exclusive dedication to economic and material progress. On the other hand, "humanity expects from the Church . . . that it aid . . . with all the means at its disposal, the construction and formation of the *Civitas Máxima* — the great universal fraternity of all men of which Vitoria speaks." Siri calls upon all Christians to raise their voices in a "clamor of faith, hope, and love," moved by the promise of the kingdom of God. "It is the hour for Christians to resolve to become the most vigorous restorers of the earthly *Civitas* right here in this world." The state has its responsibility too. It must provide the conditions of freedom within which man can be most creative. It must "assure and

8. These comments are based largely on Agustín Basave Fernández, *Teoría de la Democracia* (Monterrey, México: Universidad de Nuevo León, 1963). Other important works are *Teoría del Estado* (México: Jus, 1955), *Filosofía del Hombre* (México: Jus, 1957), *La Filosofía de José Vasconcelos. El Hombre y su Sistema* (Madrid, 1958), and *Ideario Filosófico* (México: Jus, 1961).

structure the optimal coordination of the initiatives of individuals and groups," providing the hierarchization of society.[9]

Christian Radicals

The agitated decade of the 1960's brought a number of younger priests and Christian student leaders to abandon or modify their previous Christian stance of anti-Marxism. Camilo Torres (1929–1966) of Colombia is an example. Studying sociology in the University of Louvain, Belgium, he seems to have taken up with neo-Marxist ideas there. Within just a few years after his return to Colombia, he moved from Christian reformism in the spirit of *Mater et Magistra* to a radical revolutionary position that led him to take up the class struggle and eventually to join a band of guerrillas fighting in the mountains (the Army of National Liberation). He met a martyr's death a few months later when the guerrilla band was ambushed in the mountainous province of Santander in February of 1966 by the Colombian army.[10] The spiritual heirs of Torres in Colombia are a group of Christian activists called *Galconda* who are fomenting a proletarian, anti-imperialist movement to overthrow the established order. In Argentina a similar group of "Third World Priests" reportedly collaborate with revolutionary guerrillas. G. Castillo Torres, writing in the Protestant sponsored *Cristianismo y Sociedad* (Montevideo), interprets Father Torres as a symbol of the revolutionary potentiality in Christianity.[11]

9. Carlos Alberto Siri, *La preeminencia de la civitas y la insuficiencia de la polis* (San Salvador, El Salvador: Ministerio de Educación, 1967), 172–73, 200, 212.

10. See Camilo Torres, *Revolutionary Writings* (New York: Herder and Herder, 1969), and Germán Guzmán Campos, *Camilo Torres* (New York: Sheed and Ward, 1969).

11. G. Castillo Torres, "Violencia contra Sacerdotes en Colombia, *Cristianismo y Sociedad,* Año 7, No. 21 (1969), 87–91.

Most Christian radicals stop short of the violence that Camilo Torres came to believe was inescapable. Their position is better represented by the followers of Monsignor Ivan Illich of Cuernavaca, México, and his supporter, Cuernavaca's liberal bishop; by the followers of Bishop Helder Camara of Recife, Brazil; or by the contributors to the leftist *Vispera,* published in Montevideo.

THE MISSIONARIES

Foreign missionaries, both Catholic and Protestant, seem to have stimulated some of this Christian activism, and possibly certain aspects of the neo-Christian thought. Some missionaries, of course, have been an influence for traditionalism in social thought and fundamentalism in theology. In the nineteenth century the missionary influence was generally one of this traditionalism. Thus, early nineteenth century Spanish émigré priests helped to turn the Peruvian clergy away from their earlier commitment to reform and toward traditionalism, as has recently been pointed out by Antonine Tibesar.[12] We have already seen that as late as 1910 émigré priests from Portugal were stoned upon their arrival in Brazil because they were reactionary.

But while most twentieth century missionaries, both Catholic and Protestant, were conventional Christians, a significant number advocated ideas of social Christianity. We have noted the influence of Protestant missionary W. E. Finley in the intellectual development of Jackson de Figueiredo. Hernán Siles Suazo, one of the leaders of the Bolivian Revolution of 1952, was the product of a Methodist sponsored secondary school in La Paz in which such ideas prevailed. *Christianismo y Sociedad,* referred

12. Antonine Tibesar, "The Peruvian Church at the Time of Independence in the Light of Vatican II," *The Americas,* XXVI (April, 1970), 349–75.

to above, has been published in Uruguay since 1962 by a group of liberal Protestants. It is a voice of the Protestant concern for social change. Among Catholic missionaries, the Maryknoll fathers have had an important liberalizing influence, particularly since World War II. Some of them, for example, the brothers Thomas and Arthur Melville in Guatemala, have contributed notably to the revolutionary but nonviolent mood.

Not since the days of the Independence movement have the clergy of Latin America been moved so markedly as they are today to demand rapid social change. There are those who attribute this new mood to the growing social tensions created by a population explosion and overly rapid urbanization. Others are inclined to see it as a direct result of the renewal of Christianity and the flowering of Christian social thought. The latter would say that Pope John XXIII has had an important influence. A fair appraisal would doubtless be that both social circumstances and the Christian intellectuals and activists have had a share in creating the contemporary mood. The more difficult question is whether this renewed vitality of Christian thought in the decades since World War II is a passing phase that has already run most of its course, and will surrender to a more secular outlook, or whether it has initiated a longer term trend of growth in the importance of Christian thought.[13]

13. Chapter 13 of Jorrín and Martz, *Latin American Political Thought and Ideology,* is a good discussion of the thought and ideology of the Christian Democratic parties and includes a useful select bibliography.

Some Unresolved Problems

It may be appropriate to ask whether the historical analysis of Latin American thought tentatively set forth in the introductory chapter of this book has proved valid in subsequent chapters. In the most general sense that interpretation is that Latin American thought since independence has been revolutionary and nationalist, displaying the preoccupation which Martin S. Stabb has called a quest for identity and which Leopoldo Zea has stated in dialectical form as the unsuccessful effort to reject the colonial past. The most obvious contradiction in this general interpretation might appear to be the continued strength of traditionalist and, somewhat paradoxically, internationalist thought currents. These latter streams of thought may not be as contradictory as at first appears, however. Rather, they are best understood as the virtually inevitable reaction and counterpoise to the more generally nationalist revolutionary or reform tendency.

Whether this revolutionary nationalism has Amerindian or Afro-American roots is less than clear, although some aspects of the thought suggest that this is so. Nor is it clear how far this trend in Latin American thought is distinctively American rather than universal. Certainly in the twentieth century the currents of Latin American revolutionary ideas show many close relationships to more universal revolutionary and nationalist currents, as we have seen. Many Latin Americans have insisted, of course, and this author tends to agree, that they are "walking on their own feet" and "thinking their own thoughts." Perhaps the best conclusion on this question of Americanism versus universalism is the existentialist concept of Gilberto Freyre that there is no necessary contradiction between cultures and ideas that are regional and those that are universal.

From the standpoint of the last third of the twentieth century it is also appropriate to ask what is the relevance of the intellectual heritage outlined in this brief history to the contemporary social issues and problems of knowledge. One form in which this question may be cast is this: Is this heritage a useful guide in the persistent and elusive search for an intelligible basis for a normative pattern or for some meaning in life within the contemporary intellectual atmosphere of relativism, skeptical existentialism, alienation, and anomie? The empirical evidence presented in this brief survey, or that which could be presented in a much more extensive one for that matter, cannot be expected to provide a satisfactory answer to this question, except possibly for those readers for whom the lack of empirical proof is in itself a satisfactory answer. For in general, as the reader will doubtless agree, the answer to such an inquiry depends upon the philosophical or theoretical assumptions that one brings to bear upon the question. Particularly, in this case, it will be determined by the philosophy of history one holds, and even more specifically by the degree to which this philosophy of history embraces an idealist element.

A similar comment must be made in considering the closely related question as to whether our analysis has in any way substantiated or disproved the thesis of Leopoldo Zea, as set forth in the Introduction. For the problem of interpretation posed by Zea is another of those questions that cannot be answered empirically, unless one adopts the theoretical position that all answers must be confined to the empirical. The author finds considerable validity in the Zea thesis, as the reader has seen, but this is more because of theoretical considerations than because of historical evidence. This is an overly simple way of saying that Zea gives meaning to the intellectual history of Latin America, particularly in the nineteenth century.

If one assumes the truth of the paradox stated by Zea — that Latin Americans struggling in the nineteenth century to rid their mentality of colonialism and imperialism, were unable to do so precisely because they had not themselves fully experienced this colonialism and imperialism — a further question arises. Have Latin Americans in their twentieth century anticolonialism and anti-imperialism experienced their own history sufficiently to make this ideology in any sense real? Or is this anticolonialism and anti-imperialism, like the anti-Europeanism of the nineteenth century, destined to reveal itself an empty shell?

Do the religious, social, and esthetic concepts derived from the Amerindian and Afro-American heritage have useful meaning in the present-day ethnic scene? Do they have validity in relation to present problems, or are they a limiting, restricting inheritance, standing in the way of the self-realization of Latin American peoples?

Conclusions in respect to all these questions will depend upon how one understands the continued preoccupation of Latin American thought with what is American. This preoccupation has its basis, as we have seen, in a long tradition of historical and legal thought and in literary criticism. Twentieth century tendencies have sometimes undermined and sometimes strengthened this basis. In any case, the outcome seems to be the survival of a rather general Latin American insistence upon a view of history in which man has freedom to move toward higher social goals. Many, but not all Latin American writers find its basis in some specifically American concept or set of values. Some find it in *indigenismo,* although this tendency seems to be waning.[1] A few have found it in *negritude.* Some find it in the Aprista variety of Marxism. In any case, this Americanism is likely to be identified with thought that is revolutionary, that expresses confidence in the possibility of revolutionary social change and confidence in revolutionary leadership.

The increasingly violent character of twentieth century thought raises the question of the direction in which this radicalism is going. Latin American intellectuals are increasingly accepting Trotskyism, Maoism, Castroism, and other revisionist Marxist revolutionary ideas, reconciling them with existentialism on the one hand and with Christian theology on the other. In doing so, are they preparing the "subjective conditions" for a continent-wide overthrow of the existing establishment? Is this Latin American development merely part of the more general Third World trend? Or is one to read into this phenomenon some other interpretation?

We have certainly seen a general tendency in the history of Latin America, especially in the past century, for its philosophers to display an increased degree of sophistication and an increased independence in their thought. Entirely aside from the question of the Americanism of this thought, is it also in a real sense more autonomous? Is this question any longer relevant in the late twentieth century? Or is Latin American thought rather to be judged, as suggested earlier, by some more universal standard?

In conclusion, the reader of this brief introduction to the history of Latin American thought would do well to recall that

1. See the discussion of "The Social Conscience and Indigenismo" in Jorrín and Martz, *Latin American Political Thought and Ideology,* 318ff.

it is written upon the basis of what is on the whole a meager monographic literature. The increased study of intellectual history by Latin American scholars in the 1950's was followed in the 1960's by a notable increase in the activity of scholars working in the English language, both in research and in the translation of Latin American works. But the lack is still great. We have a few good books, such as those of Bernard Moses, John Tate Lanning, Harry Bernstein, Charles Hale, Martin Stabb, the joint work of Miguel Jorrín and John D. Martz, the books of Leopoldo Zea, William Rex Crawford, and an increasing literature of scholarly articles. Generally speaking, the best works are those treating the history of thought in individual countries. We still lack a comprehensive history of thought in Latin America as a whole.

As a largely undeveloped field, the history of Latin American thought presents many challenging questions for study, questions ranging from the most general problems to those of micro-research, and from pre-Conquest thought to that of the twentieth century. The burden of this book has been to present some of the problems involved in achieving an acceptable synthesis or alternative syntheses. These problems involve the relationship of various aspects of social thought, especially since pre-Conquest days, to the more general philosophical trends of the various eras, as well as the question of the autonomy of Latin American thought—more precisely defined as the relationship of Latin American ideas to those of Europe and the United States. In this respect the Zea synthesis has probably raised more questions than it has answered. Nor is it to be expected that other scholars will agree with each other in their theoretical approach. The important thing is to achieve some kind of consensus upon what the problems for investigation are, and in this

respect Zea's synthesis provides an invaluable point of departure.

The relationship of the history of ideas in Latin America to that of Spain and Portugal is a closely related problem of interpretation. This is a controversial and on the whole little-studied area, although Spanish scholars have begun to give it some attention. The relationship of philosophical and theoretical concepts to political ideologies and the penetration of these ideologies into traditional attitudes are other questions largely unexplored.

One of the more obvious general needs is for study of the currents of ideas expressed in the Latin American labor press during the late nineteenth and twentieth centuries. This is a subject in which Carlos Rama of Uruguay and Moisés Poblete Troncoso of Chile have ploughed significant ground with their writing, including Rama's important bibliography. As we have seen, it is a subject currently engaging the interest of Soviet historians.

The influence of Spanish *krausismo* is another theme that has received little attention. The relationship of Unamuno's personalism and religious existentialism, Ortega's philosophy of law and history, and Altamira's historiography all invite further study.

Another major area calling for research is that of traditional and conservative political and social thought during and since independence. Colombians have done important work here, as in Carlos Valderrama's study of Miguel Antonio Caro and Pablo González Casanova's treatment of efforts of the Inquisition to protect traditional thought against the innovations of the Enlightenment in the eighteenth century. Studies of a sort have been made of such political figures as Rosas, Portales,

Alamán, and Bernardo de Pareira Vasconcellos; but in general
we have only a vague concept of the nature of their ideas, of
the relationship of their ideas to the problems of the eras in
which they lived or acted, or of the connections of their ideas
with contemporary trends in Europe, particularly with traditionalist thought in Spain and Portugal.

We also appear to know little of the relationship of nineteenth century liberal-radical thought in Latin America to the
European liberal Catholic trends represented in Lammenais.
The history of the penetration and spread of the concepts of
social Christianity expressed in the *Rerum Novarum* (as well as
those of Protestant missionary social Christianity) is largely untouched. The social and political ideas behind the important
relationship of the military to politics is another such undeveloped area of study. The history of legal thought is largely un-
cultivated, except for the pioneering work of the Instituto de
Historia del Derecho Ricardo Levene in Argentina and Rafael
Altamira's studies of the Laws of the Indies. Nor have we much
significant research on the history of economic thought in Latin
America. Much the same may be said for the history of Latin
American historiography, although the Commission on History
of the Pan American Institute of Geography and History has
partly remedied this lack by sponsoring a series of significant
publications in this field, and the *Hispanic American Historical
Review* and other journals have published some useful articles.

First among the more specific areas calling for research is
that of the thought of individual writers and political leaders.
Pioneering work has been done by Latin American biographers,
but critical studies which show the relationship of ideas of these
individuals to the trends of thought and the problems of their
times are rare. Beyond this initial need, the range of specific
questions for research is virtually unlimited. Studies are needed

of the thought involved in most of the important revolutions, events, and movements of change in Latin America since independence. Research has been done on a few such questions by both Latin American and United States historians, but the field is still wide open.

Finally, one of the least-explored areas is that of the nature and influence of Aztec, Maya, and Inca thought in relation to the whole panorama of Latin American thought. This need for the study of pre-Conquest thought may be the best note on which to end this historical survey, for it is also the place where this history began.

A Select Bibliography

BIBLIOGRAPHIES

Fuentes de la filosofía latinoamericana. Washington, D.C.: Organization of American States, 1967.

Los Fundadores en la filosofía de América Latina. Washington, D.C.: Organization of American States, 1970.

Handbook of Latin American Studies. Washington, D.C.: Hispanic Foundation, Library of Congress, published annually.

PRE-CONQUEST AND COLONIAL

Aldridge, A. Owen. *The Ibero-American Enlightenment.* Urbana, Ill.: University of Illinois Press, 1971.

Bitar Letayf, Marcelo. *Economistas españoles del siglo xviii.* Madrid: Ediciones Cultura Hispánica, 1968.

Herr, Richard. *The Eighteenth Century Revolution in Spain.* Princeton, N.J.: Princeton University Press, 1958.

Lanning, John Tate. *Academic Culture in the Spanish Colonies.* New York: Oxford, 1940.

————.*The Eighteenth Century Enlightenment in the University of San Carlos de Guatemala.* Ithaca, N.Y.: Cornell University Press, 1956.

Ossio, Juan. "Apuntes para una comprensión del concepto de 'Historia' entre los Incas." *Ciencias Prehistóricas y Antropológicas,* Universidad Católica, Peru, 1:58A (1965), 170–77.

Picón Salas, Mariano. *A Cultural History of Spanish America.* Translated by Irving Leonard. Berkeley: University of California Press, 1962.

Puy, Francisco. *El pensamiento tradicional en la España del siglo xvii; introducción para un estudio de las ideas jurídicas-políticas españolas en dicho período histórico.* Madrid: Instituto de Estudios Políticos, 1966.

Whitaker, Arthur P., et al. *Latin America and the Enlightenment.* 2nd ed. Ithaca, N.Y.: Cornell University Press, 1961.

————. "Changing and Unchanging Interpretations of the Enlightenment in Spanish America." *Proceedings of the American Philosophical Society,* CXIV (August, 1970), 256–71.

SINCE INDEPENDENCE

Bernard, L. L. "Latin America." *Encyclopedia of the Social Sciences.* New York: Macmillan, 1930–1935, I, 301–20.

Bernstein, Harry. *Making an Inter-American Mind.* Gainesville, Fla.: University of Florida, 1961.

Caturla Brú, Victoria. *¿Cuáles son los grandes temas de la filosofía latinoamericana?* México: Novaro, 1959.

Clissold, Stephen. *Latin America, A Cultural Outline.* London: Hutchinson, 1965.

Crawford, William Rex. *A Century of Latin American Thought.* 2nd ed. Cambridge: Harvard University Press, 1961.

Daireaux, Max. *Littérature hispano-américaine.* Paris: KRA, 1930.

Davis, Harold Eugene, *Latin American Leaders.* New York: H. W. Wilson, 1949, and Cooper Square Publishers, 1968.

————. *Latin American Social Thought.* Washington, D.C.: University Press of Washington, 1961.

————. *Social Science Trends in Latin America.* Washington, D.C.: American University, 1950.

————. "Trends in Social Thought in Twentieth Century Latin America." *Journal of Inter-American Studies,* I (January, 1959), 57–71.

————."The History of Ideas in Latin America." *Latin American Research Review,* III (Fall, 1968), 23–44.

————. "Problems in the History of Ideas in Latin America." *Duquesne Review,* XV (Fall, 1970), 243–53.

———. "Sources and Characteristics of Latin American Thought." Topic: 20 [Washington and Jefferson College] (Fall, 1970), 12–20.

Echeverría, José. *La ensenañza de la filosofía en la universidad hispanoamericana*. Washington, D.C.: Unión Panamericana, 1965.

Frondizi, Risieri. "Tendencies in Contemporary Latin American Philosophy. In *Inter-American Intellectual Interchange*. Austin, Texas: Institute of Latin American Studies, 1943, pp. 35–48.

Gaos, José. *Sobre Ortega y Gasset y otros trabajos de historia de las ideas en Espãna y la América española*. México: Imprenta Universitaria, 1957.

García Calderón, Francisco. *Latin America: Its Rise and Progress*. Translated from French (*Les démocraties latines de l'Amérique*) by Bernard Miall. London: T. F. Unwin, 1918.

Gavidia, Francisco. *La formación de una filosofía propia o sea latino-americano*. San Salvador, 1931.

Gómez Robledo, Antonio. *Idea y experiencia de América*. México: Fondo de Cultura Económica, 1958.

Halperín Donghi, Tulio. *Tradición política española e ideología revolucionaria de Mayo*. Buenos Aires: Editorial Universitaria de Buenos Aires, 1961.

Henríquez Ureña, Pedro. *Historia de la cultura en la América Hispánica*. México: Fondo de Cultura Económica, 1947.

Johnson, Kenneth F. "Latin American Political Thought: Some Literary Foundations." In Ben Burnett and Kenneth F. Johnson, *Political Forces in Latin America*. Belmont: Wadsworth Publishing Co., 1968.

Jorrín, Miguel, and John D. Martz. *Latin American Political Thought and Ideology*. Chapel Hill: University of North Carolina Press, 1970.

Kempff Mercado, Manfredo. *Historia de la filosofía en Latino América*. Santiago, Chile: Zig-Zag, 1958.

Larroyo, Francisco. *La filosofía americana*. México: Universidad Autónoma Nacional, 1958.

Mijares, Augusto. *Hombres e ideas en América: Ensayos*. Caracas: Escuela Técnica Industrial, 1940.

Nicol, Eduardo. *El problema de la filosofía hispánica.* Madrid: Tecnos, 1961.

Romero, Francisco. "El pensamiento hispanoamericano." *Philosophy and Phenomenological Research,* IV (December, 1943), 132–53.

Sánchez Reulet, Aníbal. (Selección y prólogo) *La filosofía latinoamericana contemporánea.* Washington, D.C.: Unión Panamericana, 1949. English translation by Willard R. Trask. Albuquerque: University of New Mexico Press, 1954.

Skotheim, Allen. *American Intellectual Histories and Historians.* Princeton, N.J.: Princeton University Press, 1966.

Soler, Ricaurte. *Estudios sobre história de las ideas en América.* Panama City: Imprenta Nacional, 1960.

Stabb, Martin. *In Quest of Identity: Patterns in the Spanish American Essay of Ideas, 1890–1960.* Chapel Hill: University of North Carolina Press, 1967.

Villegas, Abelardo. *Antología del pensamiento social y político de America Latina.* Washington, D.C.: Unión Panamericana, 1964.

Zea, Leopoldo. *Dos etapas del pensamiento hispano-americano.* México: El Colegio de México, 1949.

———. *The Latin American Mind.* Translated by James H. Abbott and Lowell Dunham. Norman, Okla.: University of Oklahoma Press, 1963.

———. *El pensamiento latinoamericano.* 2 vols. México: Pormaca, 1965.

Special Aspects of Thought

Anderson Imbert, Enrique. *Spanish-American Literature.* 2nd ed. Translated by John V. Falconieri. Detroit: Wayne State University Press, 1969.

Arévalo Bermejo, Juan José. *Anti-Kommunismo in Latin America: An X-Ray of the Process Leading to a New Colonialism.* Translated by Carleton Beals. New York: L. Stuart, 1964.

Agramonte, Roberto. "La sociología en Latinoamérica." *Journal of Inter-American Studies,* II (July, 1960), 209–237.

Basbaum, Leoncio. *O processo evolutivo da história*. São Paulo: Edaglit, 1963.

Bastide, Roger. "Sociology in Latin America." In G. D. Gurvitch and W. E. Moore. *Twentieth Century Sociology*. New York: Philosophical Library, 1945.

Cidade, Ernani. *Ensaio sôbre a crise moral do século xviii*. Coimbra, 1929.

Comas, Juan. *Ensayos sobre indigenismo*. Prólogo de Manuel Gamio. México: Instituto Indigenista Inter-Americano, 1953.

Echanove Trujillo, Carlos A. *La sociología en Hispanoamérica*. La Habana: Imprenta Universitaria, 1953.

Frankenhoff, Charles A. "The Prebisch Thesis: A Theory of Industrialism for Latin America." *Journal of Inter-American Studies*, IV (April, 1962), 185–206.

Gamio, Manuel. *Consideraciones sobre el problema indígena*. México: Instituto Indigenista Interamericano, 1948.

García Gallo, Alfonso. "Problemas metodológicos de la historia del derecho indiano." *Revista del Instituto de Historia del Derecho Ricardo Levene*, Núm. 18 (1967), 13–64.

González Casanova, Pablo. *Una utopía de América*. México: El Colegio de México, 1953.

González Gerth, Miguel. "The Image of Spain in American Literature, 1815–1865." *Journal of Inter-American Studies*, IV (April, 1962), 16–26.

Hayes, Carlton J. H. *Nationalism: A Religion*. New York: Macmillan Co., 1960.

Jacobini, H. B. *A Study of the Philosophy of International Law as Seen in the Works of Latin American Writers*. The Hague: Martinus Nijhoff, 1954.

Kilgore, W. J. "The Development of Positivism in Latin America." *Inter-American Review of Bibliography*, XIX (April–June, 1969), 23–42.

Kusch, Rodolfo. "Pensamiento aymara y quechua." *América Indígena*, XXI (1971), 379–96.

McNicoll, Robert E. "Hegel and Latin America Today." *Journal of Inter-American Studies,* VI (January, 1964), 129–31.

Martz, John D. "Characteristics of Latin American Political Thought." *Journal of Inter-American Studies,* VIII (January, 1966), 45–65.

Medina Echeverría, José. *Panorama de la sociología contemporánea.* México: Casa de España en América, 1940.

Mijares, Augusto. *La interpretación pesimista de la sociología hispanoamericana.* 2nd ed. Madrid: Afrodisio Aguado, 1952.

O'Gorman, Edmundo. *The Invention of America.* Bloomington: Indiana University Press, 1961.

Onís, José de. "Pan-Hispanism." *Inter-American Review of Bibliography,* XIII (October–December, 1963), 428–72.

Peralta Pizarro, Ariel. *El cesarismo en América Latina.* Santiago, Chile: Orbe, 1966.

Pike, Frederick B. *Hispanismo, 1898–1936: Spanish Conservatives and Liberals and Their Relations with Spanish America.* Notre Dame: University of Notre Dame Press, 1971.

Poviña, Alfredo. *Nueva história de la sociología latinoamericana.* Córdoba: Imprenta de la Universidad, 1959.

———. *La sociología como ciencia y como ontología.* Córdoba: Imprenta de la Universidad, 1958.

———. *Sociología.* 5th ed. Córdoba: Assandri, 1966.

Quintanilla, Luis. *Bergsonismo y política.* México: Fondo de Cultura Económica, 1953.

———. *Pan Americanism and Democracy.* Boston: Boston University Press, 1952.

Rama, Carlos M. *Mouvements ouvriers et socialistes (Vol. 1) (chronologie et bibliographie) L'Amérique Latine (1492–1936).* Paris: Les Editions Ouvrieres, 1959.

Recaséns Siches, Luis, et al. *Latin American Legal Philosophy.* Translated by Gordon Ireland and others. Cambridge: Harvard University Press, 1948.

Richards, Edward B. "Marxism and Marxist Movements in Latin

America in Recent Soviet Historical Writings." *Hispanic American Historical Review*, XLV (November, 1965), 577–94.

Río, Ángel del. *The Clash and Attraction of Two Cultures: The Hispanic and Anglo-Saxon Worlds in America.* Translated and edited by James F. Shearer. Baton Rouge: Louisiana State University Press, 1965.

Rippy, Fred J. "Literary Yankeephobia in Hispanic America." *Journal of International Relations*, XIII (1922), 350–71, 524–38.

Rodríguez Alcalá, Hugo. *Korn, Romero, Güiraldes, Unamuno, Ortega. Literatura paraguaya y otros ensayos.* México: Andrea, 1958.

Romero, José Luis. *El pensamiento político de la derecha latinoamericana.* Buenos Aires: Paidos, 1970.

Sánchez, Luis Alberto. *Proceso y contenido de la novela hispanoamericana.* Madrid: Gredos, 1953.

Sanz, Víctor. *La historia y el futuro.* Montevideo: Universidad de la República, 1962.

Sarrailh, Jean. *L'Espagne éclairée de la seconde moitié du xviiiᵉ siècle.* Paris: Imprimerie Nationale, 1954.

Schwartzman, Felix. *El sentimiento de lo humano en América: ensayo de antropología filosófica.* Santiago, Chile: Universidad de Chile, 1950.

Silva Herzog, Jesús. *Antología del pensamiento ecconómico-social, I: De Bodin a Proudhon.* México: Fondo de Cultura Económica, 1967.

Sommers, Joseph. "The Indian-Oriented Novel in Latin America: New Spirit, New Forces, New Scope." *Journal of Inter-American Studies*, VI (April–June, 1964), 249–63.

Spell, Jefferson R. *Rousseau in the Spanish World Before 1833.* Austin: University of Texas Press, 1938.

Stimson, Frederick S. *Origenes del hispanismo norteamericano.* México: Librería Stadium, 1961.

Terán Gómez, Luis. "El ocaso de socialismo." *Journal of Inter-American Studies*, II (July, 1960), 276–93.

ARGENTINA

Binayán, Narciso (ed.). *Ideario de mayo*. Buenos Aires: Kapelusz, 1960.

Furlong Cárdiff, Guillermo. *Bibliotecas argentinas durante la dominación hispánica*. Buenos Aires: Huarpes, 1944.

———. *Nacimiento y desarrollo de la filosofía en el Rio de la plata*. Buenos Aires: Guillermo Kraft, 1952.

Gandía, Enrique de. *Historia de las ideas políticas en la Argentina*. 5 vols. Buenos Aires: Depalma, 1960–1968.

Ingenieros, José. *La evolución de las ideas argentinas*. 2 vols. Buenos Aires: 1918–1920.

Jaén, Didier T. "La generación romántica argentina y el problema de Hispanoamérica." *Journal of Inter-American Studies*, VIII (October, 1966), 56–76.

Levene, Ricardo. *Las revoluciones indígenas y las versiones o idiomas de los naturales de documentos de la Independencia*. Buenos Aires, 1948 (14 page lecture before the National Academy of History, July 6, 1946).

Lombardi, Carlos M. *Las ideas sociales en la Argentina*. Buenos Aires: Platina and Stilcograf, 1965.

Mantovani, Juan, et al. *Sarmiento. Educador, sociólogo, escritor, político*. Buenos Aires: Universidad de Buenos Aires, 1963.

Mouchet, Carlos. "Alberdi y Sarmiento: Planificadores de Ciudades en Desarrollo Económico." *Journal of Inter-American Studies*, VIII (October, 1966), 87–99.

Romero, José Luis. *A History of Argentine Political Thought*. Translated by Thomas F. McGann. Stanford: Stanford University Press, 1963.

Sierra, Vicente D. *Historia de las ideas políticas en Argentina*. Buenos Aires: Ediciones Nuestra Casa, 1950.

Soler, Ricaurte. *El positivismo argentino*. Panamá: Imprenta Nacional, 1959.

Torchia Estrada, J. C. *La filosofía en la Argentina*. Washington, D.C.: Pan American Union, 1961.

Varela Domínguez de Ghioldi, Delfina. *La generación argentina del 37.* Buenos Aires: Populares Argentinas, 1956.
Weinberg, Félix, (ed.). *M. Sastre, J. B. Alberdi, J. M. Gutiérrez, E. Echeverría: El Salón Literaria.* Buenos Aires: Hachette, 1958.

BOLIVIA

Francovich, Guillermo. *El pensamiento boliviano en el siglo xx.* México: Fondo de Cultura Económica, 1956.
———. *La filosofía en Bolivia.* La Paz: Juventud, 1966.

BRAZIL

Bastos, Tocary Assis. *O positivismo e a realidade brasileira.* Belo Horizonte: Universidade de Minas Gerais, 1965.
Burns, E. Bradford. "The Enlightenment in Colonial Brazil." *Journal of the History of Ideas,* XXV (July-September, 1964), 430–38.
———. "Role of Azeredo Coutinho in the Enlightenment in Brazil." *Hispanic American Historical Review,* 44 (May, 1964), 145–60.
Carrato, José Ferreira. *Igreja, iluminismo e escolas mineiras coloniais.* São Paulo: Companhia Editora Nacional, 1965.
Coutinho, Afranio. "Some Considerations on the Problem of Philosophy in Brazil." *Philosophy and Phenomenological Research,* IV (December, 1943), 186–95.
Costa, João Cruz. *A History of Ideas in Brazil.* Translated by Suzette Macedo. Berkeley: University of California Press, 1964.
Fernandes, Floreston. *The Negro in Brazilian Society.* Translated by Jacqueline D. Skiles, A. Brunel, and Arthur Rothwell. New York: Columbia University Press, 1969.
Francovich, Guillermo. *Filósofos Brasileños.* Buenos Aires, 1943.
Gómez Robledo, Antonio. *La filosofía en el Brasil.* México, 1946.
Kahl, Joseph. *The Measurement of Modernism: A Study of Values in Brazil and Mexico.* Austin: University of Texas Press, 1968.
Lins, Ivan Monteiro de Barros. *Historia de positivismo no Brasil.* São Paulo: Companhia Editora Nacional, 1960.
Oliveira Torres, João Camilo de, *O positivismo no Brasil.* Rio de Janeiro, 1943.

Paim, Antonio. *História das idéias filosóficas no Brasil.* São Paulo: Grijalba, 1967.

Tobías, José Antonio. *O ensino da filosofía nas universidades brasileiras.* Washington, D.C.: União Panamericana, 1968.

Vita, Luis Washington. *A filosofía no Brasil.* São Paulo: Martins, 1950.

Werneck Sodré, Nelson. *Orientações do pensamento brasileiro.* Rio de Janeiro: Editora Vecchi, 1942.

CENTRAL AMERICA

Láscaris C., Constantino. *Desarrollo de las ideas filosóficas en Costa Rica.* San José: Editorial Costa Rica, 1965.

Valle, Rafael Heliodoro. *Historia de las ideas contemporáneas en Centro-América.* México: Fondo de Cultura Económica, 1960.

CHILE

Bader, Thomas. "Early Positivist Thought and Ideological Conflict in Chile." *The Americas,* XXVI (April, 1970), 376–93.

Donoso, Ricardo. *Las ideas políticas en Chile.* México: Fondo de Cultura Económica, 1946.

Eyzaguirre, Jaime. "Los presupuestos jurídicos y doctrinarios de la independencia de Chile." *Ateneo,* Tomo XCV, Nos. 291–92 (1949), 182–238.

Jobet, Julio César. "Notas sobre la historiografía chilena." *Ateneo,* Tomo XCV, Nos. 291–92 (1949), 345–77.

Molina, Enrique. *La filosofía en Chile en la primera mitad del siglo xx.* 2a ed. aumentada. Santiago, Chile: Nascimento, 1953.

Torres Rioseco, Arturo. "La novela chilena contemporánea." *Journal of Inter-American Studies,* IV, (October, 1962), 503–516.

COLOMBIA

Jaramillo Uribe, Jaime, *El pensamiento colombiano en el siglo xix* Bogotá: Temis, 1964.

Valderrama Andrade, Carlos. *El pensamiento filosófico de Miguel Antonio Caro.* Bogotá: Instituto Caro y Cuervo, 1961.

CUBA

Mestre y Domínguez, José Manuel. *Estudio preliminar, notas por Humberto Pinera Llera. De la filosofía en la Habana.* La Habana: Ministro de Educación, 1952.

Pinera Llera, Humberto. *Panorama de la filosofía cubana.* Washington, D.C.: Unión Panamericana, 1960.

DOMINICAN REPUBLIC

Cordero, Armando. *Panorama de la filosofía en Santo Domingo.* 2 vols. Santo Domingo: Impresora "Arte y Cine" and Editorial la Nación, 1962.

HAITI

MacLeod, Murdo J. "The Haitian Novel of Social Protest." *Journal of Inter-American Studies,* IV (April, 1962), 207–221.

JAMAICA

Curtin, Philip D. *Two Jamaicas; the role of ideas in a tropical colony, 1830–1865.* Cambridge: Harvard University Press, 1955.

MEXICO

Alba, Víctor. *Las ideas sociales contemporáneas en México.* México: Fondo de Cultura Económica, 1960.

Cockcroft, James D. *Intellectual Precursors of the Mexican Revolution, 1900–1913.* Austin: University of Texas Press, 1968.

Cosío Villegas, Daniel. *The United States versus Porfirio Díaz.* Translated by Nettie Lee Benson. Lincoln: University of Nebraska Press, 1964.

Cueva, Mario de la, et al. *Major Trends in Mexican Philosophy.* Translated by Robert Caponigri. Notre Dame: University of Notre Dame Press, 1966.

García Cantú, Gastón. *El pensamiento de la reacción mexicana.* México: Empresas Editoriales, 1965.

Hale, Charles A. *Mexican Liberalism in the Age of Mora, 1821–1858.* New Haven: Yale University Press, 1968.

Hernández-Luna, Juan. *Dos ideas sobre la filosofía en la Nueva España*. México: Universidad Nacional, 1959.

Ibargüengoitia, Antonio. *Filosofía mexicana en sus hombres y en sus textos*. México: Porrúa, 1967.

Johnson, Kenneth F. "Ideological Correlates of Right Wing Political Alienation in Mexico." *American Political Science Review*, LIX (September, 1965), 656–64.

León Portilla, Miguel. *Aztec Thought and Culture: A Study of the Ancient Nahuatl Mind*. Translated by Jack Emory Davis. Norman: University of Oklahoma Press, 1963.

————. *Tiempo y realidad en el pensamiento maya*. México: Universidad Nacional Autónoma de México, 1968.

López Rosado, Diego. *Historia y pensamiento económico de México*. México: Universidad Nacional Autónoma de México, 1969.

Moreno, Daniel. *El pensamiento jurídico mexicano*. México: Librería de Porrúa, 1966.

————. *El pensamiento jurídico de México en el derecho internacional*. Colegio de Abogados de México. México: Librería de Porrúa, 1960.

Raat, William D. "Agustín Aragón and Mexico's Religion of Humanity." *Journal of Inter-American Studies*, XI (July, 1969), 441–57.

————. "Leopoldo Zea and Mexican Positivism, An Appraisal." *Hispanic American Historical Review*, XLVIII (February, 1968), 1–18.

————. "Ideas and History in Mexico: An Essay on Methodology." (Paper presented at Oaxtepec Conference, Mexico, November, 1969; also published in Spanish in No. 3 of *Latinoamérica*, UNAM.)

————. "Positivism in Díaz Mexico." Ph.D. dissertation. University of Utah, 1967.

Ramos, Samuel. *Profile of Man and Culture in Mexico*. Translated by Peter G. Earle. Austin: University of Texas Press, 1962.

————. *Historia de la filosofía en México*. México: Imprenta Universitaria, 1943.

Reyes Heroles, Jesús. *El liberalismo mexicano.* 3 vols. México: Universidad Nacional Autónoma de México, 1957–1961.

Romanell, Patrick. *The Making of the Mexican Mind.* Lincoln, Neb.: University of Nebraska Press, 1952).

————. "Ortega in Mexico." *Journal of the History of Ideas,* XXI (October-December, 1960), 600–608.

Schmitt, Karl M. "The Mexican Positivists and the Church-State Question." *Church and State,* VIII (Spring, 1966), 200–213.

Silva Herzog, Jesús. *El agrarismo mexicana y la reforma agraria: exposición y crítica.* México: Fondo de Cultura Económica, 1959.

————. *El pensamiento económico en México.* México: Fondo de Cultura Económica, 1947.

Villoro, Luis. *Los grandes momentos del indigenismo en México.* México: El Colegio de México, 1950.

Zea, Leopoldo. *El positivismo en México. Apogeo y decadencia del positivismo en México,* 2 vols. México: El Colegio de México, 1944.

————. *La filosofía en México.* 2 vols. México: Libro-Mexicano Editores, 1955).

PARAGUAY

Cardozo, Efraím. *Apuntes de história cultural del Paraguay.* Asunción, 1963.

Irala Burgos, Aduano. "Nuevas corrientes de la historiografía paraguaya." *Inter-American Review of Bibliography,* XVIII (April-June, 1968), 125–41.

PERU

Barreda y Laos, Felipe. *Vida intelectual del virreinato del Perú.* 3rd ed. Lima: Universidad Nacional Mayor de San Marcos, 1964.

Chavarría, Jesús. "The Intellectuals and the Crisis of Modern Peruvian Nationalism: 1870–1919." *Hispanic American Historical Review,* L (May, 1970), 257–78.

Pike, Fredrick. "The Old and the New APRA in Peru: Myth and Reality." *Inter-American Economic Affairs* (Autumn, 1964), 3–47.

Salazar Bondy, Augusto. *Historia de las ideas en el Perú contemporánea.* 2 vols. Lima: Francisco Moncloa, Editores, 1965.

URUGUAY

Ardao, Arturo. *Espiritualismo y positivismo en el Uruguay.* México: Fondo de Cultura Económica, 1956. *La filosofía en el Uruguay en el siglo xx.* México: Fondo de Cultura Económica, 1956.

Oddone, Juan Antonio. *El principismo del setenta.* Montevideo: Universidad de la República Oriental del Uruguay, 1956.

Zum Felde, Alberto. *Proceso intelectual del Uruguay.* Montevideo: Editorial Claridad, 1941.

VENEZUELA

Leal, Ildefonso. "La aristocracia criolla venezolana y el Código Negrero de 1789." *Revista de Historia* (Venezuela), II (February, 1961), 61–81.

Mijares, Augusto. *Lo afirmativo venezolano.* Caracas: Ediciones de la Fundación Eugenio Mendoza, 1963.

Index